C.G. JUNG—THE BASEL YEARS:
A WALKING GUIDE

KATHRIN SCHAEPPI

C.G. JUNG—
THE BASEL YEARS:
A WALKING GUIDE

DAIMON

Kathrin Schaeppi
C.G. Jung—The Basel Years: A Walking Guide

Copyright © 2025 by Kathrin Ursula Schaeppi
and Daimon Verlag,
am Klosterplatz, CH-8840 Einsiedeln
First edition, 2025
ISBN 978-3-85630-391-4

Design:
Sibylle Ryser, Office for Book Design,
www.sibylleryser.ch
Fonts: Arnhem, Albula, Gotham Narrow

Printing and Binding:
Gugler DruckSinn, Melk AT

Cover image:
C.G. Jung in a *Weidling* (flat-bottomed boat)
with friends. Taken on the so-called Old Rhine
or the Haltingermoos, near Basel.
Courtesy of the Jung Family Archive

All rights reserved

For information about permission to repro-
duce selections from this book, write
to Kathrin Schaeppi, Bachlettenstrasse 33,
4054 Basel

Copyright received from Penguin Random House
to reprint the vision and dreams from *Memories,
Dreams, Reflections* by C.G. Jung,
edited by Aniela Jaffé (Vintage Books, 1989)

CONTENTS

8 FOREWORD
by Sonu Shamdasani

11 INTRODUCTION

20 TOUR 1
CARL'S EARLY YEARS IN KLEINHÜNINGEN

82 TOUR 2
CARL'S WALK FROM KLEINHÜNINGEN TO THE GYMNASIUM IN BASEL

152 TOUR 3
YOUNG ADULTHOOD: FROM THE GYMNASIUM TO UNIVERSITY

212 TOUR 4
BOTTMINGER MÜHLE: SÉANCES AND ENCOUNTERS WITH THE FEMININE

250 TOUR 5
INTERLOCKING SPHERES: JUNG, HESSE, AND NIETZSCHE

265 END MATTER
266 FAMILY TREES
272 WHO LIVED WHERE
274 ABBREVIATIONS
274 LIST OF MAPS
274 LIST OF TABLES
275 IMAGE CREDITS
277 ENDNOTES
283 REFERENCES
285 MAIN INDEX
292 FAMILY NAME INDEX
294 ABOUT THE AUTHOR
295 ACKNOWLEDGMENTS

TOUR 1

BRIDGE OVER THE RIVER WIESE
Carl's Lifelong Connection to Water

ENTRANCE TO DORFSTRASSE
Village Life

PARSONAGE, DORFSTRASSE 19
The Interior Sphere: The House Where Carl Grew Up

FISHER HOUSE AND SILO, SCHULGASSE 16
Modernity Knocks on Kleinhüningen's Door

CEMETERY, FRIEDHOFSGASSE
Encounters with Death

PROTESTANT REFORMED CHURCH, DORFSTRASSE 39
Faith, Fishermen, Farmers, and Factory Workers

PRIMARY AND SECONDARY SCHOOL, BONERGASSE 30
Where Knights Battle and Slay Dragons

BÜRGIN FISHER HOUSE, BONERGASSE 71

CLAVEL ESTATE, BONERGASSE 71
Juxtaposition of Old and New

FORTRESS HÜNINGEN
A Well-Fortified Castle

TOUR 2

WIESENDAMM / UFERSTRASSE
Leaving Kleinhüningen to Walk Along the Rhine to Basel

HOLZPARK KLYBECK, UFERSTRASSE 40
15th-Century Castle and Father Rhine

TOUR 2A: THE GROSSBASEL ROUTE

JOHANNITERBRÜCKE
A Citizen-Led Initiative

ERLACHERHOF, ST. JOHANNS-VORSTADT 15/17
Silk Ribbons for the Global Fashion Industry

TOTENTANZ 17
The Dance with Death

BÜRGERSPITAL, PETERSGRABEN 4

JUNGSTRASSE

FRIEDMATT ASYLUM, WILHELM KLEIN-STRASSE 27
Basel's Sick and Impoverished Citizens

ERIMANSHOF, PETERSGRABEN 1
Art Salon in the Erimanshof

TOUR 2B: THE KLEINBASEL ROUTE

KASERNE, VIEWED FROM UNTERER RHEINWEG
Military Barracks and Cloister

KLOSTER KLEINES KLINGENTAL, UNTERER RHEINWEG 26
Medieval Masterpieces and Miniatures

MITTLERE BRÜCKE AND KÄPPELIJOCH
A Place of Grim Reckoning

CONVERGENCE OF ROUTES A&B

LÄLLEKÖNIG, SCHIFFLÄNDE 1
Trickster at the Gate

OLD UNIVERSITY, RHEINSPRUNG 9
The Jung Family Medical Legacy

AUGUSTINERBRUNNEN, RHEINSPRUNG 21
A Pagan Creature Holds the Bishop's Staff

NATURHISTORISCHES MUSEUM, AUGUSTINERGASSE 2
Carl Discovers All Manner of Things

GYMNASIUM, MÜNSTERPLATZ 15
Nine Years of Study

ST. ALBAN PFARRHAUS, MÜHLENBERG 12
Where Isemännli Lives

TOUR 3

BASEL MÜNSTER
A Towering Edifice

ANTISTITIUM, RITTERGASSE 2
A Family of Pastors

BISCHOFSHOF, RITTERGASSE 1
An Opulent Past

MÜNSTER KLOSTERGARTEN, ENTRY OPPOSITE RITTERGASSE 2
Young Carl's Faith Is Tested

HISTORISCHES MUSEUM BASEL, BARFÜSSERPLATZ
Inspiration: Knights and the Grail Legend

LEONHARDSKIRCHPLATZ 1
At a Threshold: Major Life Choices

VESALIANUM, VESALGASSE 1
Carl Studies Medicine

PETERSPLATZ
The Culmination

HAUS ZUM SESSEL, TOTENGÄSSLEIN 3
Individuation and Alchemy

TOUR 4

ZOFINGIA STUDENT FRATERNITY, STEINENVORSTADT 36
Carl Finds His Voice and Place in a Community of Peers

NACHTIGALLENWÄLDELI
Spooky Nights in the Forest Along the Birsig

MARGARETHENSTRASSE 19
A Bustling and Loved Extended Family Home

MARGARETHEN-BRÜCKLEIN
Family Ties Between Church and Mill

BINNINGER SCHLOSS, SCHLOSSGASSE 5
Castle Near the Woods

BOTTMINGER MÜHLE, BOTTMINGERSTRASSE 68, BINNINGEN
The Mill's Many Incarnations

THE PREISWERK SISTERS' DRESS SHOP, ST. ALBAN-ANLAGE 5
Les Demoiselles Helene & Valerie Preiswerk: *Robes et Manteaux*

BRUDERHOLZ, MARGA BÜHRIG-WEG
Broader Horizons:
The Colorful Hills of Binningen

ST. MARGARETHENKIRCHE, FRIEDHOFSTRASSE, BINNINGEN
Leaving Basel for Zürich

TOUR 5

BASEL MISSION, MISSIONSSTRASSE 21
Hesse's Basel and Path to Individuation

RESTAURANT ZUM TELL, SPALENVORSTADT 38
Hesse's Analysis and Creative Outpouring

NIETZSCHE FOUNTAIN

**NIETZSCHE'S BASEL HOMES: SCHÜTZENGRABEN 47
SPALENTORWEG 48
SPALENTORWEG 5
SPALENTORWEG 2**
The Baumannhöhle and Other Homes

FOREWORD: FROM BASEL TO ZURICH

In 1900, toward the end of his medical studies, Jung made one of the most decisive choices of his life. He decided to emigrate from Basel to Zürich, taking up a position as an assistant doctor at the Burghölzli hospital, at the invitation of the director, Eugen Bleuler. For the rest of his life, Jung would live as an outsider, a Basel émigré, in self-imposed exile in Zürich. Decades later, he reflected on what Basel and this move meant to him, in the interviews with Aniela Jaffé that formed the basis of *Memories, Dreams, Reflections*.[1] Jung recalled:

> *In Basel you are defined once and for all: there, I was the son of Jung, the parson. I belonged in a certain set, a sort of "pious set," and there, you could only sense resistance towards it. I did not wish, nor was I able, to allow myself to be pinned down.*[2]

In Basel, Jung experienced a cultural and social embeddedness and belonging. He noted: "You were able to take a classical education for granted in any conversation. We could debate about the different styles in Cicero, even among medical students. That was simply a part of how it was."[3] Readers of Jung's works – who often encounter untranslated quotations from Greek and Latin – will be familiar with this presupposition. These were books for the cognoscenti. At the same time, Jung experienced this atmosphere as constricting: "I wanted to get right away from Basel. One was so stuck in tradition there. It was also a very conservative element in me as well, it suited me, but at the same time I also feared it."[4] Moving to Zürich heralded freedom from the past, and a quest for the new.

Jung reflected on the differences between Basel and the mercantile world of Zürich:

And yet, all in all, there was a cosmopolitan and international atmosphere in Basel at that time. I saw the difference when I came to Zurich. It felt as if I had relocated to a village. The relationship of Zurich to the world is not one of spirit, but of trade. In Basel too there were tradesmen, the Bändeliherren [...] They made the necessary money for the others who were intellectually connected to the world. One section of the Baselers were proper hucksters and money makers, but then this money flowed profitably to the university. One must also not forget that Basel is a border town, so this extraordinary syncretic spirit developed between France, Germany, and Switzerland.[5]

Clearly, Jung's mindset was shaped by this cosmopolitan, internationalist spirit, which is so central to the ethos of his work. He considered this to be a privilege: "being from Basel, I was terribly spoiled. There, I belonged to a sort of aristocracy, also of the spirit. There was a highly cultured tradition discernible in conversation and in people's background, sensed as cultivated."[6] At the same time, Zürich provided Jung with the space and freedom to fulfil his calling, and allowed his creativity to come to full expression. He recalled:

It's typical for Basel that they said of someone whose house was located a small distance from Basel that they were from "beyond the Birs." Whoever does not in live in Basel, lives in "misery." When I went to Zurich, they asked me: "So, when are you coming back? Can you really live in Zurich then?" That's Basel! – Even today I still have a painful weakness for Basel but it's no longer what it once was. I myself still belong in that time where there was a Bachofen and a Burckhardt.[7]

In 1943, Jung was appointed as a professor in medical psychology at the University of Basel. However, fate was cruel, and following his heart attack the following year, he had to resign his chair. On September 6, 1955 he wrote to Werner Kuhn, Rector of the University of Basel, of the "joy I felt when the University of my home town did me the honour of appointing me to a professorship, and on the other hand of those bitter drops that fell into the beaker of joy when severe illness prevented the continuation of my teaching activity in Basel. But such is the fate of the pioneer: he himself is too early, and what he longs for comes too late."[8] For Jung, the recognition by his alma mater was the ultimate homecoming.

In 1927, Jung wrote an essay entitled "The Earth-Conditioning of the Psyche."[9] The earth that conditioned him was that of Basel, and its surroundings. *C. G. Jung—The Basel Years* takes readers back to Jung's upbringing and student days in and around Basel—back to the time of Burckhardt and Bachofen—enabling them to follow in his footsteps, as well as those of his eminent forebears. At the same time, it allows them to see what he took with him, when he made the fateful decision to leave Basel for Zürich, and how this furnished him with essential prerequisites for his opus.

Sonu Shamdasani

INTRODUCTION

This tour guide honors the eminent Swiss psychiatrist and psychoanalyst Dr. med. Carl Gustav Jung (1875–1961), in commemoration of his 150th anniversary. This man, who established the field of analytical psychology and left a major imprint on the Swiss and international psychic landscape, was once a boy. For 21 years spanning the turn of the century (1879–1900), Carl was a citizen of Basel, like both of his parents. He remained there until passing the *Staatsexamen* (federal exams) in medicine at the University of Basel. However, the Basel dialect remained with him throughout his life, serving as a reminder of his formative years. This book guides readers to locations that were integral to Carl's early life—places where he played, studied, worshipped, and wandered—shedding light on his struggles and experiences as a youth. Walking in his footsteps, you will experience Kleinhüningen and Basel through his younger eyes.

By the time Carl completed his medical studies, he had already encountered and personally experienced many of the concepts he would later explore and develop, both professionally and personally. Indeed, the origins of analytical psychology can be traced back to his childhood visions and dreams, which revealed to him the personal and collective unconscious. His experiences with religion and parapsychology point toward his lifelong desire for a relationship with the numinous and the symbolic. Moreover, his medical studies intensified a tension he would struggle with all his life, between his training as an empirical scientist and his natural orientation toward the creative and unknown. For Carl, this tension lived within him, granting him the insight, curiosity, and courage to explore the borderlands of the unconscious and develop tools to bring its contents into awareness. Thus, it is precisely in this tension between the experiential-mystical and the experimental-empirical that the field of analytical psychology lies.

What You Will Learn on These Tours

What will you learn about Carl's early years by taking these walking tours in Basel? Beyond discovering his connection to the city, its people, and its unmatched spiritual, philosophical, and historical character, you will also gain insight into his personal development. By connecting specific sites to Carl's visions, dreams, and drawings, you will experience them in a deeper—more lived—sense. You will also discover the societal turbulence Carl witnessed during his youth, driven by Basel's rapid modernization and population growth at the turn of the century. Additionally, you will learn about his family dynamics during this period. Both his paternal grandfather and his father were actively engaged in the burgeoning field of psychiatry in the mid-19th century, and his relationships with his mother, aunts, and cousins—often overlooked in biographical accounts—provide valuable context for his enduring interest in the unconscious and the feminine.

Tour 1 starts in Kleinhüningen, where you will visit important sites in Carl's early childhood and family life. In **Tour 2,** you will follow in Carl's footsteps along his daily walks from home to school in Basel. Perhaps you will choose to take his route along the Rhine and over the Johanniterbrücke, or perhaps you will opt for the walk over the Mittlere Brücke, instead. In either case, the scenes Carl would have also seen along these paths will come fully alive. This tour also includes details about Carl's adolescent experience at the Gymnasium (high school). **Tour 3** begins at Basel Münster and explores sites connected to Carl's religious and spiritual awakening, including his efforts to reconcile Personality No. 1 and Personality No. 2 (respectively, the "spirit of the times" and the "spirit of the depths"). This tour spans his university and medical school years and his participation in a student fraternity, revealing his early interest in alchemy. **Tour 4** takes you to Binningen, where Carl resided following his father's death. Here, you will learn about the many séances he attended and the feminine influences that shaped his life during this period. **Tour 5** highlights the intersections between Carl's life and the lives of Hermann Hesse and Friedrich Nietzsche in Basel, revealing the cultural and intellectual milieu that shaped his thinking.

Jung's Imprint on the International and Swiss Landscape

As the tours in this book show, Jung's early years coincided with the infancy of psychiatry—a time when many new theories were emerging from the successes and failures of early exploratory work. Jung's profound influence on the psychological and cultural landscape of Switzerland and the broader world is evident in the vast number of his concepts that have organically found their way into common parlance. Terms such as "midlife crisis," "unconscious," "complex," "persona," "projection," "compensation," "anima/animus," "shadow," "psychological types," "individuation," "transcendent function," "synchronicity," and "Self" are now commonly used, yet rarely recognized as Jung's original contributions. Two hallmark ideas that distinguish Jung's analytical (or depth) psychology from Freudian psychoanalysis are the "collective unconscious" and "archetypes." These groundbreaking concepts, which shaped much of Jung's work over his lifetime, took root during his early years in Basel.

Today, Jung's legacy is carried forward by the International Association of Analytical Psychology (IAAP), which was founded in 1955 by a group of Jungian analysts to preserve and promote his work. The IAAP now recognizes 69 Group Members (societies) throughout the world, and approximately 3,500 analysts have been trained in accordance with its rigorous standards. In Switzerland, three institutes offer training for Jungian analysts: the C.G. Jung-Institut (established in 1948), das Forschungs- und Ausbildungszentrum für Tiefenpsychologie nach C.G. Jung und Marie-Louise von Franz (Research and Training Center for Depth Psychology According to C.G. Jung and Marie-Louise von Franz, established in 1994), and ISAPZURICH (International School of Analytical Psychology Zurich, established in 2002). Additionally, Switzerland is home to two professional associations supporting Jungian analysis: the Psychological Association Basel (established in 1933) and the Psychology Club Zurich (founded in 1916). Jung's family home in Küsnacht, where much of his scholarly and domestic life unfolded, has since been transformed into a historic house museum.

Shortly before his break with Freud, Jung experienced a profound "house dream," in which his dream-ego moved downward through the layers of his personal living space, descending deeper into increasingly ancient structures. At each level, he encountered an earlier time in history, thereby successively uncovering the strata of humanity's shared past. At the deepest layer, he discovered scattered bones, fragments of pottery reminiscent of the "remains of a primitive culture," and human skulls. In many ways, this book mirrors that dream, inviting readers to embark on a similar journey through Jung's life, tracing his development within the historical and cultural context of Basel. The archival research behind this work was itself a kind of excavation—an uncovering of forgotten artifacts, overlooked stories, and unseen relationships that reveal the depth of Jung's roots. My process of discovering where he lived, walked, studied, and formed memories as a child and adolescent allowed me to uncover the deeper layers of his ancestral line and personal development, which inspired his revolutionary theories and practices. As an analyst and resident of Basel, I invite you to partake in this shared journey of discovery. I encourage you to immerse yourself in the places and stories, allowing yourself to drop into the depths to uncover the sites and structures that influenced Jung's life and work.

Some Practical Considerations for Your Time in Basel

It is possible to complete two tours in a single day, depending on your energy level and the walking distances involved. Tours 2 and 4, for example, involve longer routes and may be more challenging to pair with another tour on the same day. Each tour has been estimated to take approximately 90 to 120 minutes, allowing you ample time to immerse yourself in the atmosphere of the Basel of Jung's formative years. While the tours may be spread across multiple days (I would recommend at least three days to complete them all), some combinations—such as Tours 1 and 2 or Tours 2 and 3—may be comfortably completed in a single day for those with sufficient time and energy. Basel's efficient public transport system makes navigating the city straightforward, and the SBB website (https://www.sbb.ch/en) offers a reliable resource for travel instructions and timetables.

This book also includes a range of supplementary materials—a chronology, family trees, maps, and plentiful photographs—to support the self-guided walks and provide a vivid context for readers exploring the material from afar. Also sprinkled throughout the text are key concepts central to Jung's approach to psychology, many of which have become integral to mainstream psychological understanding.

Naming Conventions Used in this Book

Family Names
Carl and Jung. C. G. Jung is referred to as "Carl" in this tour guide when discussing his childhood. He is referred to as "Jung" upon becoming an adult, following the completion of his medical studies at the University of Basel and his relocation to Zürich to begin professional work.

Karl and Carl. During his years at the Gymnasium, Jung changed the spelling of his name from "Karl" to "Carl." To maintain consistency, this book systematically adopts the spelling "Carl." However, references to Jung's grandfather, Karl Gustav Jung, retain the spelling with a "K" in order to distinguish the elder from the younger.

Samuel and Samuel Gottlob. The significant presence of Carl's maternal grandfather Samuel and maternal uncle Samuel Gottlob in Jung's formative years is reflected in their frequent mention in the tours. The use of the younger Samuel Preiswerk's middle name (Gottlob) is used to distinguish them.

Alliance Name. The historic Basel marital naming convention that has been adopted in this book to help clarify identities is adjoining the wife's family name to the husband's with a hyphen. In Carl's early years, his extended family was large, and given names were repeated across generations and lineage. Likewise, Basel was a small, interrelated community with many common family names. For example, Jung's maternal uncle Gustav is identified as Gustav Preiswerk-Vetter. Because a special case has already been made for paternal grandfather Karl, maternal grandfather Samuel, and maternal uncle Samuel Gottlob, the marital alliance is not indicated unless it is specifically germane to the context.

Family Branch Name. To help clarify the lineage of never- or not-yet-married family members, the family branch is sometimes given parenthetically to foster clarity about identity. For example, Jung's maternal cousin Wilhelm might be referred to as Wilhelm Preiswerk (Allenspach branch) as a child and becomes Wilhelm Preiswerk-Zumstein after marrying.

Given Names. When an individual has multiple given names, the name used most commonly is underlined the first time it appears in a tour and then used exclusively for the remainder of the tour. Thus, Johann Paul Achilles Jung-Preiswerk becomes Paul Jung-Preiswerk.

Nicknames. When an individual was known primarily by their nickname, the nickname is given in quotation marks with first mention in a tour and then used exclusively for the rest of the tour. For instance, Helene "Helly" Preiswerk becomes Helly Preiswerk.

The Elder and the Younger. When a child shares a parent's name, the parent is designated as the Elder and the child as the Younger. For example, Rudolf Preiswerk-Allenspach (the Elder) and Rudolf Preiswerk (the Younger). This is akin to the designations "Senior" and "Junior" in the English language.

Place Names
Sites Not Visited. Some sites are too far away to be comfortably included in the tour, and they may also no longer exist. The station number for these sites is given in a box **2** rather than a circle **2**, and has no color fill, only a color outline.

Historic Site. In some instances, a site is visited but the original structure no longer exists. This is indicated by the designation "Historic Site".

Table 1
A Brief Chronology

1875	July 26: Carl Gustav Jung is born in Kesswil, Canton Thurgau, on Lake Constance, to Johann Paul Achilles Jung and Emilie Preiswerk. He holds Basel *Heimatrecht* (citizenship).
1875	August 29: Carl is baptized in Kesswil. His godfathers are Ernst Jung and Robert Fiechter, and his godmother is Auguste "Gusteli" Preiswerk.
1876	The Jung family moves to Laufen, Canton Zürich, near the Rheinfall (Rhine Falls).
1879	The Jung family moves to Kleinhüningen, a farming and fishing village next to Basel on the Rhine.
1884	July 17: Carl's younger sister, Johanna Gertrude ("Trudi"), is born.
1882–1886	Carl attends primary school at Krautgasse 1 in Kleinhüningen (ages 7–11). His teacher is Joh. Thalmann (academic year 1986/87). Trudi later attends the same school (1891–1895).
1886–1891	Carl attends the Unteres Gymnasium at Münsterplatz 15, Basel (ages 11–16). Due to a fall and subsequent absences, he repeats class 2B during the academic year 1888/89.
1891	March 27: Carl is confirmed on Good Friday by his father, Pastor Paul Jung, in the church at Kleinhüningen.
1891–1895	Carl attends the Oberes Gymnasium at Münsterplatz 14, Basel (ages 16–20).
1895	April 18: Carl enrolls in Natural Sciences and Medicine at the University of Basel, where he studies for five years (ages 20–25).
1895	May 18: Carl becomes a member of Breo, the Basel chapter of the Zofingiaverein, a Swiss male student association (short name: Zofingia).
1895–1899	Carl attends séances and experiments with spiritualism (particularly in 1898 and 1899).
1896	January 28: Carl's father, Paul Jung, dies. Carl is 20 years old and Trudi is 11.
1896	Emilie, Carl, and Trudi move to Bottminger Mühle in Binningen, near Basel.
1896–1899	Carl delivers five Zofingia lectures.
1897–1898	Carl serves as president of Zofingia.
1900	March: Carl completes his tenth semester of medical studies at the University of Basel.
1900–1909	December 10, 1900: Jung begins work as an assistant medical doctor at the Psychiatric Clinic Burghölzli, Zürich, a position he holds throughout this period.
1901	Easter Sunday: Trudi is confirmed.
1902–1903	Trudi resides in Château-d'Oex at the home of the village priest, from whom she takes French and English lessons.

1902	Jung completes his dissertation in psychiatry, titled "On the Psychology and Pathology of So-Called Occult Phenomena," at the University of Zürich.
1903	Jung marries Emma Rauschenbach, with whom he will have five children.
1904	Following the death of Aunt Gusteli, Emilie and Trudi move to Küsnacht, near Jung's home with Emma.
1906–1908	Trudi works as a warden at the Burghölzli, where she assists Jung with patient observations.
1908	Jung builds a new home in Küsnacht on Lake Zürich, which also becomes the site of his private practice.
1923	Jung purchases land and begins constructing the tower in Bollingen on the upper shore of Lake Zürich.
1923	January 9: Emilie Jung dies.
1933	February 20: Psychologische Club Basel is founded, spearheaded by Dr. Schmid-Guisan and Dr. Kurt von Sury, with strong support from Jung. Dr. von Sury presides over the organization for 18 years. In 1944 it was renamed to Psychological Association Basel.
1934	October 1–6: Jung presents a series of seminars in Basel.
1935	Jung conducts extensive research at the University of Basel, focusing on alchemy.
1935	May 30: Trudi Jung dies, following complications from a minor operation.

1943	October 15: Jung is appointed full professor at the University of Basel, with a teaching assignment in "Medical Psychology with Special Consideration of Psychotherapy." Only a limited number of lectures are delivered.
1944 & 1946	Jung suffers a near-death experience (1944) and heart attack (1946).
1955	November 27: Emma Jung-Rauschenbach dies.
1961	June 6: Jung dies at his home at Seestrasse 228, Küsnacht, following a brief illness.
1975	Simultaneous exhibitions are held at the Kunstmuseum Basel and Helmhaus (Zürich) to commemorate the 100th anniversary of Jung's birth.
1977	Jung's childhood home and the church in Kleinhüningen are recognized as historically valuable and placed under preservation.
1986	The parsonage in Kleinhüningen is renovated and Psychologische Gesellschaft Basel installs a commemorative plaque on its façade to mark Jung's birthplace.
2025	October: An exhibit is held at the Landesmuseum Zürich to commemorate the 150th anniversary of Jung's birth, featuring a range of his personal artifacts.

TOUR 1

CARL'S EARLY YEARS IN KLEINHÜNINGEN

Tour 1 opens the door to Kleinhüningen, a small fishing and farming village with just over 700 inhabitants when the Jung family moved there in 1879. On this tour, you will get to know Carl's childhood environment through glimpses into his family life and interior world.

Taking a leisurely stroll through the village, you will encounter the places where Carl played, attended school, and went to church. You will also learn about his love of drawing, his early encounters with death, and his boyhood secrets. All of this will be situated against the backdrop of Kleinhüningen's transition from a rural village to an industrialized community.

TOUR 1 OVERVIEW

① **BRIDGE OVER THE RIVER WIESE**
Carl's Lifelong Connection to Water

② **ENTRANCE TO DORFSTRASSE**
Village Life

③ **PARSONAGE, DORFSTRASSE 19**
The Interior Sphere:
The House Where Carl Grew Up

④ **FISHER HOUSE AND SILO, SCHULGASSE 16**
Modernity Knocks on Kleinhüningen's Door

⑤ **CEMETERY, FRIEDHOFSGASSE**
Encounters with Death

⑥ **PROTESTANT REFORMED CHURCH, DORFSTRASSE 39**
Faith, Fishermen, Farmers, and Factory Workers

⑦ **PRIMARY AND SECONDARY SCHOOL, BONERGASSE 40 (HISTORIC SITE)**
Where Knights Battle and Slay Dragons

⑧ **BÜRGIN FISHER HOUSE, BONERGASSE 71**

⑨ **CLAVEL ESTATE, BONERGASSE 71**
Juxtaposition of Old and New

⑩ **FORTRESS HÜNINGEN (HISTORIC SITE)**
A Well-Fortified Castle

START
The tour starts at the Kleinhüningen tram stop.

GETTING THERE
Board tram 8 from central Basel (direction Kleinhüningen or Weil am Rhein). Exit at the Kleinhüningen stop.

TOUR LENGTH
Allow three to four hours, including the tram rides to and from Kleinhüningen.

RETURN
Follow Dorfstrasse back toward the River Wiese, reflecting on some of the trades and places described in ❷ **Village Life**. Cross the river and return to the Kleinhüningen tram stop. From there, take tram 8 in the direction of Neuweilerstrasse. For up-to-date tram schedules, visit https://www.sbb.ch/en

 Scan to follow the tour on Google Maps

This Google Map is also accessible at www.kschaeppi.ch/book

23

Map 1
Kleinhüningen in 1882

Note Klybeck Schlössli, Klybeck Insel, and the border between Germany and Switzerland. Across the Rhine, the territory now part of France belonged to the German Empire following the Franco-Prussian War of 1870–1871 and was only ceded back to France in 1920.

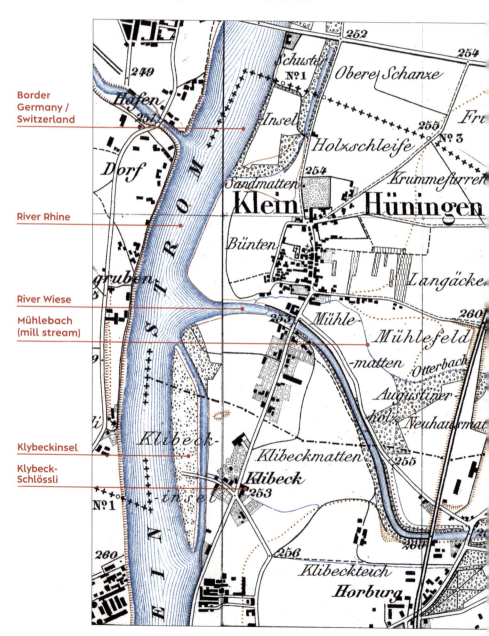

1 BRIDGE OVER THE RIVER WIESE

CARL'S LIFELONG CONNECTION TO WATER

We begin our tour by taking tram 8 from Bahnhof Basel to the Kleinhüningen tram stop. From there, head to the bridge over the Wiese, a tributary of the Rhine, and pause to take in the surroundings.

Jung once reflected on his early life in Basel, remarking, "without water, I thought, nobody could live at all."[1] Indeed, water wove a continuous thread through his life. Born in 1875 in Kesswil on Lake Constance in Canton Thurgau, Carl Gustav Jung, the son of Reformed Protestant pastor Johann Paul Achilles Jung-Preiswerk (1842–1896) and Emilie Jung-Preiswerk (1848–1923, both citizens of Basel), spent his childhood surrounded by lakes, rivers, and streams. When he was just 6 months old, his family moved to Laufen in Canton Zürich near Schaffhausen, at the edge of the Rheinfall (Rhine Falls). Three years later, in 1879 (when Carl was 4 years old), they relocated to Kleinhüningen, a small fishing and farming village nestled along the confluence of the Wiese and the Rhine.

Carl spent much of his childhood near these waterways and local streams, both in Kleinhüningen and, later, in Binningen. As an adult, he built his family home with his wife Emma on the shores of Lake Zürich. Later in life, he constructed his iconic tower in Bollingen, on the edge of Lake Zürich's Obersee (Upper Lake) basin. At age 85, he died in his bedroom on Seestrasse, overlooking the same lake.

In 1887, when the Jung-Preiswerk family arrived in Kleinhüningen, the Rhine at this location bordered Germany. Across the Rhine lay Alsace, which, following the Franco-Prussian War (1870–1871), had been part of the German Empire for eight years. It would only return to France after World War I, transforming the region once again into the border triangle of Switzerland, Germany, and France.[2] The Rhine originates in the Alps of Canton Graubünden, meanders through Lake Constance,

TOUR 1

and forms the border between Switzerland and Germany before flowing through Basel. Beyond Basel, it marks the border between France and Germany before continuing through the Netherlands to empty into the North Sea.

Although the Wiese is now tame, in the late 19th century, it was torrential and unpredictable. When the Jung-Preiswerk family took up residence in the parsonage near the mouth of the Wiese on the east bank of the mighty Rhine, they lived behind the Bünten—a low-lying floodplain prone to seasonal inundation. During Carl's childhood, the Wiese was a wild river, teeming with fish. The silt carried from its source in the Feldberg region of the Black Forest enriched the surrounding flats, providing fertile soil for fruit trees, vegetable gardens, and grazing livestock. Together with the plentiful fish, these natural resources sustained Kleinhüningen's identity as a farming and fishing village.

When Carl was 7 years old, in 1882, the Wiese flooded with such force that it destroyed the oldest bridge over the river.[3] In *Memories, Dreams, Reflections* (*MDR*), Jung recalled:

> And once there was a great flood the river Wiese, which flowed through the village, had broken its dam, and in its upper reaches a bridge had collapsed. Fourteen people drowned and were carried down by the yellow flood water to the Rhine. When the water retreated, some of the corpses got stuck in the sand. When I was told about it, there was no holding me. I actually found the body of a middle-aged man, in a black frock coat; apparently, he had just come from church. He lay half covered by sand, his arm over his eyes.[4]

1 View North from the River Wiese toward Dorfstrasse (c. 1900)
From near to far on the right: Sawmill Herbst, followed by Carpentry Greiner with its distinctive stepped tower. On the left: Restaurant Schiff, the Horse-Coach Transport Glockner, the parsonage wall, and Restaurant Krone.

2   Village Idyll on the Kronenplatz (c. 1890–1894)
Under the village linden tree in front of the post office, all of Kleinhüningen gathered, from the village youth to the cattle. This scene depicts Dorfstrasse around 1890–1894, with the parsonage located just out of frame to the left.

② ENTRANCE TO DORFSTRASSE

VILLAGE LIFE

Finish crossing the bridge and continue through the roundabout along Dorfstrasse, Kleinhüningen's main street. On the corner of Hochbergerstrasse 134 and Dorfstrasse stands Restaurant Schiff, with murals painted by the Swiss artist Burkhard Mangold around 1923. These colorful depictions of fishing activities—added long after Carl left the village—celebrate Kleinhüningen's heritage as a fishing village and its guild of fishermen.

Imagine the small fishing and farming community in the late 19th century, with only 740 inhabitants. Dorfstrasse (Village Street), known then as Dorfweg (Village Way), was the village's main thoroughfare. Unlike today, the road was unpaved, and the clatter of horse hooves could often be heard emanating from the Fuhrhalterei Glockner (horse-coach transport) located next to the present-day Restaurant Schiff. Continue along Dorfstrasse, noting the bend as the roadway rolls away from the Wiese. On the left, at the intersection with Pfarrgasse (Parsonage Alley), stands the parsonage at 19 Dorfstrasse, where the Jung-Preiswerk family lived. Just before reaching the high garden gate at the back of the house, look for a small gully. This is the remnant of the *Mühlebach* (mill stream)—a manmade waterway that once powered the mill, which no longer exists (originally situated diagonally on the opposite side of Dorfstrasse). The stream drew its waters from the Wiese.

Let us imagine the atmosphere of Kleinhüningen in 1879. This small village, or *Dorf,* was primarily inhabited by workers, including a mix of tradespeople, artisans, and laborers. Among them were butchers, carpenters, fishermen, farmers, millers, restaurateurs, tailors, weavers, washerwomen, and, of course, a pastor.

A large, shade-giving linden tree stood across from the parsonage entrance, and behind the tree was the town's pump well and fountain. It is somewhat unusual that the church and parsonage were not located

Map 2
Trades and Places
Along Young Carl's Dorfstrasse

side by side. Instead, the village center, closer to the parsonage than to the church, naturally evolved around the fountain and well, which became a central meeting place for *"tout Kleinhüningen*, from the village youth to the cattle."[5] To the left of the linden tree was the post and telegraph office, and to the right stood the fountain and an advertising pillar. Also on the right, but nearer to the parsonage than to the tree, was Sawmill Herbst, powered by the *Mühlebach*. This large sawmill with a stepped roof and tower featured numerous workshops. Adjacent to it was Autino, a general grocery store, and across the road stood Carpentry Greiner.

Further along Dorfstrasse, the Reformed Church at Dorfstrasse 39 anchored this social hub. Between the parsonage and just beyond the church were three restaurants: Die Krone, Dorfstrasse 27, first mentioned in 1689, was demolished in 1960 to make way for the Kronenplatz playground at Pfarrgasse; Restaurant Turnerstübli (Gymnasts' Parlor Restaurant) at Dorfstrasse 37 offered a cozy gathering spot for food and drinks; and Gasthaus Drei Könige (Guesthouse of the Three Kings) at Dorfstasse 46, located just past the church. A popular Sunday excursion for families from Basel was a visit to Kleinhüningen to enjoy a meal of fresh fish—such as *salmon à la bâloise* (Basler-style salmon), blue trout, or baked *nasen* (nosegill)—paired with a regional white wine from Baden.

Village life was visceral and hands-on. Carl grew up in daily contact with tradespeople earning their livelihoods through manual labor. Along Dorfstrasse, the butcher (Dorfstrasse 31) and the dairy (Dorfstrasse 33) served the community between Gasthaus Krone and the church. Other road names reflected local trades and products, such as Schneidergasse (Tailor Alley; now Friedhofsgasse (Cemetery Alley)), Schulgasse (School Alley), Krautgasse (Herb Alley), Schäfergasse (Shepherd Alley), Rebgasse (Vineyard Alley), and Salmengasse (Salmon Alley).

3 (above) Kleinhüningen Town Square
A view along Dorfstrasse looking south toward the Wiese. On the left are the town's water pump, a linden tree, and a pillar for public notices. Farther down, behind the trees, stand Autino general grocery store and the stepped tower of Sawmill Herbst. On the right is the parsonage, situated just before Dorfstrasse curves toward the river.

4 (below) Hospitality in Kleinhüningen
Looking north along Dorfstrasse from the parsonage, one of the town's three restaurants, Gasthaus zu den Drei Königen, appears on the left. Just beyond the restaurant is an old schoolhouse (not attended by the Jung-Preiswerk children), which blocks the view of the church further down the road.

Until the 1930s, fishing was the most common profession. In 1640, in a move to secure fishing rights on the Rhine, Basel bought Kleinhüningen at the price of 3,500 Reichstaler from the Margraviate of Baden.

Fishing families in Kleinhüningen, despite the abundance of fish before 1930, endured grueling work. In order to survive, they needed to catch 100 kilograms of fish per week to sell at markets and to local restaurants. Common fish at the mouth of the Wiese were salmon, barbel, alet, carp, eel, tench, and bream. However, nosegill was most prolific.[6]

Washerwomen pushed wheelbarrows of laundry through the streets, serving wealthy Basel families who preferred their linens to be washed in either the Wiese or the Bachrain (a river nearer to the border), rather than the Rhine, as the lime in the water left fabrics smoother to the touch.

In later years, as Jung rose in social status, he retained great respect and appreciation for tradespeople and artisans. He connected easily with them, perhaps inspired by his childhood observations of their work. His own pursuits in wood carving and stone sculpting may have been outgrowths of his early experiences.

On the return leg of the tour, you will have the opportunity to explore some of these sites in greater detail. For now, let us turn our attention to Carl's years at the parsonage.

KLEIN-HÜNINGEN

5 Fishermen Fishing at the "Lachsweid" (c. 1918)
Fishermen casting a net from a *Weidling* at the so-called "Lachsweid" (Salmon Meadow), where the Wiese and Rhine meet. Regularly in May, for three to four days, the river would be swarmed with nosegill fish.

6 Fishermen's Working Area at the Mouth of the Wiese (1910)
Fishing nets hung to dry, with two men in a *Weidling*. Across the Rhein is the tower of the Evangelical Church, Hüningen.

7 Rhine Ferry in Kleinhüningen
Passengers standing aboard the ferry and onlookers on shore. Note there are no seats on the ferry!

8 Washer Women on the Wiese Wash Platform
The foremost woman strikes a piece of laundry against a *Waschbank* (wooden plank).

9   Kleinhüningen Fishermen Holding Their Catch (c. 1918)
On average, a fish weighed 9 kilograms.

10 Young Carl Looking Out from an Upstairs Window of the Parsonage (c. 1895)

③ PARSONAGE, DORFSTRASSE 19

THE INTERIOR SPHERE: THE HOUSE WHERE CARL GREW UP

Secrets in the House and Garden

When Carl's father, Paul Jung-Preiswerk (1842–1896), became pastor of the Reformed Church in Kleinhüningen, a benefit of the position was residency in the handsome two-story house with a large, walled garden.[7] Built in 1754 as a farmhouse (most likely as a tenant building of a long-established Basler family), it first served as a parsonage in 1808 and partly continues in this capacity today.[8] Neighboring the large parsonage were modest fisher houses,[9] while the back of the house, with its enclosed balcony, looked toward the Rhine. (However, it was set back far enough to be secure from overflow and potential flooding—also from the Wiese.) Carl lived in the parsonage for sixteen years, between the ages of 4 and 20. Today, a plaque on the large façade reads: "Carl Gustav Jung, 1875–1961, founder of analytical psychology, lived in this house from 1879 to 1896."

The exterior of the house remains largely unchanged since 1879, when the family moved in. At that time, a large wooden door opened onto Dorfstrasse. Behind the garden wall, large deciduous trees stood (and still stand), likely shading a spacious garden replete with fruit trees, shrubs, and flowers. The property also included a stall and barn—remnants from the previous owners, the Iselin family—which have since been converted into workspaces. From the upper floors, the Jung family would have enjoyed unobstructed views of the Rhine over the Bünten. While the house largely retains its historical character, two windows on the north face and a winter garden on the balcony have been added. The interior has also been renovated to meet contemporary standards for rental properties.

37   TOUR 1

11 (above) Parsonage, Dorfstrasse 19
Northeast side of the parsonage.

12 (below) Parsonage Garden

During Carl's childhood, while his mother tended to the flowers in the garden, he engaged in unconscious rituals,[10] which he later recalled in *MDR:* "In our garden, there was an old wall built of large blocks of stone, the interstices of which made interesting caves. I used to tend a little fire in one of these caves with other children helping me." Carl also had a "secret relationship" with a particular stone embedded in the garden wall that slightly jutted out.[11] Later in life, he identified these instinctual actions and rituals as archetypal patterns expressing deeper human needs and desires.

In *MDR*, Jung also described another ritual from this time:

> I will tell you a story about an experience of my own when I was quite a little boy, before I went to school. Every Sunday I was allowed to spend the morning with an old aunt who had a quaint old room with beautiful engravings on the wall. I always looked at these with intense interest. One was a picture of a vicarage in the country, and the parson was coming out in his robes to go to the Sunday service; he was just shutting the door and about to go down the steps to the street. I looked at him very hard because he was such an interesting old chap, and once I discovered that he began to walk down the stairs. I called to my aunt: "He is walking!" Of course, she said it was impossible. "But I have seen him, sure enough he is walking down the stairs!" And every Sunday thereafter, that was my great pleasure—to stare at the old parson till he walked down the steps.[12]

Jung devoted three pages of *MDR* to describing a ritual he performed at the parsonage, which he described as the "climax and the conclusion of my childhood."[13] In this ritual, Carl carved the end of a ruler into a small manikin, about 2 inches long, dressing it in a frock coat, top hat, and shiny black boots. Once completed, he inked the manikin black and placed it in his pencil case alongside a smooth, blackish stone that he had painted with watercolors to serve as its "company." He then took the pencil case to the attic, where he had once hidden after

13 (left) *Atmavictu* (1920)
Sculpture in the garden of the C.G. Jung House Museum in Küsnacht, made of shell-limestone.

14 (right) *David with the Head of Goliath* (1600s)
Reproduction of an oil-on-canvas painting by Guido Reni once displayed in the dining room of the parsonage, now located in the dining room of the C.G. Jung House Museum in Küsnacht.

15 (far right) *Basel Landscape* (1835)
Painting by Sebastian Gutzwiller (1798-1872).

seeing a man in town wearing a black frock, whom he suspected to be a Jesuit. This same attic was connected to Carl's memory of witnessing a drowned corpse in a black frock after a flooding incident. Even his father wore a black robe when performing church services. The manikin, causing Carl anxiety and perhaps awe, may have represented a shadow for Carl, hidden twice—once within the pencil case and a second time on a beam in the attic. Carl seemingly took comfort in this secret and the associated ritual. The manikin, itself, has never been recovered. The current pastor of the parsonage explained that, even if the manikin were still in the attic, the walls have long been covered with wood paneling, and even prior to this renovation, she personally washed each beam and found no trace of a pencil case or manikin.[14] Later in life, Jung identified the manikin as an archetypal image corresponding to Telesphorus, the cloaked god found on monuments to Asclepius, the Greek god of healing. He later (1920) commissioned a sculptor to carve a stone figure based on his more recently carved wood figure (1919) that he described as unconsciously based on this childhood experience. He named the sculpture *Atmavictu*, meaning "breath of life." This stone figure currently resides in the garden at the C.G. Jung House Museum on Seestrasse in Küsnacht.[15]

In *MDR,* Jung recalled a print of Reni's *David with the Head of Goliath* that hung in the dining room of the parsonage, describing it as "a mirror copy from the workshop of Guido Reni; the original hangs in the Louvre."[16] In the parlor, however, Carl was particularly drawn to another painting, titled *Basel Landscape.* Jung reflected, "Often I would steal into that dark, sequestered room and sit for hours in front of the pictures, gazing at all that beauty. It was the only beautiful thing I knew."[17] Reading this, one wonders whether beauty was scarce in young Carl's surroundings, and whether the Protestant Reformation's Bildersturm (Picture Storm of 1528) had stripped public spaces of their icons, leaving only formal spaces like parlors as rare refuges where beauty and art could still be enjoyed.

Basel Landscape offers a unique perspective, depicting a view from an attic window. The painting presents a vista toward the hills to the south of Basel, as viewed from the home of Carl's grandfather, Karl Jung, at Elisabethenstrasse 9. Painted in the early 19th century by Alsatian artist Sebastian Gutzwiller, the work is presumed to have been commissioned by Karl and later gifted to his son, Paul, who ultimately passed it on to Jung. In the painting, the steep nose of the Gempenstollen is recognizable, along with both towers of Basel Münster.[18]

Parents

Carl's mother, Emilie, came from a poor branch of the prestigious and long-established Preiswerk family, who had formed part of Basel's patrician elite for more than 500 years. When Carl was just 3 years old, and thus still living in Laufen, his mother left the family several times for extended stays at a rest home near Basel.[19] In *MDR,* Jung wrote:

> *My illness in 1878 must have been connected with a temporary separation of my parents. My mother spent several months in a hospital in Basel, and presumably her illness had something to do with the difficulty in the marriage. An aunt of mine, who was a spinster and some twenty years older than my mother, took care of me. I was deeply troubled by my mother's being away. From then on, I always felt mistrustful when the word "love" was spoken. The feeling I associated with "women" was for a long time that of innate unreliability. "Father," on the other hand, meant reliability and—powerlessness. That is the handicap I started off with.*

16 Carl's Parents, Emilie and Paul
(1876)

17 Johanna Gertrude "Trudi" Jung,
Estimated 6–8 Years Old (1890–1892)

Before Carl was born, Emilie had two miscarriages and suffered the loss of a newborn son, Paul. During Emilie's absences, Carl was cared for by a maid, his unmarried Aunt Gusteli (Auguste "Gusteli" Preiswerk, 20 years older than Emilie), and a "younger girl" who would later become his mother-in-law, Bertha Rauschenbach.[20] Aunt Gusteli managed the household and played a significant role in Carl's life. On the back of a photograph, it is briefly noted, "Emilie, suffered from depressions, then Aunt Gusteli helped out."[21] Aunt Gusteli became a second mother figure to Carl during his formative years.[22] She nurtured his curiosity, pointing out the evening alpenglow in the mountains (a memory Jung would later describe as one of his earliest and most vivid) and taking him to the museum on Augustinergasse (see Tour 2). However, despite the care Carl received from his aunt, he experienced his mother's absences as deeply troubling.

Looking back on this time as an adult, Jung described his relationships with both parents as complicated and often ambivalent, and he recalled struggling to reconcile their outward behaviors and attitudes with what he suspected were their more private, underlying concerns. Jung later attributed his mother's illness to hysteria: "Also, my parents' marriage was not harmonious. My mother was sometimes hysterical. She lived in a fantasy world and had every possible medical condition. I always had the feeling that these illnesses were not real. After my father's death she was better. ... The traces of hysteria in my mother were so repulsive to me." He described his mother's hospitalization in similar terms: "At that time, my mother was in hospital in Basel for some months. Presumably with hysteria due to disappointment with her husband, whose heroic period had expired with his final exams."[23]

18 Carl's Extended Family (1891)
Uncle Rudolf, Aunt Célestine, and 15 cousins of the Preiswerk-Allenspach Family at Christmas. Uncle Rudolf was the fifth child of Antistes Samuel Preiswerk.

Top row (left to right): Emilie, Friedrich, Clara, Bertha, Wilhelm, and Louise.
Lower row (left to right): Valerie, Rudolf, Mathilde, Ottilie, Célestine with baby Sophie, Rudolf with Esther, Célestine, Ernst, and Helene (Jung's Medium).
(See also Table 11: Carl's Close Cousins)

While Carl considered Emilie a good mother, he also felt that her true personality remained hidden. By this, he was likely referring to her dark, uncanny side—the aspect of her that appeared with nightfall. Since her youth, Emilie had believed she possessed mediumistic powers and could communicate with the dead.

During his mother's illness, Carl developed eczema—an ailment that, later in life, he attributed to this "temporary separation" from his mother during her stays at the rest home. At the age of 7, he became "sick with pseudo-croup accompanied by choking fits." He later related these symptoms to the atmosphere at home, which "was beginning to be unbreathable" as a consequence of the growing unhappiness in his parents' marriage.[24]

When Carl was 9 years old, his sister Gertrude "Trudi" was born. In *MDR,* Jung reflected on his mother's pregnancy: "I had thought nothing of [her] lying in bed more frequently than usual, for I considered her taking to her bed an inexcusable weakness in any case." Thus, Carl was taken utterly by surprise when his mother gave birth to a baby girl. However, already at this young age, he had developed a means of self-healing:

> *If things became too bad I would think of my secret treasure in the attic, and that helped me regain my poise. For in my forlorn state I remembered that I was also the "Other," the person who possessed that inviolable secret, the black stone and the little man in frock coat and top hat.*[25]

This was his valuable secret: "I had a vague sense of relationship between the 'soul-stone' and the stone which was also myself."

When he was 9 or 10 years old (1884–1885), Carl became deeply troubled by the idea that his father, a pastor, did not truly "know" God. Rather, he perceived his father's religious practice as mechanical and devoid of spiritual meaning, and saw him as trapped in the performance of meaningless rituals.

Friend, Sister, Cousins

The childhood Jung described in *MDR* is so solitary and introspective that it is almost a surprise to discover the presence of a childhood friend, a sister, and an abundance of cousins (64, to be precise).

Carl's earliest friend was Albert Oeri, a boy his age whose family was acquainted with the Jung-Preiswerks. Their fathers had been old school friends, which naturally brought Carl and Albert together to play in Laufen, where Carl lived as a young child. Albert, born in Schaffhausen and raised with several siblings, recalled Carl as a boy who did not pay the slightest attention to him, describing him as an "asocial monster."[26] At the time, Carl was an only child, with little opportunity to develop the kind of social or playing skills that Albert, surrounded by siblings, naturally possessed. However, the Oeri family occasionally visited the parsonage in Kleinhüningen on Sunday afternoons, and a friendship developed between the two boys. Interestingly, Albert's father was Johann Jakob Oeri, Carl's teacher at the Gymnasium.

What do we know about Carl's sister Trudi? In *MDR,* Jung reflected, "At bottom she was always a stranger to me, but I had great respect for her." He described her as composed, sensitive, and possessing a remarkable personality, adding that he admired her attitude. Given their nine-year age difference, it is no wonder that Carl found her a stranger. While Trudi attended the same primary and secondary school as Carl in Kleinhüningen, her courses focused on practical skills specified for girls, such as cooking, sewing, mending, and knitting. By this time, Carl had already left for the Gymnasium in Basel.

Although Carl had many cousins, the ones he interacted with most were close in age—namely Louise "Luggy," Helene "Helly," and Wilhelm from the Preiswerk-Allenspach family, which included a remarkable 15 children! The family lived in a baroque country house at Margarethenstrasse 19, near the new main train station in Basel.

This cousin connection was particularly strong because Carl's mother was good friends with her sister-in-law of almost the same age, Carl's Aunt Célestine Preiswerk-Allenspach. Célestine's husband, Carl's Uncle

19 Carl in a *Weidling* (flat-bottomed boat) with friends
Taken on the so-called Old Rhine or Haltingermoos, near Basel.

Rudolf Preiswerk-Allenspach, attended Carl's confirmation, offering proof of the family bond. These relationships provided Carl with ample opportunities to play with Wilhelm, who was one year younger. Together, they roamed the meadows of the estate, affectionately called "d'Margarete" in Swiss German. This area, along with the walled garden of the parsonage in Kleinhüningen and the Bünten behind Carl's home, served as their "children's paradise." Over time, Carl developed an attraction to Luggy, who was one year his senior and his so-called *Jugendschatz* (childhood crush). Meanwhile, Helly, another cousin, grew fond of Carl. The dynamics of Carl's relationship with Helly are discussed in greater depth in Tour 4.

The conflicts Carl experienced with classmates during his childhood and early adolescence eventually softened into friendlier rivalries. One activity that fostered camaraderie among Carl and his peers was boating, using *Weidling* boats. In shallower waters, poles were used to push the boats along the riverbank, while oars were used in deeper waters. Before there were bridges, *Weidling* boats were used to traverse the Rhine. Sometimes, the young men would fish from the boats, throwing nets off the side and later hauling them back in with a catch of fish. However, the boats were also used for leisure, as seen in the photograph of Carl and his friends on the so-called Old Rhine or the Haltingermoos. Rhein-Club Basel, founded in 1883, now fosters this tradition as a local sport.

When Carl was 18 years old, he experienced a troubling incident that, many years later, he would reference in a letter to Freud: an unwanted sexual advance by a family friend—a man he admired and respected as a fatherly figure. There is a further account that substantiates this. It was reported that the incident influenced him to resist being placed in subordinate roles, and when Freud later wanted to designate Jung as his successor, Jung reportedly responded with: "No, no, no, I don't want to belong to anybody. I don't want to be embraced."[27]

4 FISHER HOUSE AND SILO, SCHULGASSE 16

MODERNITY KNOCKS ON KLEINHÜNINGEN'S DOOR

When the Jung-Preiswerk family moved to Kleinhüningen in 1879, industrialization and population growth had already begun to transform the village. From the southern Klybeck quarter, industries and factories were starting to spread, encroaching upon Kleinhüningen's pastoral character. To the east of the village, dye works were multiplying along the banks of the Wiese, and the population soon tripled as workers were drawn to the area to fill positions in these and other factories. However, this rapid growth came at a steep cost. Air, water, and ground pollution skyrocketed, creating immense challenges for the village's infrastructure and way of life. The tranquil fishing and farming community that had long defined Kleinhüningen began to give way to an industrialized landscape with accompanying hardships.

Industrial Transformation
Crossing Kronenplatz and walking down Schulgasse (School Alley, though not the location of Carl's primary school), you will encounter a stark example of Kleinhüningen's transformation. The Rhine, once visible from this point, is now hidden by a massive silo constructed in 1923 to serve the new harbor. The silo creates a dead end and towers over one of only three remaining fisher houses from Carl's time, built in 1825. This humble cottage, now overshadowed by the silo, captures a pivotal moment in the village's history. During Carl's childhood, fishing families made their living from the Rhine, and historical photographs often show nets left to dry outside their homes. However, industrial development cut these families off—literally and figuratively—from their traditional livelihood. As factories grew, they were forced to adapt, and many shifted to work as laborers in the burgeoning industries. The fishermen's cottages were modest and lacked modern amenities such as warm water, central heating, toilets, and baths. To address this, a public bathhouse was built on the Wiese.

20 (left above) Fisher House, Schulgasse 16
This typical fisher house remains at its original site.

21 (left below) Fisher House, Friedhofsgasse 10
Built in continuity with the church wall.

22 (right) The Silo Insignia: Kleinhüningen Coat of Arms
A detail revealing the village's storied origins. This grain silo and the Bernoulli building beside it were the first high-rises in Basel.

Insignia on the Silo

Take another look at the grain silo to see the Kleinhüningen coat of arms. The insignia features Attila, King of the Huns, draped in a red cape and standing in front of a nomad tent. According to local legend, Attila once camped at the mouth of the Wiese and founded Kleinhüningen, giving the village its name. However, more recent research challenges this story, suggesting that the Huns were likely confused with invaders from Hungary (German: Ungarn), who plundered the region in 917. This reinterpretation aligns with the etymology of Hüningen, which derives from *Hun/Huno* and the suffix *-ingen,* meaning "belonging to a family or group." Thus, the name can be translated as "the clan of Huno."[28]

The unpaved path between the first fisher house and the silo leads to what was previously a cemetery when the Jung-Preiswerks arrived. Nearby stands the second of the three surviving fisher houses: a single-story cottage built in 1773, situated along the wall bordering the church at Friedhofsgasse 10. From here, enter the church courtyard through the side entry.

23 A Somber Funeral Procession on Kleinhüningerstrasse (1918)
Only a few villagers could afford such a funeral with the row of *Droschken* (carriages). During the approximately four months of mourning, entertainment was avoided.

5 CEMETERY, FRIEDHOFSGASSE

ENCOUNTERS WITH DEATH

Death and loss were pervasive in Carl's early life, particularly within his family. As described above, his mother, Emilie, endured significant losses, including two miscarriages and the death of an infant born before Carl. Similarly, Carl's father, Paul, experienced the loss of three brothers: Rudolf and Fritz succumbed to tuberculosis while they were medical students in their early 20s, and Max passed away when Carl was only 13.

For Carl, encounters with death were part of everyday life. As a child, he was fascinated by the corpses of drowned townspeople he discovered in Laufen and Kleinhüningen, as well as a pig slaughter he witnessed years later ("To the horror of my mother, I watched the whole procedure").[29] While death is an ever-present feature of life, we might ask how being a pastor's son and growing up in this particular time and place influenced Carl's unique perception of it.

From Carl's home, it was only a 5-minute walk to the church and cemetery called Gottesacker (God's Field). The cemetery was contained within the church courtyard, partially surrounded by a roofed wall with houses bordering the outer wall. In the 19th century, death was a more intimate and visible part of daily life. People typically died at home, rather than in a hospital, as life expectancy was shorter and mortality rates among the young were higher. With limited medical treatments available, death often came quickly, and its rituals were woven into the fabric of community life. After a person's death, their body would be washed and prepared in the family home, often with great care and dignity. Relatives, neighbors, and friends would visit the bereaved to express their condolences, frequently bringing flowers or wreaths.

Funerals in Kleinhüningen were conducted by Carl's father, Paul. At these proceedings, as on Sundays, Paul would wear his ceremonial long black robe, often referred to by Carl as a frock. The rites would begin at the deceased's home, where Paul would collect the coffin and lead the funeral procession to the church. After performing the funeral service there, he would then lead the mourners in another procession to the cemetery, where the body would be buried. These rites were usually followed by a reception, at which mourners would share a light meal or luncheon. Through his father's visible role in these events, Carl would have been acutely aware of deaths in his community and their impact on the public sphere.[30]

In 1882, another unusual task fell to Paul, reflecting the challenges posed by the village's rapid growth and industrialization. By this time, the Jung-Preiswerk family had been in Kleinhüningen for three years, and Carl was 7 years old. The cemetery behind the Reformed church, established in 1849, had become severely overcrowded. Coffins were stacked in two layers, with graves dug so shallowly that the fetid stench of putrefying bodies became a serious problem. Paul was tasked with presiding over what we might imagine was a very grim exhumation of the cemetery and the relocation of its remains to a new burial ground closer to the German border, behind the Hiltalingerbrücke.[31] Ten years later, in 1892, Schneidergasse, the road leading to the cemetery, was renamed Friedhofgasse (Cemetery Alley). Over a century later, in 2022, the site of the old cemetery underwent a "soft" renovation, transforming the small, rather neglected space into a small park. While this offered a small gesture of acknowledgment for the displaced remains, in 1931, the government decided that the old cemeteries in Kannenfeld, Wolf, Horburg, and Kleinhüningen would be shut down due to the opening of the new forest cemetery Hörnli in 1932. Therefore, the bodies that had already been relocated were *again*, in 1931, given a chance for relocation upon request, before storage tanks were placed on the cemetery site at the end of 1951. Only four requests to relocate the remains of ancestors were received. One of these requests came from Jung, with instructions to relocate his father's remains.[32]

Carl had one more deeply personal death to navigate as the pastor's son: that of his own father, Paul. After many years of declining health, Paul became bedridden in 1895. Carl, just 20 years old at the time, cared for his father, whom he later described as having wasted away

24 Jung Family Portrait Shortly Before Paul's Death (1893)
Taken in the parsonage garden. Paul and Emilie Jung-Preiswerk are pictured with Carl (age 18), Trudi (age 9), and their little dachshund.

into a "heap of bones."[33] Paul died in 1896, likely of pancreatic cancer, when Carl was in his second year of university studies.[34] His death left the family destitute. Paul was buried in the church courtyard in Kleinhüningen. However, years later, his remains were transferred to the family grave in Küsnacht, where Emilie, Carl, and Trudi would later be buried.[35] Six weeks after his father's death, Carl had a vivid dream in which his father appeared to him, saying he was coming home. This dream had a profound impact on Carl's understanding of death, and life after death.[36]

Carl's contemplation of mortality continued throughout his life and appeared prominently in his later writings. In *MDR,* Jung reflected that an aging person "ought to have a myth about death, for reason shows him nothing but the dark pit into which he is descending."[37] In 1916, while in his 40s, Jung wrote "Seven Sermons to the Dead" (*Septem Sermones ad mortuos*)—a gnostic text that he initially distributed only privately, among friends. This work, which later became a section ("Scrutinies") of *The Red Book,* is considered a summative revelation of Jung's spiritual insights.[38] Reflecting on this work, Jung commented: "From that time on, the dead have become ever more distinct for me as the voices of the unanswered, unresolved and unredeemed."[39]

Tuberculosis: Most Prominent Cause of Death

At the turn of the century, tuberculosis (TB) was the leading cause of death, making hygiene a critical public concern. The rapid urbanization and overcrowding that accompanied industrialization contributed significantly to the spread of this disease. By 1876, Swiss statistics attributed one in every five deaths to TB, underlining its devastating impact on society. As mentioned above, this illness struck Carl's family, as well. His uncles Rudolf (1836-1857) and Max (1837-1888) both succumbed to TB, as did his cousin Helly (1881-1911) at the age of 30. Although the causal bacteria was discovered in 1882, effective treatment only became available in 1943 with the introduction of the antibiotic streptomycin. The connection between TB and poor living standards was recognized in the late 19th century, spurring social reforms. Efforts were made to improve public health, enforce Sunday rest, and establish convalescent homes, including sanatoriums for children (such as the one in nearby Langenbruck). However, access to fresh, alpine air—often associated with places such as Davos—was typically limited to the wealthy, leaving many of the working class unable to access the same level of restorative care.[40]

25 Protestant Reformed Church (1937)
This historic photograph, taken years after Paul Jung-Preiswerk's death, shows renovations described on the plaque at the church entrance: "Built in 1710 by master builder Peter Racine in a simple baroque style to replace a medieval predecessor destroyed in the Thirty Years' War (1618–1648). Protestant hall church with a flat, west porch and polygonal tower choir. Restored in 1847 by Amadeus Merian. 1910 raising of the bell tower by four meters, bells renewed at that time."

26 Protestant Reformed Church
The plaque at the church entry reads: "[There were] comprehensive renovations inside and outside in 1975 and 2010."

6 PROTESTANT REFORMED CHURCH, DORFSTRASSE 39

FAITH, FISHERMEN, FARMERS, AND FACTORY WORKERS

Church and Congregation

As Kleinhüningen transformed from a rural village to an industrialized factory town, its congregation reflected this transformation. On Sundays, farmers, fishermen, factory workers, and tradespeople would make their way to the church. Historically, the congregation had a burly reputation. Following the destruction of the original church during the Thirty Years' War (1618–1648), villagers were reassigned to St. Theodor's Church in Basel. However, the unruliness of the farmers and fishermen traveling to St. Theodor's prompted Basel authorities to construct a new church in Kleinhüningen in 1710.[41]

The current church may be built on the ruins of a medieval church, likely consecrated to Saint Margaret before being destroyed in the Thirty Years' War, though this has not been archeologically verified. Today, the church remains the only Baroque-style church in Basel dating from the post-Reformation period. Parts of Kleinhüningen and its church were damaged again during the Napoleonic Wars in 1814, shortly before Napoleon's defeat at Waterloo in 1815.[42] The fortress across the Rhine was dismantled stone by stone in 1815, but not before the bombardments and fires caused extensive damage to the church's western façade, organ, and altar.[43] When the church was rebuilt, four cannonballs were left embedded in the north wall (left of the main entrance, high on the wall) as a reminder of the damage.

Presently, the church features large windows that allow natural light to flood the white, minimalist interior. There is a pulpit and organ, but no iconic imagery, in keeping with the Reformed Protestant tradition. Earlier photographs show dark pews and a few paintings, but the simplicity of the space remains intact. The church tower, topped with an eight-cornered onion-shaped cap, was heightened by 4 meters in 1910

27 Protestant Reformed (Evangelical) Church Interior
View of the church interior prior to modern renovations, possibly showing the pulpit as it appeared during Paul Jung-Preiswerk's tenure as pastor.

28 Protestant Reformed (Evangelical) Church Interior

29 Gravestone Commemorating Paul Jung-Preiswerk
Located in the church courtyard, the inscription reads: *Dem Andenken an Paul Jung Preiswerk | Pfarrer in Kleinhüningen von 1879–1896* ("In Memory of Paul Jung Preiswerk | Pastor in Kleinhüningen from 1879–1896").

to accommodate a new bell. Outside, the church courtyard features a round trough fountain adorned with relief images of men and women, depicting fishermen and farmers at work. This Jubilee Fountain was erected in 1940 to honor the original inhabitants of Kleinhüningen and commemorate 300 years of belonging to Canton Basel-Stadt.[44] Since 1945, both the church and the parsonage have been protected as historical monuments.

The church is surrounded by a wall. Within its courtyard, shaded by trees and blanketed with ivy, stands a simple, solitary gravestone commemorating Paul Jung-Preiswerk (visible from the path on your right as you exit).

Ritual and Service:
Pastor Paul Wore a Black Robe and Many Hats

In May 1892, just three years after the Jung-Preiswerk family arrived in Kleinhüningen, Paul was elected as a member of the synod. In the Protestant Church, the synod is a local assembly of elected congregational representatives (both clergy and laity) that holds legal authority to govern matters of doctrine, church order, discipline, and administration.[45] Paul's responsibilities extended well beyond his role as pastor. That same year, he was appointed president of the school commission, tasked with overseeing primary education and hiring village schoolteachers.[46] Additionally, he was confirmed for another term as chaplain at Friedmatt Asylum in Basel (now the site of the University Psychiatric Clinics Basel).[47] On a local level, Paul participated in council meetings and played a vital role in community life. As pastor, his duties included leading Sunday services, officiating marriages and funerals, counseling members of the congregation, and providing religious instruction to the youth—including his son, Carl. Among his students were also the "Schoren Girls," whose connection to the church is explored further in Tour 3. During Sunday services, we can imagine young Carl sitting with his mother in the front row of pews.

30 Carl at Age 6 (November 18, 1881)
At this age, Carl began primary school and started receiving Latin instruction from his father.

Carl the Pastor's Son

At age 16, Carl—also called "Pastor's son Carl"—was confirmed by his father, Paul, in the church at Kleinhüningen. Sitting beside him during the ceremony was his uncle, Rudolf Preiswerk-Allenspach, who was also a synod member. According to the large confirmation register,[48] Carl was confirmed on Good Friday, March 27, 1891, alongside seven boys and five girls, all born in 1875. The register also lists the professions of the fathers of the children being confirmed, offering a glimpse into the social fabric of Carl's peers. Occupations included a blacksmith, factory worker, gardener, mechanic, day laborer, swimming instructor, town president, cobbler, and church warden, and of course, a pastor. For one girl whose father had passed away, her mother, listed as a washerwoman, represented the family.[49] This diverse mix of trades highlights the working-class composition of Kleinhüningen during Carl's formative years.

7 PRIMARY AND SECONDARY SCHOOL, BONERGASSE 30
(HISTORIC SITE)

WHERE KNIGHTS BATTLE AND SLAY DRAGONS

At the age of 6 (1880–1881), Carl attended the "Primary and Secondary School for Boys and Girls," located just around the corner from the church. The street name of the school changed three times: from Krautgasse 1 in 1837 to Hinterer Dorfweg, and later to Bonergasse in 1860 (officially recognized as such in 1896).[50] This representative public school, built in 1874 to 1875—just four years before the Jung-Preiswerk family arrived—was a direct result of the introduction of universal, free, and compulsory schooling, marking education as a new democratic fundamental right. From 1873 to the end of the 19th century, eighteen such public school buildings were constructed in the Canton of Basel-Stadt. Carl's school was demolished in 1966 and replaced by the present-day primary school with a swimming pool.

In his day, Carl's school was a three-story building with a neoclassical façade, round entrance, and twelve classrooms in which 54 students were taught.[51] Although girls and boys both attended, classes were generally segregated by gender, with differing subjects taught to each group.

In *MDR,* Jung recounted: "Soon after I was six my father began giving me Latin lessons, and I also went to school. I did not mind school, it was easy for me, since I was ahead of the others and had learned to read before I went there."[52] He also described himself as "introverted"—a term he later formalized in his theory of psychological types. Reflecting on his early years, he characterized himself as sensitive, vulnerable, and lonely. His semi-rural, transforming environment presented numerous challenges, including authoritarian schooling and bullying. However, it also provided opportunities for adventure in the landscape. Until the age of 9, when his sister Trudi was born, Carl remained an only child. Solitary play and drawing were significant pastimes, as he would later recall:

31 Carl's Primary and Secondary School (c. 1875)
Built in 1874–1875, this school for boys and girls had 12 classrooms and was located at Bonergasse 1. It replaced the first school in Kleinhüningen, built on Schulgasse.

32 Carl's (Karl-Gustav's) Report Card from his First Class in Kleinhüningen (Academic Year 1882/83)

My first concrete memory of games dates from my seventh or eighth year. I was passionately fond of playing with bricks, and built owers which I then rapturously destroyed by an 'earthquake.' Between my eighth and eleventh years I drew endlessly—battle pictures, sieges, bombardments, naval engagements. Then I filled a whole exercise book with ink blots and amused myself giving them fantastic interpretations. One of my reasons for liking school was that there I found at last the playmates I had lacked for so long.[53]

Young Carl's creativity was often expressed in drawings of battles and castles.[54] One such sketch from his childhood notebooks, titled *3rd and 4th Grade Students in Kleinhüningen* (1884), depicts his classmates as knights battling and slaying dragons. This imagery bears a strong resemblance to the sandstone sculpture on the façade of Basel Münster depicting Saint George thrusting a lance into the mouth of a small dragon. Notably, this motif later reappears in *The Red Book,* in Jung's painting of a man dismembering a dragon. This many-armed dragon painted by Jung is a variation of Atmavictu.[55]

33 Man Dismembering a Dragon, Jung (1914–1930)
"The damned dragon has eaten the sun" ("Der verfluchte Drache hat die Sonne gefressen"), from *The Red Book* (image 119).

Dragons, Archetypes, and the Collective Unconscious

The dragon is an archetypal image. As such, it resides in the collective unconscious and appears across cultures in fairytales, myths, dreams, fantasies, artistic expressions, and popular culture. The specific form that the dragon archetype assumes is colored by its cultural and historical context.

In 1919, Jung borrowed the term "archetype" from classical sources and thinkers such as Jacob Burckhardt, who used the term *Urbilder* (primordial images) to define recurring mythical patterns.[56] Jung conceptualized archetypes as universal human instincts expressed through imagery.[57]

In his seventh "Zarathustra Lecture" (November 1934), Jung interpreted Nietzsche's depiction of the authoritative word of the Christian God as a dragon, describing this transformation as an "enantiodromic cycle" through which something originally perceived as good became transformed into a symbol of evil.[58]

When Jung applied the archetypal myth of the knight slaying the dragon to psychology, he interpreted the knight as a symbol of the hero fighting for independence and freedom.[59] Within Christian mythology, this narrative may serve as a metaphor for the conscious ego overcoming the unconscious "shadow" (which may manifest as an evil dragon), which is often projected outward.[60] However, Jung later argued that the ultimate psychological task is to "slay the hero" (the ego) in order to place the ego in service of the Self.

As a symbol, the dragon may represent negative forces, including evil, chaos, danger, and the untamed. Killing (or taming) the dragon thus signifies the elimination of imminent danger as a means of establishing or maintaining order. Psychologically, the dragon may represent that which is repressed or suppressed, and thus not yet conscious. Such unconscious elements, if unexamined, may cause havoc in the individual psyche. Confronting and integrating unconscious conflicts and complexes, rather than projecting them outward, is thus essential for achieving greater awareness and consciousness.

It is possible that the statue of Saint George slaying the dragon outside Basel Münster inspired Jung's childhood drawings of dragons. However, it is also plausible that these images arose spontaneously as archetypal symbols from the collective unconscious.

TOUR 1

34 Carl's Early Drawing of Dragon-Slaying (c. 1884)
Image titled *3rd and 4th Grade Students in Kleinhüningen*, from a pupil number booklet.

35 Saint George Slaying the Dragon (1372)
A red sandstone sculpture on the west façade of Basel Münster.

36 Fisher House (c. 1900)
Bürgin's house on Schulgasse 27, before being relocated to Bonergasse in 1905.

37 Fisher House
Bürgin's relocated house in the garden of the Clavel Estate, against an industrial backdrop.

TOUR 1

BÜRGIN FISHER HOUSE, BONERGASSE 71

CLAVEL ESTATE, BONERGASSE 71

JUXTAPOSITION OF OLD AND NEW

Opposite the school stands the third and final surviving fisher house, now situated adjacent to the impressive Clavel Estate. This house, originally belonging to the Bürgin fishing family, was spared demolition when it was relocated to Bonergasse 71.

The contrast in these neighboring structures illustrates the industrial transformation that was not only shaping Kleinhüningen and greater Basel at the time, but also establishing the economic foundation for all of Switzerland. A significant industrialist associated with this transformation was Alexander Clavel I (1805–1873). In 1859, two decades before the arrival of the Jung-Preiswerk family, Clavel purchased the baroque country estate before you, once adorned with an expansive and magnificent park. He resided there with his family,[61] becoming a symbol of the emerging urban economic elite. By the second generation, the Clavel family had ascended into the patriciate through strategic marriages.

Despite the wealth and prestige brought to the village by the Clavel family, Kleinhüningen remained largely impoverished, while air, water, and soil population increased alarmingly. Bindschedler & Busch faced mounting pressure to either expand their operations or relocate entirely. Community assembly records reveal that both options sparked heated debate among residents. Villagers voiced concerns over pollution and potential water contamination, while proponents of expansion argued that the most hazardous dyes were produced only at night, thereby limiting exposure. They also noted that the factory had improved economic livelihoods by increasing employment from 30 workers to 250.

In 1892, the decision was finalized to construct a chemical factory in Kleinhüningen on Neuhausweg and Mühlefeld. By 1893, Bindschedler & Busch had begun to produce dyes and pharmaceuticals there. Within a single year, fifteen new factory buildings were erected.

TOUR 1

Table 2
Population of Canton Basel-Stadt
The population of Kleinhüningen tripled between 1870 and 1910.

Year	Canton Basel-Stadt	Basel-City without Kleinhüningen	Basel-City with Kleinhüningen	Kleinhüningen
1870	47,100	44,180	44,920	740
1880	64,300	60,640	61,830	1,190
1888	73,720	69,780	71,100	1,320
1900	112,240	107,290	109,170	1,880
1910	136,170	130,280	132,500	2,200

The Chemical Dyestuff Industry Begins to Dominate Kleinhüningen

Clavel hailed from a family of silk dyers and traders in Lyon, who later settled in Basel. During this period, technological advancements made it possible to synthesize dyes. Clavel's development of the red synthetic dye fuchsin (aniline red)—a formula brought from Lyon—was one of the pioneering innovations that sparked the growth of Basel's chemical and pharmaceutical industries, making it the city's most significant economic sector.

In 1859, Clavel began producing dyes in a laboratory in Kleinbasel (below Rebgasse 4/6). The dyes were derived from aniline, a compound extracted from coal tar, which generated toxic waste and fumes during manufacturing. In 1864, after complaints from neighbors, Basel's Small Council banned the production of aniline red within the city center, forcing Clavel to relocate his operations to the outskirts of town. He moved his "laboratory for the production of aniline and other colors" to Klybeckstrasse 198, near the Rhine,[62] while operating a separate dye works at Gärtnerstrasse 22, then part of Kleinhüningen.

Clavel's enterprise combined two trades: dyeing silk fabrics and yarns and manufacturing the dyes, themselves. However, his son, Alexander Clavel-Merian II (1847–1910), saw greater potential in an exclusive focus on dye production. Just weeks before his father's death in 1873, the dyestuff production unit was sold to Bindschedler & Busch, a company that later became the Gesellschaft für die Chemische Industrie in Basel (Society for the Chemical Industry in Basel), known from 1945 onward as CIBA. Thus, Alexander Clavel I may be regarded as an industrial pioneer of Basel's founding era.

In 1873, Bindschedler & Busch took over Clavel's dye factory on Klybeckstrasse. By 1893, the firm had expanded operations to Kleinhüningen (Neuhausweg, Basler Chemische Fabrik Bindschedler).[63] Together with firms such as Geigy, these early factories laid the groundwork for the globally influential CIBA-Geigy, which, along with Roche, became one of the region's most transformative multinational corporations. Today, Novartis (a successor to CIBA-Geigy) and Roche remain two of Basel's most formative companies, shaping the area's economic, social, and cultural development.

38 Clavel Estate (1880–1900)
Industrialist Alexander Clavel purchased this country estate with its magnificent park in 1859 as his family home.

39 Three Women in a Boat on Clavel Pond (c. 1880–1900)
This striking feature of the estate no longer exists.

40 Contemporary Sign Marking the Historic Boundaries of Kleinhüningen
These signs, bearing the insignia of Kleinhüningen, demarcate the larger village boundaries of Kleinhüningen prior to its incorporation into Basel. This sign is found near Wiesenstrasse.

Incorporation of Kleinhüningen into Basel

The sweeping changes in Kleinhüningen were connected to its eventual incorporation into Basel in 1893. Discussions about the merger began in 1891. Paul Jung-Preiswerk, who was actively involved in these talks, observed that some villagers were more invested than others.[64] Paul participated in the planning of a celebration to mark the incorporation, though he and teacher Meier noted a general lack of enthusiasm for the event. Community meetings and minutes documenting the merger process ceased once the village was formally absorbed into Basel. A photograph of a celebration exists, but it was taken much later, after Paul's death.[65]

Kleinhüningen became an official district of Basel between 1907 and 1908. A new city plan was implemented, redefining quarter and church boundaries, with the result that Kleinhüningen significantly reduced in size. Only the area north of the Wiese remained part of the Kleinhüningen district, while the southern portion—previously extending roughly to Ackerstrasse and encompassing what is now the Klybeck quarter—was excluded.

Since that time, community organizations have sought to preserve the memory of the former village. Today, plaques bearing the insignia of Kleinhüningen—visible from the tram—serve as reminders of the village's historical geography and identity.

Kleinhüningen's radical transformation from an agrarian to an industrial village redefined its community as primarily working class. Areas such as Klybeck (which remained part of Kleinhüningen until 1903) and the banks of the Wiese became crucial hubs for industry. Basel, in turn, became an important node in an increasingly interconnected global network. The development of transportation infrastructure played a key role in this transformation. Railroad connections were continually expanded, modern shipping along the Rhine flourished, and construction projects began to make the Upper Rhine navigable from the North Sea to Basel. These developments were well underway by the time Carl turned 20.

Art and Life: *Quadrated Circle in the Sky*
The *Quadrated Circle in the Sky* image (no. 125) from *The Red Book* (painted between 1916 and 1930) contains many elements of Carl's childhood experiences in Kleinhüningen. It depicts a port, farmland, train tracks, factories spewing smoke, and a fortress, juxtaposed by industry, military, and tranquil pastoral life, evoking a sense of nostalgia.[66] Dominating the composition is an enormous, fiery, quadrated circle in the sky. Below it, a meditative figure sits cross-legged on a cushion, holding a container above their head. This figure appears to reconcile the tension between the mundane activities of the small town below—where daily business continues uninterrupted—and the immense, fiery powers above. The figure's calm presence suggests a capacity to hold the tension of these opposites.

In the 1930s, Jung revisited Kleinhüningen and was deeply unsettled by its transformation. His once-idyllic fishing and farming village had become a poor, industrialized, urban harbor.[67] The village center was, by then, fully enclosed and cut off from the Rhine, its green spaces lost to development, and the traditional ways of life of farmers and fishermen extinct due to pollution and industrial encroachment. Despite his dismay at the changes, could *Quadrated Circle in the Sky* offer a symbolic pathway toward reconciliation with "progress"? The painting appears to suggest that, while the unfolding of events on the ordinary plane often results in tension and loss, a transcendent presence prevails—a higher order likely unnoticed by the figures on the ground. Could this tension and balance also represent Jung's personal reckoning with the "spirit of the times" and the "spirit of the depths"?

41 Quadrated Circle in the Sky, Jung (1919–1920)
Image 125 from *The Red Book*.

42 Chemical Factory Bindschedler & Busch (1897)
The industrial landscape of Kleinhüningen resembles the town in Jung's *Quadrated Circle in the Sky* from *The Red Book*.

Map 3
Kleinhüningen in 1918
This map shows the Old Rhine filled in.
Klybeckinsel no longer exists.

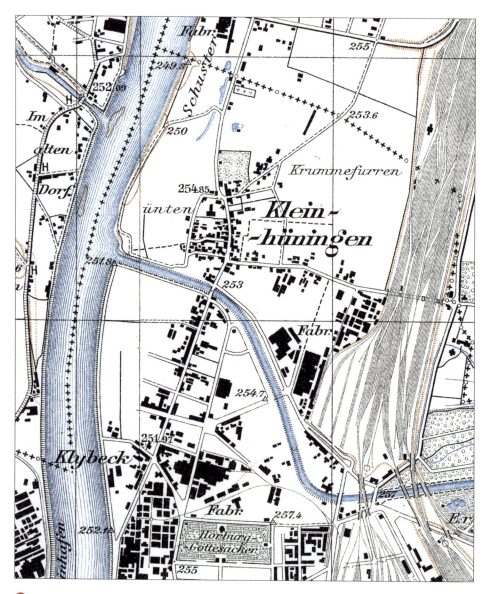

Map 4
Kleinhüningen in 1932
This map depicts the area's increased population density. The train tracks and new harbor cut Kleinhüningen off from direct access to the Rhine.

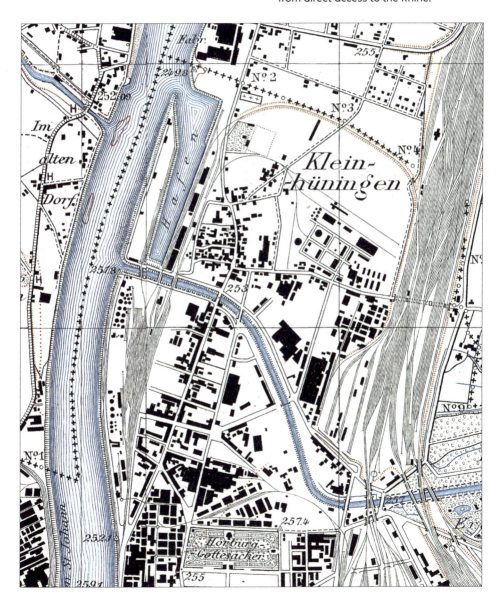

TOUR 1

43 Fortress at Hüningen by Architect Sébastian le Prestre de Vauban (1700s)
A bird's-eye view from the north shows the fortress (front lower right), the confluence of the Rhine and Wiese rivers, the village of Kleinhüningen (center), and the city of Basel (background).

10 FORTRESS HÜNINGEN (HISTORIC SITE)

A WELL-FORTIFIED CASTLE

Before leaving the Clavel Estate, let us consider another notable structure, now long gone, that would have been visible from the property: the Fortress at Hüningen. Located diagonally downstream along the Rhine from Kleinhüningen, this fortress, dismantled in 1815, seems to have captured Carl's imagination. A glance at the historical map reveals the fortress's proximity to the Wiese. Possibly, this fortress (along with another like it that Carl encountered in his youth) inspired Carl's games and depictions of castles, fortresses, and battle scenes. Could the triangular border at Hüningen—where distinct countries converge—have also planted the seed for Jung's later focus on the coming together of "parts" within a unified whole? Might it have shaped his fascination with mandalas, which he conceptualized as diagrams of the Self? Later in life, Jung's library included a book on Kleinhüningen containing an engraving of the Fortress at Hüningen by Emanuel Büchel.[68]

As a youth, Carl also visited another fortress: the Citadel in Belfort, France (now a UNESCO World Heritage Site). Both the Fortress at Hüningen and the Citadel in Belfort were designed by the same architect.

The Fortress at Hüningen was built during the period of French possession by the renowned military engineer Sébastian le Prestre de Vauban, under the direction of King Louis XIV. Together with the builder Jacques Tarade, Vauban constructed the pentagonal fortress between 1679 and 1682, over a century before the Jung-Preiswerk family arrived in the region. Its primary purpose was to defend France's border and control traffic on the Rhine. Construction of the fortress required the evacuation of residents living on a small island in the Rhine, who were relocated to Aoust. The site of the fortress was chosen as the narrowest part of the Rhine, enabling a bridge to be built between the island and the opposite bank, where a smaller fortification was erected to complete the defensive system.[69] The fortress was a key stronghold during the sieges of 1796, 1814, and 1815, the latter of which left lasting marks

44 Aerial View of the Fortress in Neuf-Brisach Taken During a Balloon Flight

on the region. Cannonballs from the 1815 siege damaged the church in Kleinhüningen, and these were later embedded into its reconstructed façade, remaining a visible testament to the area's turbulent history. In the aftermath of the Napoleonic Wars, the fortress was dismantled between 1815 and 1817 at the request of the Swiss government, which advocated for its removal in the name of peace. Today, a model of the fortress can be seen in the Historical and Military Museum Hüningen (Musée historique et militaire).[70]

Consider the similarities between the Citadel at Belfort, the fortified town Neuf-Brisach, and Jung's *The Golden Well-Fortified Castle* painting from *The Red Book* (image 163).[71] In Jung's painting, we see a town fortified by walls and a moat, with an additional second moat enclosing a central castle. The castle, adorned with golden roofs, features a golden temple with sixteen towers arranged in a mandala-like configuration.[72] Jung later identified mandala shapes as symbols of the Self—an archetype of orientation, wholeness, and meaning—using this picture as an example of the mandala's psychological significance.[73]

Follow Dorfstrasse back toward the Wiese, passing by some of the trades and businesses described earlier in station ❷ Village Life. Cross the Wiese and head to the tram stop diagonally to the left of Restaurant Schiff. Take tram 8 in the direction of Neuweilerstrasse, back to central Basel.

45 *The Well-Fortified Golden Castle*, Jung (1928)
Image 163 from *The Red Book*. Jung noted: "When I was painting this picture, which shows the golden well-fortified castle, Richard Wilhelm in Frankfurt sent me the Chinese, thousand-year-old text of the yellow castle, the germ of the immortal body. *Ecclesia catholic et protestantes et seclusi in secreto. Aeon finitus.* (The Catholic church and the Protestants and those secluded in secret. The end of an aeon.)"

46 Map of Belfort with Fortress Belt (1780)
In his childhood, Carl visited the Citadel Belfort, designed by architect Vauban and built in 1687.

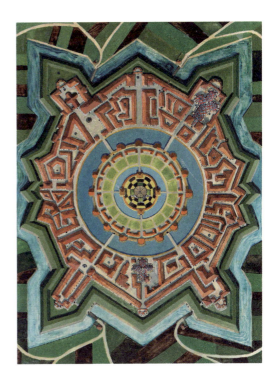

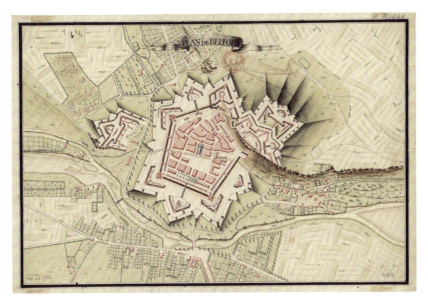

TOUR 2

CARL'S WALK FROM KLEINHÜNINGEN TO THE GYMNASIUM IN BASEL

For nine years, while attending the Gymnasium in Basel (ages 11 to 20, 1886–1895) and during his first year at university, Carl walked 4 kilometers daily from his home in Kleinhüningen to Münsterplatz and back This tour features two alternative routes, defined by the choice of bridge to cross the Rhine, but they share a common starting point in Kleinhüningen.

Along the way, you will encounter reminders of Basel's rich spiritual and scholarly traditions, as well as the presence of Carl's paternal (Jung) and maternal (Preiswerk) lineage in academic, medical, religious, and civic realms. You will also explore places and things that captured young Carl's imagination.

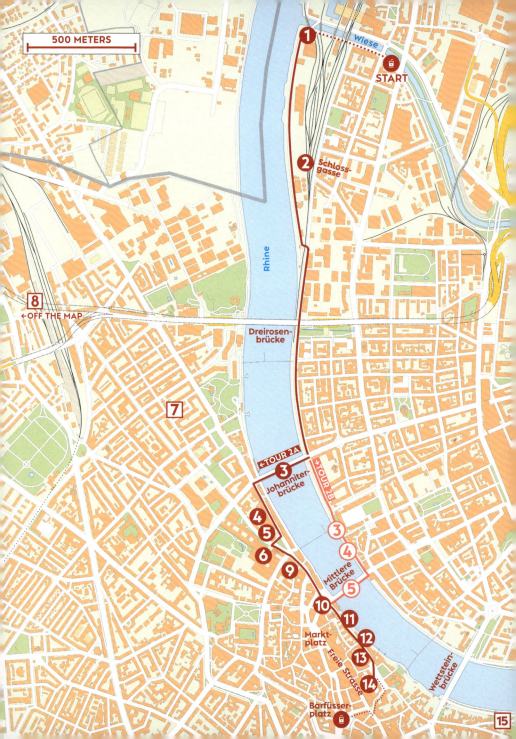

TOUR 2 OVERVIEW

① WIESENDAMM / UFERSTRASSE
Leaving Kleinhüningen to Walk Along the Rhine to Basel

② HOLZPARK KLYBECK, UFERSTRASSE 40
15th-Century Castle and Father Rhine

TOUR 2A: THE GROSSBASEL ROUTE

③ JOHANNITERBRÜCKE
A Citizen-Led Initiative

④ ERLACHERHOF, ST. JOHANNS-VORSTADT 15/17
Silk Ribbons for the Global Fashion Industry

⑤ TOTENTANZ 17
The Dance with Death

⑥ BÜRGERSPITAL, PETERSGRABEN 4 (HISTORIC SITE)

⑦ JUNGSTRASSE

⑧ FRIEDMATT ASYLUM, WILHELM KLEIN-STRASSE 27
Basel's Sick and Impoverished Citizens

⑨ ERIMANSHOF, PETERSGRABEN 1 (HISTORIC SITE)
Art Salon in the Erimanshof

TOUR 2B: THE KLEINBASEL ROUTE

③ KASERNE, KLYBECKSTRASSE 1B
Military Barracks and Cloister

④ KLOSTER KLEINES KLINGENTAL, UNTERER RHEINWEG 26
Medieval Masterpieces and Miniatures

⑤ MITTLERE BRÜCKE AND KÄPPELIJOCH
A Place of Grim Reckoning

CONVERGENCE OF ROUTES A & B

⑩ LÄLLEKÖNIG, SCHIFFLÄNDE 1
Trickster at the Gate

⑪ OLD UNIVERSITY, RHEINSPRUNG 9
The Jung Family Medical Legacy

⑫ AUGUSTINERBRUNNEN, RHEINSPRUNG 21
A Pagan Creature Holds the Bishop's Staff

⑬ NATURHISTORISCHES MUSEUM, AUGUSTINERGASSE 2
Carl Discovers All Manner of Things

⑭ GYMNASIUM, MÜNSTERPLATZ 15
Nine Years of Study

⑮ ST. ALBAN PFARRHAUS, MÜHLENBERG 12
Where Isemännli Lives

START
The tour starts at the Kleinhüningen tram stop.

GETTING THERE
Board tram 8 from central Basel (direction Kleinhüningen or Weil am Rhein). Exit at the Kleinhüningen stop.

TOUR LENGTH
Allow two to three hours for this tour.

RETURN
It is a 5- to 10-minute walk from the Gymnasium to the tram stops (Kunstmuseum, Bankverein, and Barfüsserplatz). For up-to-date tram schedules, visit https://www.sbb.ch/en.

Scan to follow the tour on Google Maps

This Google Map is also accessible at www.kschaeppi.ch/book

1   A View Across the Rhine Showing Kleinhüningen and Klybeck Island (1855)
Looking downstream from St. Johann, the Blauen mountain in the southern Black Forest, Germany, is visible in the distance. This romantic setting would soon undergo significant change.

① WIESENDAMM / UFERSTRASSE

LEAVING KLEINHÜNINGEN TO WALK ALONG THE RHINE TO BASEL

From the tram stop, follow the Wiese as it flows toward the Rhine, then turn left onto Uferstrasse (Riverbank Road), the promenade along the Rhine. Here, you will encounter a long stretch where you can let your imagination flow, much as Carl did during his daily walks to school. In *MDR*, Jung twice recalled the tedium of this daily journey. To break the monotony, he would immerse himself in vivid fantasies. As he walked along the Rhine, he would imagine the Alsace transformed into a vast lake or an open sea, with sailboats, a grand steamer, and two-masted schooners floating or docked at port. On a rocky outcrop, he would envision a well-fortified castle with a watchtower, a library, weapons, and bastions armed with cannons. This imaginary castle concealed a great secret laboratory—one shared also with nature—dedicated to the making of gold. The kilometers would pass effortlessly as his imagination carried him forward. When one fantasy grew stale, he would find another, constructing mental models of castles. He wrote, "I stepped out of my fantasy as out of a carriage which had effortlessly driven me home."[1]

While many of the Klybeck landmarks that would have caught young Carl's eye no longer exist, we can pause along the Rhine and envision them as they might have been. Walking briskly, Carl might have reached the Gymnasium in 45 to 60 minutes.

2 Fishermen at the Mouth of the River Wiese (1618–1624)
Castle Klübin stands at the center, with a panoramic view of Basel on the right. Today, only the road named Schlossgasse (Castle Way) remains as a reminder of the castle and its moat.

TOUR 2

② HOLZPARK KLYBECK, UFERSTRASSE 40

15TH-CENTURY CASTLE AND FATHER RHINE

Carl likely alternated his school route, walking through Klybeck on some days and along the river on others. Today, in Holzpark Klybeck, it feels as though one of Carl's childhood fantasies has come to life: the striking red lightship Gannet, once stationed outside Dublin, now sits beached here, where it has transformed into a vibrant nightclub and dining venue.

Nearby, Carl would have passed by or through the grounds of Klybeck Schlössli (Klybeck Castle), also known as Klübin. The site, now located at Klybeckstrasse 248, is commemorated by the small street Schlossgasse (Castle Way), which is the only remaining trace of the once-impressive estate. Facing away from the Rhine, Schlossgasse lies just beyond the park. The castle, first documented in the 15th century (c. 1438), stood until its demolition in 1955.[2] Let us pause to imagine what Carl would have seen: a grand castle adorned with allegorical frescoes of "Father Rhine"—complete with beard and trident—clasping hands with the Wiese on its tower. Created by the owner, Georg Abt (1860–1886), the castle was surrounded by extensive vineyards, trees, and meadows. Nearby was a manmade mill stream, drawing water from the Wiese, which powered a sawmill, two paper mills, and an oil mill, while also filling the estate's fish ponds. This stream eventually flowed off into the Old Rhine. At one time, the estate also included Klybeckinsel, a small island in the Rhine. While the island no longer exists, its presence is hinted at by Inselstrasse, located just before Schlossgasse.

Let us stay with the image of the castle and estate, which had many owners over the years. What local castles, fortresses, and citadels may have fueled Carl's fantasies and inspired his early drawings? Several examples in the vicinity echo his depictions, including the aforementioned Schloss Klybeck, Schloss Horburg (practically around the corner), and Burg Rötteln (near Lörrach, Germany, which may have been visible even from Kleinhüningen). There were also castles in the quarter where his Preiswerk-Allenspach cousins lived, as well as the Augustinian cloister in the center of Basel.[3] Additional castles were situated a bit further away: Schloss Münchenstein (Münchenstein), Burg Reichenstein (Arlesheim), Ruin Château de Landskron (Alsace, overlooking Cloister Mariastein), and Schloss Wartenberg (Muttenz, where Carl's maternal grandfather once lived). The tower in Bollingen, Jung's later creation, bears similarities to some of these fortifications.

The Klybeck quarter, named after the castle, was rapidly transforming during Carl's youth. As early as 1858, the first synthetic dyes were being manufactured there. Over the nine years that Carl walked to the Gymnasium, he witnessed the gradual disappearance of grazing cattle, sprawling orchards, and vegetable gardens. By 1895, when Carl was 20 years old, the small island of Klybeckinsel had also disappeared. The arm of the Rhine separating it from the mainland had filled with residue, stagnating to the point that, in summer, the water often ceased flowing entirely. In the following year (1896), the castle ponds were also filled in to create land for industrial construction.

The Klybeck quarter became home to a growing number of factories, including a fertilizer plant, the region's first industrial mill, and a manufacturer of coffee substitutes, which emanated an intense odor.[4] While unpleasant, the smell was at least less harmful than the exhaust fumes emanating from the chemical plants. The Gesellschaft für Chemische Industrie Basel (Society for Chemical Industry Basel, later known as CIBA) and residential buildings expanded significantly. The Rhine itself was polluted by waste materials from the factories, and the growth of the dyestuff industry produced dramatic effects on the local landscape and people. Workers in the dye factories, often referred to as *Papageien* (parrots) by locals such as Carl, had brightly stained blue, yellow, or red hair, mustaches, and hands from the chemicals they handled. Even the Rhine occasionally ran blue, yellow, or red, depending on the dye being produced at the time.

3 Klybeck Castle (c. 1900)

This large estate featured mills and vineyards. Note the fresco of Father Rhine on the castle tower.

4 Landscape and Town (c. 1898)
Graphite on paper drawing by Jung.

In 1869, Basel introduced its first factory law following the 4th General Congress of the International Workingmen's Association (IWA). Held in Basel, the Congress was attended by 75 delegates representing socialist and labor movements. The Factory Act marked the beginning of modest improvements in workers' conditions, though their overall situation remained precarious.

In the years that followed, Basel's population ballooned to 100,000, with the most rapid growth occurring in the final quarter of the 19th century. New tenements (*Mietskasernen*)—three-, four-, and even five stories high—were built to accommodate the influx of people from not only Basel and its surrounding countryside, but also other parts of Switzerland, as well as Germany, France, and Italy. The Catholic community, once a marginal population, began to grow significantly. Alongside this population boom, new business centers emerged, with shops and ateliers—such as hatters, photographers, and grocery stores—opening to meet the daily needs of the working and middle classes. Carl also observed the rise of the Allgemeiner Consum-Verein (General Consumer Cooperative), which opened numerous shops throughout the city. Members of the cooperative enjoyed greater purchasing power compared to the past, when shops were small and privately owned. Additionally, the stores created new job opportunities, with young women often employed as shop assistants—a modern and progressive role for women at the time.[5]

Continuing along the Rhine on Uferstrasse, cross the railroad tracks and eventually pass beneath the Dreirosenbrücke (Dreirosen Bridge) at Feldbergstrasse. This bridge did not exist in Carl's day.

5 Bird's-Eye View of St. Johann's Quarter Shortly After the Inauguration of the Johanniterbrücke (c. 1882)
St. Johann's Quarter is on the right bank, while the smokestacks of Kleinbasel are on the left (looking north, upstream).

TOUR 2A: THE GROSSBASEL ROUTE
JOHANNITERBRÜCKE

A CITIZEN-LED INITIATIVE

Imagine young Carl choosing to cross the Rhine by traversing the brand-new Johanniterbrücke (Johanniter Bridge), inaugurated in 1882—just four years before he began his studies at the Gymnasium. The bridge connects the Matthäus quarter of Kleinbasel (Small Basel) on the northeast bank of the Rhine with the St. Johann quarter of Grossbasel (Greater Basel) on the southwest side. To cross the bridge, take the stairs to your left before passing beneath it.

Pause for a moment on the bridge to reflect on its historical significance. The Johanniterbrücke was Basel's first major project born of a citizen-led initiative, made possible by the constitutional reform of 1875. Among its advocates was the prominent industrialist Alexander Clavel, who, along with others, championed the bridge despite fierce resistance from political leaders who viewed it as an unnecessary drain on the state treasury. Undeterred, the proponents collected 1,450 signatures to force a public vote. In 1877, Swiss male citizens (women, unfortunately, would not gain suffrage for nearly another century) cast their ballots in favor of the new bridge, overcoming government objections. With public support secured, the dream of the bridge was soon realized.

Before turning left at the end of the bridge to walk along St. Johanns-Vorstadt, Carl's attention on warm summer days may have been drawn to the newly built Rheinbadanstalt (Rhine Bathing Center) on his right. This popular spot offered swimming lessons to children, while proving adults a place to cool off and refresh themselves in the river. We might imagine that, as Carl continued, a few carriages passed by, carrying farming women from Hüningen or Village Neuf (Neudorf) in France. These women would have been on their way to Marktplatz (Market Square) to sell fruits and vegetables grown in their fields in Alsace.

6 Women Heading to Market in a Horse-Drawn Carriage
Traveling from Alsace along Elsässerstrasse (Alsace Road).

7 Market Women from Alsace with Baskets on Their Heads
The gasworks are visible in the background.

Others may have been walking the long distance, carrying large baskets full of their wares. The street would have presented a contrast of landscapes: on one side, stately homes with beautifully maintained parks, and on the river side, newer residential buildings designed to accommodate the growing population.

8 St. Johanns-Vorstadt 3–29 (1868)
No. 17 housed a Preiswerk family silk ribbon factory.

TOUR 2A: THE GROSSBASEL ROUTE
ERLACHERHOF, ST. JOHANNS-VORSTADT 15/17

SILK RIBBONS FOR THE GLOBAL FASHION INDUSTRY

The legacy of Carl's maternal (Preiswerk) and paternal (Jung) lineages would have been reflected in many of the sites he passed on his walk to school. For example, Lucas Preiswerk-Forcart (1788–1848) once resided in the stately home at St. Johanns-Vorstadt 17. Today, the factory site is still visible at 15/17 St. Johanns-Vorstadt, on the right. The ensemble of houses, known as the Erlacherhof and first mentioned in 1414, remains almost completely intact and is now occupied by contemporary creatives, including architects and graphic designers.

During Carl's time, the factory at this site produced vibrant, high-quality silk ribbons—essential components of the global fashion industry and Basel's most significant export. The factory remained in the Preiswerk family for 82 years (1817–1899), until ownership formally passed from Lucas Preiswerk-Forcart to Friedrich and the factory was renamed Senn & Co.

In the late 19th century, many women worked long hours in the factory. During lunch breaks, they would run home to care for their families before returning to work in the afternoon. Despite their hard work, women earned significantly less than men, as their labor was undervalued. However, even the higher wages earned by men were often insufficient to support a family, making women's income essential for survival. This presented a social dilemma, as the bourgeois ideal dictated that the husband should work while the wife managed the household.

9 Bürgerspital on Petersgraben (c. 1840–1850)
Basel's new hospital.

TOUR 2A: THE GROSSBASEL ROUTE
TOTENTANZ 17

THE DANCE WITH DEATH

On his walk to school, Carl likely passed two notable landmarks: the new Bürgerspital[6] (Citizens' Hospital) on Petersgraben, and the site of the *Totentanz* (*Dance of Death*) mural, which had been removed in 1805. Today, the former location of the *Totentanz* is marked by a park and sculpture. Historically, this site housed the publicly accessible cemetery of a Dominican monastery (founded in 1440), surrounded by a 60-meter-long, 2-meter-tall wall. On this wall, a mural—the *Totentanz*—depicted people of all ages and social classes dancing with death, portrayed as a skeleton. The artwork served as a striking visual reminder of the inevitability of death, encapsulated in the phrase: "All men must die, without distinction, from the emperor to the beggar."

Although the mural eventually succumbed to the elements (true to its message), nineteen fragments were preserved and are now housed in the Historical Museum Basel. The mural was also copied and published, making it a popular tourist attraction and a frequent subject of travelogues. Carl would not have seen the wall, but he may have remembered the story as he passed by.

10 Friedmatt Asylum (1925)
Located at Wilhelm Klein-Strasse 27 (previously designated Mittlere Strasse 300 until 1956).

6 TOUR 2A: THE GROSSBASEL ROUTE
BÜRGERSPITAL, PETERSGRABEN 4 (HISTORIC SITE)

7 JUNGSTRASSE

8 FRIEDMATT ASYLUM, WILHELM KLEIN-STRASSE 27

BASEL'S SICK AND IMPOVERISHED CITIZENS

Just beyond the *Totentanz,* Carl would have seen the Bürgerspital on Petersgraben. Today, this location is where St. Johanns-Vorstadt converges with Spitalstrasse (Hospital Street) and Petersgraben, framing the University Hospital Basel (though the larger hospital complex extends beyond this area). Here, pause to reflect on the significant contributions Carl's father and paternal grandfather made to the care of Basel's mentally and physically ill, despite their different professional orientations.

Carl's paternal grandfather, Karl Jung (1795–1864), was a physician and educator who, in 1832 (fifty-four years before Carl began walking this route), recognized the urgent need for a larger facility to house the infirmary and asylum, then located at Barfüsserplatz. Karl also advocated for a home for destitute citizens at the new site. Two years later, in 1834, the City Council approved the use of the Markgräflerhof on Hebelstrasse (a city-owned property) for this purpose, thereby avoiding additional costs to the cantonal budget. The initial idea was to house impoverished townspeople in the existing building, while constructing an adjoining facility for the infirmary and asylum. By 1842, the relocation of patients from the old Barfusserplatz infirmary to the new 588-bed Bürgerspital was complete. However, by 1857 (a mere 15 years later), the hospital had already reached full capacity, necessitating further expansion. Thanks to a generous donation, the Christoph-Merian-Wing was added at the end of Spitalgraben and St. Johanns-Graben. In 1865, eight years later, the Bürgerspital was officially designated as a teaching hospital. It continues to serve in this capacity today.

In addition to his contributions to establishing a modern hospital and a home for Basel's impoverished residents, Karl also encouraged the

11 Friedmatt Asylum (1930)
This southeast view shows the vast scale of the property and its relatively isolated location.

founding of the Sonderschulheim zur Hoffnung (Institute of Good Hope) in Basel in 1857. This facility provided care and education for children with mental and/or physical disabilities, and it was relocated to Riehen in 1904, where it continues to serve this mission.[7] In 1897, when Carl was 22, a street in St. Johann quarter was named Jungstrasse in honor of Karl's service to Basel.

In 1882, 18 years after Karl's death, the Basler Grosse Rat (Great Council), the Bürgerspital, and the Sanitätsdepartment (Department of Health) decided to construct a new asylum on a "friendly meadow" outside of town. The 214-bed Friedmatt Asylum opened its doors in 1886, providing extended care to those with mental illnesses. In 1888, Carl's father, Paul Jung-Preiswerk, became the asylum's chaplain and counselor. In 1899, the institution's name was changed to the Kantonale Heil- und Pflege Anstat Friedmatt (Cantonal Sanatorium and Nursing Home). Today, the Friedmatt site houses the University Psychiatric Clinics Basel, continuing its legacy of mental healthcare on the outskirts of Basel.

TOUR 2A: THE GROSSBASEL ROUTE
ERIMANSHOF, PETERSGRABEN 1 (HISTORIC SITE)

ART SALON IN THE ERIMANSHOF

There is one more site to take in at the intersection of Blumenrain and Petersgraben, opposite the Seidenhof (Silk Court): the Erimanshof. The Seidenhof, first mentioned in 1363, was historically home to wealthy cloth and silk merchants.[8] During Carl's time, the Erimanshof was the residence of his great-uncle, the painter Ernst Stückelberg (1831–1903).[9] Baptized as Johann Melchior Ernst Stickelberger, he later adopted the name Ernst Stückelberg. Stückelberg was a cousin of Carl's paternal grandmother, Sophie Jung-Frey (1812–1855), though nearly 20 years her junior. After the death of his father, Stückelberg's education was overseen by his uncle, Melchior Berri, architect of the museum on Augustinergasse 2. Stückelberg became known for his historical paintings and portraits. In 1856, he created the model for a stained glass window featuring Kaiserin Kunigunde (Empress Kunigunde) and her husband Kaiser Heinrich II of Germany (Emperor), the benefactor of Basel Münster. Heinrich and Kunigunde were later crowned Holy Roman Emperor and Empress. While only Stückelberg's painting of Kunigunde has been preserved, the window is visible from inside the Münster, on the right side of the west façade.

As a youth, Carl may have lingered for a moment at Erimanshof, aware of his great-uncle's artistic legacy. Inside, the salon was adorned with Stückelberg's monumental, sensitive wall paintings of figures such as Prudentia (Prudence), depicted as a young girl draped in red and holding an oil lamp; Sapientia (Wisdom), depicted as a woman reading with a child and an owl at her feet; and Caritas (Compassion/Love), depicted as a mother holding a child with her other two children clinging to her (1875). Stückelberg's painting *The Painter's Family* (1872), which he worked on in his studio at the house, was displayed at the World Exhibition in Vienna in 1873, earning him the Knight's Cross of the Imperial Order of Franz-Joseph. Following this recognition, Stückelberg became a professor at the University of Zürich.

9 TOUR 2A

12 (left, above) Erimanshof (1931)
On the right, partially hidden by trees, is the home of Carl's great-uncle and painter Ernst Stückelberg. The Seidenhof stands on the left, while on the far right one can see the tower overlooking the atelier.

13 (left, below) Erimanshof Main Building and Tower (c.1850)
The atelier roof is in the foreground, with the window on the right.

14 (below) Erimanshof Salon (c. 1840)
The ornate decor of the salon's south and east walls presented a stark contrast to life in Kleinhüningen.

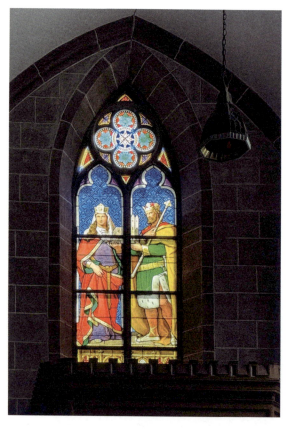

TOUR 2A

15 Kaiserin Kunigunde (1856)
A chalk and gouache drawing by Ernst Stückelberg prepared as the model for a stained glass window at Basel Münster. The complementary image of Kaiser Heinrich II is now lost.

16 (left, below) Kaiser Heinrich II and Kaiserin Kunigunde (1859)
Stained glass by Franz Xaver Egger, produced in the stained glass workshop of Heinrich Burckhardt in Munich. Installed at Basel Münster.

Stückelberg also won a competition to decorate the newly constructed Tell Chapel in Sisikon (on Lake Lucerne) with a series of frescoes. Inaugurated in June 1883, the four-part cycle depicts *The Rütli Oath, Tell's Apple Shot, Tell's Leap,* and *The Death of Gessler.* One figure in the fresco was modeled after Ernst Jung, Paul's older brother (Carl's uncle) and the architect of Tell Chapel.[10]

After turning onto Blumenrain and continuing three blocks along the Rhine toward the center of Basel, Carl would have passed the city's finest hotel, the majestic Drei Könige (since 1681, Les Trois Rois or the Three Kings, Blumenrain 8). This grand establishment served as the first address for wealthy and distinguished guests, including European aristocracy and politicians. Today, it remains a hotel of distinction, and a peek inside reveals its rich history. While reservations are necessary for lunch, weekend brunch, and high tea, it is often possible to enjoy a drink at the bar or the terrace, where one can take in the riverside views.

Two blocks beyond the hotel lies the Mittlere Brücke (Middle Bridge), where Tour 2, Route A rejoins Tour 2, Route B. Blumenrain transitions to Schifflände (Ship's Landing) for the final block, with the boat terminal adjacent on the bank of the Rhine. Before the end of the street, turn right onto Rheinsprung. Pause at the Lällekönig, then skip ahead in Tour 2 to station ❿.

TOUR 2A

17 The Kaserne (c. 1860–1880)
These barracks were actively used for military exercises during the years Carl walked this route.

TOUR 2B: THE KLEINBASEL ROUTE
KASERNE, AS VIEWED FROM UNTERER RHEINWEG

MILITARY BARRACKS AND CLOISTER

On some days, Carl may have elected to remain on the Kleinbasler side of the Rhine beyond the Johanniterbrücke, later crossing the Rhine by way of the Mittlere Brücke. We may follow in his footsteps beneath the Johanniterbrücke, continuing on Unterer Rheinweg as it transitions from a roadway to a riverside promenade after two blocks.

Just a bit further along, as Carl would have approached the imposing red stone fortress of the *Kaserne* (barracks), he may have heard the bark of commands echoing from the parade grounds or caught the scent of horses in their stalls. Built in 1860 for the Swiss Army military training, the *Kaserne* served this purpose for more than 100 years, until 1966. In 1980, the historic site was repurposed as a cultural center, open to the public.

18 Klingentalkloster and Lower Kleinbasel (1856)
Viewed from the St. Martin's Church spire, downstream.

TOUR 2B: THE KLEINBASEL ROUTE
KLOSTER KLEINES KLINGENTAL, UNTERER RHEINWEG 26

MEDIEVAL MASTERPIECES AND MINIATURES

Beyond the *Kaserne,* Carl would have encountered the remains of Kloster Klingental, founded in 1274 by twelve Dominican nuns from Alsace. The convent originally consisted of two distinct parts: Kleines Klingental and Grosses Klingental, named after its patron, the knight and troubadour Walter von Klingen.

Kleines Klingental was the original convent, housing essential spaces for community life, including a chapel, dormitory, dining hall, and kitchen. When the nuns moved to Grosses Klingental, the smaller complex was transformed into a residence and workspace for lay brothers. Grosses Klingental, constructed later, served as the main convent and reached its peak with 52 nuns living there. Renowned for its wealth, noble patronage, and comfort, it was the grandest of Basel's ten cloisters. However, the Reformation in the 16th century led to the convent's dissolution. By 1860, the residential buildings of Grosses Klingental were demolished to make way for the *Kaserne,* and the enclosed grounds were repurposed for Swiss military usage.

Today, Kleines Klingental stands as a testament to the convent's spiritual and cultural heritage. Its Gothic cloister, with pointed arches and ribbed vaults, exudes tranquility and reflects the Dominican ideals of humility and devotion. The preserved stonework, fragments of medieval frescoes, and inscriptions offer glimpses into its storied past.

The site now houses the Museum Kleines Klingental, which contains the original medieval sculptures from Basel Münster, protecting them from weathering. Visitors can also admire two detailed miniatures: one depicting Kloster Klingental as it appeared in the 16th century and the other showcasing 17th-century Basel, highlighting its churches, monasteries, public buildings, and guild houses.

19 Matthäus Merian (the Elder), *Small Basel-City View* (1642)
The Mittlere Brücke is prominently shown spanning the Rhine in this copperplate engraving.

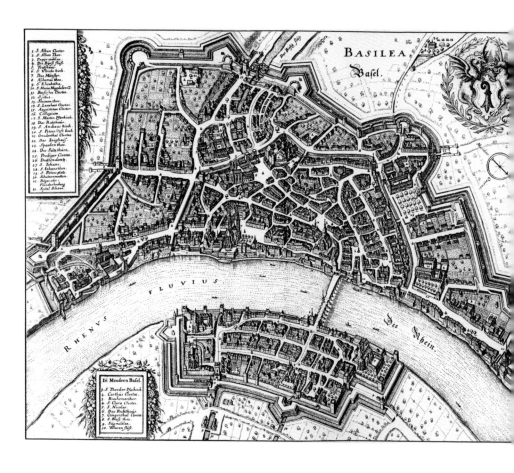

TOUR 2B: THE KLEINBASEL ROUTE
MITTLERE BRÜCKE AND KÄPPELIJOCH

A PLACE OF GRIM RECKONING

Shortly, Carl would arrive at the Mittlere Brücke and cross the Rhine. Built in 1225, this bridge was constructed from two materials, as the strong current and greater depths on the Grossbasel side made stone construction impractical.[11] On the Kleinbasel side, Carl would have stepped onto the stone portion of the bridge, while stepping off from the wooden section on the Grossbasel side. In 1899, the decision was made to decommission and replace the bridge with a new structure—a project that took place between 1903 and 1905.

At the center of the bridge, Carl would have passed Käppelijoch, a small chapel dating back to the 1300s. Until 1634, this chapel was used as a site for punishing thieves, adulterers, prostitutes, accused witches, mothers convicted of infanticide, and Anabaptists. Those condemned were sentenced to death by drowning and thrown into the Rhine from the chapel. Legend tells that nuns from Kloster Klingental and local fishermen occasionally rescued the condemned, pulling them from the river. If they managed to survive the 800 meters to the height of St. Johanns-Tor, they could be pulled to land and their lives would be spared. Today, the *Hexentafel* (witches' plaque) serves as a memorial to those accused of witchcraft and put to death at this spot.

20 Lällekönig as it Once Hung on the Basel Rheintor (c. 1650–1823)

21 As One Moves Off the Mittlere Brücke into Grossbasel One Enters Eisengasse (1901) Today the Lällekönig sticks out its tongue at passersby from the façade of Schifflände 1.

**TOUR 2, CONVERGENCE OF ROUTES A&B
LÄLLEKÖNIG, SCHIFFLÄNDE 1**

TRICKSTER AT THE GATE

The Lällekönig mask was first mentioned in 1658, when it was part of a clock adorning the Basler Rheintor (Rhine Gateway), the city gate between Grossbasel and the Mittlere Brücke. In Basel dialect, *Lälli* is the word for tongue.

Because the Lallekonig represented a king, it was removed during the Helvetic period. Its reinstallation as part of an 1801 attempt to return to the old order drew much attention to the mask. When the Rheintor was demolished in 1839, the Lallekonig found a new home in the Historical Museum of Basel.

Alas, Carl did not get to enjoy the Lällekonig during his walks to and from school. A motionless, stone replica was mounted at Schifflände 1 in 1914. This was supplanted in 1941 by the animate, mechanical Lällekonig that is visible today with its oversized, colorfully painted, crowned head, eyes that flick side-to-side in a 1-second cadence, and tongue that protrudes 10 cm at the newcomers and residents who regularly cross into Grossbasel from Kleinbasel. While the original meaning of the Lällekonig remains a mystery, legend has it that the king stuck his tongue out at Kleinbasel.

Carl would have passed the pharmacy at Schifflände 1, as shown in the adjacent photograph. Today, the Lällekonig shares the wall with the entrance to the Alchemist, a unique food and drink venue in the former pharmacy.

22 The Old University on the Rheinsprung 9/11 (c. 1860)
Founded in 1460 with papal privilege, then rebuilt and raised in 1859–1860 by Johann Jakob Stehlin (the Younger). The Old University served as the university headquarters until 1939 and now houses several university institutes.

11 OLD UNIVERSITY, RHEINSPRUNG 9

THE JUNG FAMILY MEDICAL LEGACY

Turning left, Carl would have ascended the steep Rheinsprung (Rhine Jump), rising 16 meters above the river and offering a stunning bird's-eye view of the Rhine flowing above and below. While climbing, he would have passed the yellow façade of the Old University, where his grandfather Karl previously served on the Faculty of Medicine. Carl, too, would later study medicine, though in different buildings spread across the city (see Tour 3). The Old University of Basel is the oldest university in Switzerland and one of the longest continuously operating universities in Europe. It has been a prestigious seat of learning since its inauguration with a mass in Basel Münster by Bishop Johann von Venningen on April 4, 1460. Bishop von Venningen, the university's first dean, oversaw its rapid rise to prominence in the fields of theology, medicine, law, and philosophy. The university also became home to the Theatrum and Museum Anatomicum.

Theatrum and Museum Anatomicum

In Carl's paternal lineage, three generations of men preceded him in the study of medicine: his great-grandfather Ignaz, his grandfather Karl, and his two uncles (both of whom tragically succumbed to tuberculosis in their 20s). While Carl would soon become the fourth generation to undertake medical training, he had no inkling of this as he walked to the Gymnasium. With the exception of his great-grandfather, all of the family physicians had studied or taught at the University of Basel. His grandfather Karl's many significant contributions to the Old University deserve particular attention.

Professor Dr. med. Karl Gustav Jung (1794–1864) began his studies in natural sciences and medicine at Heidelberg University in Germany.[12] He later assisted with ophthalmologic surgery at the Charité in Berlin and served as a chemistry lecturer at the Royal Military Academy. Continuing his studies in Paris, he worked as a surgeon and met the

23 Museum Anatomicum Iron Inscription (1824)
This plaque, once displayed on the walls of the Unteres Collegium on Rheinsprung at the Theatrum Anatomicum, now hangs in the Anatomical Museum, Pestalozzistrasse, Basel.

German naturalist and explorer Alexander von Humboldt, who had connections to Swiss universities. Impressed by Karl's talents, Humboldt recommended Karl for a professorship of anatomy, surgery, and obstetrics at the University of Basel—a position that Karl engaged in 1822. However, Karl's influence as a professor reached far beyond teaching. He spearheaded the expansion and reorganization of medical and anatomic studies at the School of Medicine and made significant strides in improving medical care delivery in Basel, earning the title "The Reanimator of Basel Medicine." Karl's impact eventually grew to encompass the entire university. Over nearly 30 years, he played a pivotal role in modernizing the medical facilities, increasing student enrollment, and raising the academic standards of the medical school faculty. He was elected dean of the medical faculty and, in 1828, appointed president (rector) of the university. Karl was also highly regarded for his civic service as a member of the town parliament.[13]

Vesalius and Plattner's Skeletons, Jung's Wax Models

When Karl assumed his academic role at the Old University, he became part of a rich tradition of anatomical studies. One of the most renowned figures in this history is the Belgian anatomist and physician Andries van Wezel (1514–1564)—later Latinized as Andreas Vesalius—considered the founder of modern anatomy. Known in Basel as Vesal, he traveled to Basel to have his groundbreaking anatomy textbook printed by Johannes Oporin. During his time in the city, he conducted

24 Wax Anatomical Model of the Head and Neck Nerves (1860)
Crafted by Christian Grimm.

25 Wax Anatomical Model of the Vegetative Nerve System (1850)
Crafted by Christian Grimm.

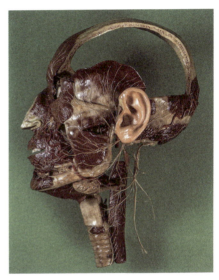

public demonstrations at the university, including a well-documented dissection of a criminal who had been decapitated for brutally attacking his wife in Allschwil (she survived). Prior to his departure, Vesalius gifted the criminal's skeleton to the university. The skeleton is now considered the oldest historical anatomical preparation in the world.[14]

Decades later, Felix Plattner (1536–1614) continued the tradition of public dissection at the Unteres Kollegium (Lower College; subsequently renamed the Alte Universität, or Old University). In 1590, the first dissections were performed in the *Theatrum Anatomicum* (anatomical theater), a modest 7×7 square meter dissection room. With poor heating and a door and windows on the north wall, the theater was made primarily of wood and had standing room for approximately 100 spectators and students.[15] By the time Karl arrived in the 19th century, Basel's reputation for medical innovation was well established. However, one of Karl's early contributions was founding the Museum Anatomicum, as indicated by an iron plaque dated 1824, which once hung on the outer walls of the Old University. The museum showcased Basel's long history of medical exploration.

Because knowledge of disinfection and preservation was limited at the time, it was not possible to retain soft tissue specimens. Recognizing the challenges of preserving human dissection specimens for teaching purposes, Karl introduced wax modeling as an innovative presentation technique.[16] His wax models eventually became part of the anatomical collection housed at the Alte Universität. This collection, originally called the Anatomical Kabinett, was later relocated to Pestalozzistrasse 20 and renamed the Anatomical Museum of the University of Basel. Today, the museum preserves many invaluable exhibits, including the skeletons prepared by Andreas Vesalius (1543) and Felix Platter (1573), as well as Karl Jung's wax models (1850–1860). Basel's contributions to modern anatomy are further recognized by the street name Vesalgasse (Vesal Street) in the Spalenvorstadt, honoring Vesalius' pioneering work.

Hortus Medicus

The *hortus medicus,* a medicinal herb garden, was recently replanted on the terrace below the Old University. For 100 years, the garden was carefully tended at the Old University before it was moved to various other locations within the city. Ultimately, it became the model for the University of Basel Botanical Garden at Petersplatz.

Freemasons and Symbols

Carl's grandfather, Karl, besides being a medical doctor, a member of Basel's parliament, and an original thinker (his early poems were published in the *Teutsches Liederbuch*[17]), was also a Freemason.[18] In his 30s, Karl was admitted to the Lodge "Friendship and Constancy" in 1825, becoming its Master of the Chair in 1838. He later fostered an understanding with the Zürich Brothers that became a precondition for founding the Grand Lodge Alpina (1844), one of Switzerland's grand lodges of Freemasons. Finally, he served as Grand Master of Alpina from 1850 to 1856.[19]

The Swiss Lodge of Freemasons, a secret society, was based on the medieval building trade of the stonemasons, emphasizing self-development and the embodiment of values such as humanity and morality.

Members were tasked with training the "disposition" of the mind, learning the meanings of symbols, upholding virtues, and participating in specific initiation rituals.[20]

It is tempting to draw parallels between Karl's Masonic values and Carl's later focus on symbols and rituals. Carl's interest in sculpting stone, his autodidactic approach to architecture and masonry, and his construction of a stone house in Bollingen may also resonate with Freemasonry. Notably, Freemasons viewed carving and cutting stone as a metaphor for refining one's character and smoothing one's "sharp edges."

Finally, as an interesting aside, the Old University in Basel is now home to eikones – Center for the Theory and History of the Image (with the Greek word *eikones* meaning "image" or "symbol").

26 A Basilisk Atop The Augustinerbrunnen Carrying Basel's Coat of Arms. Münster spires superimposed in the background.

AUGUSTINERBRUNNEN, RHEINSPRUNG 21

A PAGAN CREATURE HOLDS THE BISHOP'S STAFF

As Rheinsprung became Augustinergasse, Carl would pass the Augustinerbrunnen on his left, presided over by a basilisk. The basilisk, typically carrying Basel's coat of arms—a black bishop's staff against a white background—represented a symbol system that emerged a few years before the founding of the University of Basel (1460).

Carl would have regularly seen this fountain, where the current basilisk was installed in 1846. The fountain itself dates back to 1468, though a basilisk was only added to the top of the pillar in 1530, one year before the death of Johannes Oekolampad (1482–1531). Shortly before, in 1529, Oekolampad had been appointed Basel's first Antistes (leader of the Protestant Church). It is worthwhile to ponder the basilisk and its significance, as 72 Basilisks can be found around Basel, with approximately 28 of them adorning fountains. They appear in the context of religion, alchemy, medicine, and art—all fields relevant to Carl's later life and work.

A Basler historian has catalogued and classified 28 distinct types of basilisks in the city. The Basel Basilisk or *Draco Helveticus* (Helvetic Dragon) is a chimera of a rooster and a dragon, featuring two wings, two legs, a rooster's head with comb (known in German as a "crown"), and a feathered body. Its wings are scaled like those of a bat (but partly feathered), its claws are three-pronged like a bird's, and its long, dragon-like tail ends with an arrow.[21]

A curious historical record testifies that, on August 4, 1474, an 11-year-old rooster in Basel that had allegedly laid an egg thought to be capable of hatching a basilisk was put on trial in Basel, as officially documented:

27 Close-up of the Basilisk
Draco Helveticus adorns the fountain pillar

During the proceedings it was shown that cock's eggs were of use in mixing certain magical preparations and that sorcerers were therefore eager to get them. The defendant's lawyer frankly admitted this, but contended that the laying of the egg in this particular case had been entirely unpremeditated and involuntary... [Nonetheless] the cock was condemned and was actually burned at the stake before a great crowd of onlookers.[22]

Three eyewitness accounts provide variations on this story. Paraphrasing, Johannes Knebel, the university notary, reported that after the rooster was beheaded, two additional eggs were discovered inside. The rooster's body was then burned in front of the executioner's home on Kohlenberg. Konrad Schnitt reported widespread fear that a worm might hatch from the three eggs found inside the rooster. This resulted in the bird being sentenced to be burned on Kohlenberg. A third report mentions that the executioner was paid three schillings for carrying out the rooster's execution.[23]

The Basel Basilisk holds a range of alchemical meanings, primarily symbolizing the melding of opposites. As both rooster and dragon, it unites dualities: the rooster relates to air, the dragon to earth, and fire is present in its poison and petrifying gaze. As a fountain figure, the basilisk is also linked to water.[24] Like the fountain, the basilisk can represent both evil and Mercurius, the philosopher's stone, or gold.

28 Museum at Augustinergasse 2, later called the Natural History Museum (c. 1906)
"Jung's interest in art blossomed during his youth in Basel and throughout his education."
(*The Art of C. G. Jung*, p. 20)

29 Augustinergasse (c. 1850–1880)
Lithograph showing the museum,
Augustiner Fountain, and
Basel Münster in the background.

NATURHISTORISCHES MUSEUM, AUGUSTINERGASSE 2

CARL DISCOVERS ALL MANNER OF THINGS

Just beyond the fountain, Carl would have passed the classically styled Museum der Stadt (Museum of the City), now known as the Naturhistorisches Museum Basel. During his childhood, the museum served as a multipurpose institution, housing an extensive osteological collection with bones from more than 1,000 animal species, including fossils. It also featured ethnological displays in its showcases. At the museum's opening in 1849, the *Öffentliche Kunstsammlung* (public art collection) was housed on the second floor, where Carl was captivated by the paintings on display. In later life, Jung recounted a visit to the museum at the age of 6, accompanied by his godmother, Aunt Augusta "Gusteli" Preiswerk. She had taken him to see the taxidermy collection, and as the museum was closing, Carl could not tear himself away from the displays. The attendants eventually locked the room, and Carl and Aunt Gusteli were forced to exit by another staircase. On their way out, Carl suddenly found himself standing in front of something he described as extremely beautiful. Before he could fully take in the sight, his aunt reacted with horror, pulling him away and shouting, "Disgusting boy, shut your eyes; disgusting boy, shut your eyes!" Carl had stumbled upon figures wearing nothing but fig leaves. He recalled, "My aunt was simmering with indignation, as though she had been dragged through a pornographic institute."[25]

Carl was particularly interested in the works on display of two of Basel's greatest painters: Hans Holbein the Younger (1497/8–1543), celebrated for his masterful portraits, and Arnold Böcklin (1827–1901), a leading figure of Symbolism. Three of Böcklin's monumental wall paintings—*Magna Mater, Flora,* and *Apollon* (1868–1879)—can still be seen in the museum's stairwell.[26] They are the only suviving frescoes by Arnold Böcklin.

During his formative years, Carl's exposure to these works, along with paintings by Ferdinand Hodler (1853–1918), a prominent Swiss painter, and Hans Sandreuter (1850–1901), a Swiss Symbolist, likely influenced his early artistic endeavors (1900–1904).[27]

The Jung family shared a connection to Arnold Böcklin through Ernst Stückelberg, who was a close friend of the Symbolist painters. Also housed in this museum is an oil portrait of Karl Jung, Carl's grandfather, which can be viewed today in the museum auditorium. This auditorium, still used by the university for ceremonial events, features a portrait gallery of Basel's intellectuals. Upon entering, visitors can find Karl Jung's portrait on the right. Depicted as a professor of medicine, he is shown with one hand resting on a skull placed on his thigh.

30 (left) Arnold Böcklin Fresco *Magna Mater* (1886) with T-Rex Head
A whimsical juxtaposition of Arnold Böcklin's fresco and a dinosaur head in the stairwell of the Natural History Museum Basel on Augustinergasse, illustrating the museum's multifaceted nature.

31 Portrait of Karl Gustav Jung (Carl's Grandfather), Age 54 by Heinrich Beltz (1854)
Displayed in the auditorium of the Natural History Museum Basel.

32 Picture Gallery of the Public Art Collection, Museum Augustinergasse (c. 1860–1880)

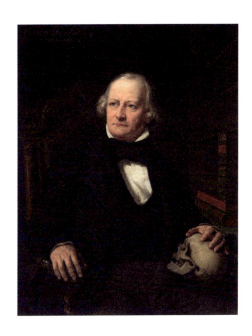

TOUR 2

Over the years, this auditorium has hosted lectures by many distinguished scholars. For example, as a new faculty member, Nietzsche delivered his inaugural lecture, "Homer and Classical Philology," on May 28, 1869. He later wrote to his sister that two of his lectures in 1870 drew "a packed audience," and that a series of five public lectures on education, delivered over several months, attracted more than 300 attendees—a remarkable achievement at the time.[28]

Dialects Heard in the Basel Region: An Auditory Journey

As Carl made his daily journey from Kleinhüningen to the Gymnasium, a subtle auditory transition would have taken place as the sounds of the rural farming and fishing village gradually gave way to the more "cultured" environment of the Gymnasium on Münster Hill. Kleinhüningen, with its high immigrant population—particularly from southern Baden and Alsace—reflected a working-class atmosphere distinct from the refined language and culture of the school.[29]

Jung later wrote that, in his Gymnasium, "a refined German and French" was spoken.[30] For schoolchildren across Swiss German–speaking regions, the spoken language shifted to High German upon entering the classroom, as Swiss German is not an officially written language. Both High German and French were compulsory subjects in the curriculum.

Both of Carl's parents were originally from Grossbasel, so he grew up learning the Basel dialect. However, he also took on the more working-class dialect of Kleinhüningen, which he humorously referred to as "Waggis-Basel," poking fun at his own speech.[31]

14 GYMNASIUM, MÜNSTERPLATZ 15

NINE YEARS OF STUDY

As the imposing buildings on Augustinergasse gave way, Carl would have arrived at the expansive, cobblestoned Münsterplatz, dominated by Basel Münster. Behind the Münster lay the Pfalz, a raised terrace offering an unobstructed view of the Rhine and its surroundings.

Carl's final destination would have been located just before the Münster: the Unteres Gymnasium (middle school) and Oberes Gymnasium (high school). A large, heavy, arched wooden door opened into the courtyard of the school buildings where Carl spent nine formative years. His report cards indicate that he attended the Unteres Gymnasium for five years (ages 11 to 16)—one year longer than usual due to an accident and prolonged illness that necessitated his repeat of a year. After completing the full five years, Carl advanced to the Oberes Gymnasium (ages 16 to 20), engaging in four years of study there, culminating in a total of nine years at the Gymnasium.

Since the 11th century, a clerical Latin school under the Bishop's authority has existed at this location. In 1529, the Great Council transferred oversight of education from the church to the city of Basel. The school, formally founded in 1589, is stately yet overshadowed by the adjacent Münster. Over the centuries, it has been known by various names: Schule auf Burg, Münsterschule, Pädagogium, Oberes und Unteres Gymnasium zu Basel, and the Gymnasium. Since 1997, it has been called the Gymnasium am Münsterplatz. During Carl's time, only young men were enrolled and, between 1600 and 1900, it was recognized as one of the most prestigious schools in the German-speaking world, with both Friedrich Nietzsche and Jakob Burckhardt teaching there at various times. When Carl attended, the school was also referred to as the Gymnasium. Above the grand arched threshold with its mighty wooden door, the Latin inscription *Moribus et litteris sacrum* ("Consecrated to character formation and scholarship") is engraved in golden letters against a black background.[32]

33 Gymnasium Courtyard
Basel Münster is visible in the background. Corner of photograph missing due to a broken glass plate.

34 Unteres and Oberes Gymnasium (c. 1904)
View from the Basel Münster spire.

Unteres Gymnasium

Jung described his initiation to higher education in Basel as follows:

> *Thus I was taken away from my rustic playmates, and truly entered the "great world," where powerful personages, far more powerful than my father, lived in big, splendid houses, drove about in expensive carriages drawn by magnificent horses, and talked a refined German and French. Their sons, well dressed, equipped with fine manners and plenty of pocket money, were now my classmates.*[33]

The elite Gymnasium primarily educated the wealthiest and most privileged children in the city, and Carl felt embarrassed by the fact that he had received a stipend for his studies.[34] Reflecting on this period as an adult, he wrote that he had become "aware how poor we were, that my father was a poor country parson and I, a still poorer parson's son who had holes in his shoes and had to sit for six hours in school with wet socks."[35] While Carl's family belonged to a relatively better-off class in Kleinhüningen due to his father's position as a pastor, he experienced himself at the bottom of the social hierarchy compared to his classmates at the prestigious school on Münsterplatz.

At the end of Carl's first year at the Gymnasium, around the age of 12 or 13, a classmate pushed him headfirst into the cobblestones. At that moment, Jung recalled thinking, "Now you don't have to go to school anymore."[36] He lay on the ground a bit longer than necessary and was subsequently excused from school to recuperate. What a relief this must have been. As a pre-pubescent, Carl found himself with a newfound space in which his inner world, imagination, and soul were free to unfold. Released from the daily pressures of school and its confrontations, he experienced fainting spells whenever he was expected to return or complete his homework. During this time of retreat, he found the freedom and time to draw. He later recalled: "I was free, could dream for hours, be anywhere I liked, in the woods or by the water or draw. I resumed my battle pictures and furious scenes of war, of old castles that were being assaulted or burned, or drew page upon page of caricatures."[37] Many of these images have been preserved.[38]

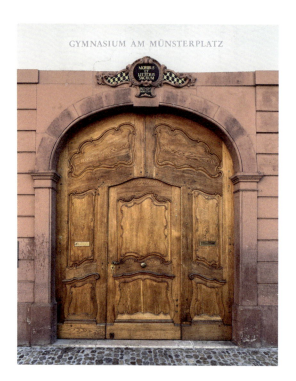

35 Entrance to the Oberes Gymnasium
The inscription above the door at Münsterplatz 15 reads: *Moribus et litteris sacrum* ("Consecrated to character formation and scholarship").

36 (right) Basel Münster Square with Cobblestones
The Gymnasium entrance lies across from the Münster.

It was only when Carl overheard his father express concern that he lacked the finances to care for an invalid son that Carl willed himself to overcome the fainting spells and return to school.[39]

He was not alone in having to repeat his second year at the Unteres Gymnasium. Ten of his male classmates from classes 1B (1886) and 2B (1887) also repeated year 2B (1988) alongside him, while two students failed out completely. It appears that this was not an unusual occurrence and perhaps not as shameful or isolating as being held back might seem in modern times. Carl's repeated year introduced him to a new mix of classmates, including some with whom he had already studied during the previous two years. However, he was separated from his good friend Albert Oeri, who had advanced to the next level. The Gymnasium had four class levels, each divided into "A" and "B" streams (1A, 2A, 3A, and 4A, with corresponding "B" classes), with an average of 35 to 40 students per class. While some students came and went, the structure remained fairly consistent.

37 Carl's Quarterly Report Card from the Oberes Gymnasium (April–July, 1894) Signed by Rector (principal) Dr. Burckhardt, with commentary: *"Er hat sich wegen eigenmächtigen Verhaltes und wegen Theilnahme an Störung, auf dem Schulspaziergang, Tadel zugezogen"* ("He has been reprimanded for unauthorized behavior and for participating in a disturbance on the school walk").

A few notable anomalies are evident in Carl's academic record. During August to October 1888, the words *"unerlaubte Mittel"* (unpermitted materials) were written next to his name, possibly referencing the infamous plagiarism charge that so outraged him. Later, in Class 4B (June to July 1891), his performance in "Religion" was marked with a grade "1" (the highest score), followed by three red "X"s, as if to indicate enthusiastic appreciation for his work. His cumulative grade for these months was also a "1."

What were the classes taught at those ages? Religion was listed first, followed by Greek, Latin, French, and German—four languages. Other subjects included mathematics, history, geography, and the natural sciences. English was an optional class. Singing was also optional, and Carl regularly opted out. Most of the students took sports, but Carl was predominantly excused from these, possibly due to some lingering effects of his accident or because his daily 90-minute walk to and from school provided sufficient physical activity.

Carl's start at school proved challenging. He began his studies in April, but by the winter of his first year, he had already missed twelve days of school. In the following January and February, his absences increased dramatically to 58 days, and a line was drawn behind his name to indicate that he received no grade. By April, Carl had returned to school, attending classes regularly and excelling academically. Between April and September, he earned the highest cumulative grade, ranking second in his class, with minimal absences. However, from October to December, he missed another 32 days and again received no grades. These irregular absences, totaling approximately four months, resulted in Carl having to repeat class 2B.

Despite these early struggles, Carl demonstrated strong academic performance throughout his education. His cumulative grades were most often "1"s, with the occasional "2." His overall average never fell below a "2" on the grading scale, which ranged from "1" (highest) to "4" (failing). His class ranking was consistently high—often second—though it fluctuated during the year he repeated, when his ranking shifted from sixteenth to fifth, then to thirteenth, second, eleventh, and back to second.

Table 3
Carl's Classmates at the Unteres Gymnasium (1886–1891)
Carl repeated Class 2B during the 1888/89 academic year.

Class 1B	1886/87	Class 2B	1887/88	Class 2B	1888/89	Class 3B	1889/90	Class 4B	1890/91
Bär	Louis	Bär	Louis	Buser	Walter	Bächlin	Jakob	Bächlin	Jakob
Brennwald	Emanuel	Bruckner	Rudolf	Cockburn	David	Bär	Louis	Bär	Louis
Bruckner	Rudolf	Dolt	Edward	Dreifus	Edmund	Dreifus	Edmund	Bloch	Max
Dolt	Edward	Enslin	Eugen	Eppler	Theophil*	Finninger	Wilhelm	Bossart	Arthur
Duthaler	Heinrich	Fäsch	Fritz	Frey	Heinrich*	Fleig	Oskar	Cockburn	David
Enslin	Eugen	Fininger	Wilhelm	Futterer	Gustav	Gautschy	Wilhelm	Dreifus	Edmund
Eppler	Theophil	Frey	Carl	Gautschy	Wilhelm*	Guggenheim	Sally	Eppler	Theophil
Fäsch	Fritz	Frey	Georg	Gentsch	Otto	Hay	Percy	Finninger	Wilhelm
Fininger	Wilhelm	Frey	Heinrich	Guggenheim	Sally	Heman	Erwin	Fleig	Oskar
Frey	Carl	Gräber	Paul	Herman	Erwin	Huber	Oskar	Glatz	Theodor
Frey	Georg	Hagenbach	Rudolf	Huber	Oskar	Jörin	Wilhelm	Gonsor	Rudolf
Frey	Heinrich	Hay	Percy	Jenny	Eduard	Jung	Carl	Guggenheim	Sally
Gautschy	Wilhelm	Herzer	Hugo	Jörin	Wilhelm*	Kestenholz	Hans	Hay	Percy
Gouber	Prosper	Hill	Karl	Jung	Carl	Kollmann	Emil	Jorin	Wilhelm
Gräter	Paul	Hoffmann	Albert	Kestenholz	Hans	Müller	Rudolf*	Joos	Albert
Hagenbach	Rudolf	Hübscher	Hans	Kollmann	Emil	Oser	Adam	Jung	Carl
Hay	Percy	Johner	Hermann	Lichtenhahn	August	Oswald	Ernst	Lichtenhahn	August
Herzer	Hugo	Joos	Albert	Merian	Walter*	Preiswerk	Mathis*	Lichtenhahn	Hans
Hill	Karl	Jung	Carl	Müller	Rudolf*	Rinderspacher	Wilhelm	Müller	Rudolf
Hoffmann	Albert	Karcher	Gustav	Oser	Adam	Ronus	Max	Oswald	Ernst
Johner	Hermann	Katz	Henri	Ostermeyer	Leo	Rudin	Caesar	Preiswerk	Adolf
Joos	Albert	Kübler	Alfred	Oswald	Ernst	Sauerbeck	Ernst	Ramus	Karl
Jung	Carl*	Lutz	Max.	Preiswerk	Mathis*	Scheuermann	Beda	Ronus	Max
Karcher	Gustav	Merian	Walter	Preiswerk	Peter*	Schläpfer	Paul	Rudin	Caesar
Katz	Henri	Müller	Arnold	Riesterer	Robert	Steib	Julius	Sauerbeck	Ernst
Köchlin	Max.	Müller	Rudolf	Rodemeyer	August	Stumm	Karl	Scheuermann	Beda
Lutz	Max.	Niethammer	Theodor	Ronus	Max	Vischer	Hans	Schultze	Otto
Merian	Walter	Preiswerk	Mathis*	Rudin	Caesar	Wächter	Nathanael	Spindler	August
Meyer	René	Preiswerk	Peter*	Sauerbeck	Ernst	Weynert	Arno	Spinnler	Fritz
Müller	Arnold	Raupp	Karl					Steib	Julius
Müller	Rudolf	Riggenbach	Lukas					Stumm	Karl
Tappolet	Peter	Sandreczki	Otto					Weitnauer	Emil
		Schaffner	Edward					Weynert	Arno
		Schuler	Fritz						
		Seiler	Adolf						
		Steib	Julius						
		Stöcklin	Paul						
		Stumm	Karl						
		Tappulet	Peter						

Table 4
Carl's Classmates at the Oberes Gymnasium (1891–1895)

						Graduation Year	
Class 1B	**1891/92**	**Class 2B**	**1892/93**	**Class 3B**	**1893/94**	**Class 4B**	**1894/95**
Berner	Fritz	**Berner**	Fritz	**Berner**	Fritz	**Berner**	Fritz
Brennwald	Emanuel	**Brennwald**	Emanuel	**Degen**	Isaak	**Degen**	Isaak
Degen	Isaak	**Degen**	Isaak	**Glatz**	Theodor	**Frith**	Paul
Glatz	Theodor	**Glatz**	Theodor	**Gonsor**	Rudolf	**Glatz**	Theodor
Golay	Eug. Emil	**Gonsor**	Rudolf	**Gough**	Charles	**Gonsor**	Rudolf
Gonsor	Rudolf	**Gough**	Charles	**Guggenheim**	Sally	**Gough**	Karl
Gough	Charles	**Guggenheim**	Sally	**Hay**	Percy	**Hay**	Percy
Guggenheim	Sally	**Hay**	Percy	**Jung**	Carl	**Jung**	Carl
Hay	Percy	**Jung**	Carl	**Lichtenhahn**	August	**Oswald**	Ernst
Jung	Carl	**Lichtenhahn**	August	**Miescher**	Gerhard	**Pfisterer**	Heinrich
Lichtenhahn	August	**Miescher**	Gerhard	**Oswald**	Ernst	**Rusterholz**	Heinrich
Lichtenhahn	Hans	**Oswald**	Ernst	**Pfisterer**	Heinrich	**Sauerbeck**	Ernst
Miescher	Gerhard	**Pfisterer**	Heinrich	**Rusterholz**	Heinrich	**Scheuermann**	Beda
Oswald	Ernst	**Rusterholz**	Heinrich	**Sauerbeck**	Ernst	**Vontisch**	Reinhard
Pfisterer	Heinrich	**Sauerbeck**	Ernst	**Scheuermann**	Beda		
Sauerbeck	Ernst	**Scheuermann**	Beda	**Vontisch**	Reinhard		
Scheuermann	Beda	**Vontisch**	Reinhard				
Steib	Julius	**Weynert**	Arnold				
Weynert	Arnold						

Notes for Tables 3 and 4
- The academic year consolidates multiple student evaluation periods. As a rule, students who failed throughout the year were removed from the list.
- The spelling of a student's name varied in some cases (e.g., Henri, Henry, Heinrich). The most frequently used form has been standardized. For example, Carl's name appeared as both "Karl" and "Carl"; for consistency, "Carl" has been used throughout.
- The average number of students represents those enrolled and those who left during a given year. The values show considerable variation.
- An asterisk * denotes students who repeated a year.

Oberes Gymnasium

Diverse sources show that Carl was an intense, engaged, and emotional youth. As a student at the Upper Gymnasium, he learned the classical languages Latin and Ancient Greek, which were considered foundational for understanding European culture and essential for a comprehensive education. His report cards show that he also studied German, French, history, geography, mathematics, physics, chemistry, natural history, religion, and sports, receiving top grades in most subjects.[40] He showed particularly strong proficiency in Latin, and his Latin teacher, recognizing his advanced abilities, assigned him special tasks: "So, instead of making me sit in class, this teacher would often send me to the university library to fetch books for him, and I would joyfully dip into them while prolonging the walk back as much as possible."[41]

A transcript from Carl's four years at the Oberes Gymnasium reveals that his class began with nineteen students and dwindled down to only fourteen by the end of his studies. Advancement was strictly dependent on performance, and not all students met the rigorous standard. This undoubtedly created immense pressure for young Carl, whose academic records show consistent excellence. Later in life, Jung recalled two significant events from his time at the Oberes Gymnasium, both leaving a lasting impression and a sense of injustice that lingered into his 80s. The first was being accused of plagiarism—an allegation he adamantly refused—and the second was being told that he could not draw. Ironically, Jung became an accomplished painter, yet he firmly rejected being labeled an artist.[42]

Carl was an autodidact, reading voraciously and immersing himself in whatever materials he could access. See Table 5 at the end of this tour for a list of what Carl was reading. Many records in the table refer to a Folio draft compiled by Sonu Shamdasani, based on handwritten library records documenting books Carl (and others) borrowed from the University of Basel. In a personal communication (Feb. 2025), Shamdasani wrote: "The bulk of the books taken out were by the professors and lecturers. Of the students, it is interesting to see Jung's friends and

38 Oberes Gymnasium
Schüler-Buch 2 (Pupil Book 2).
Cover and class list.

 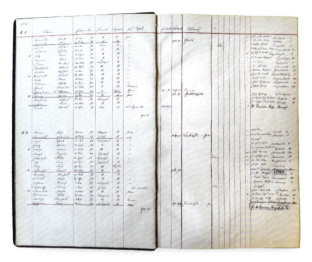

fellow Zofingians, such as Oeri, Steiner, Senn, Vischer (a number of other students were also Zofingians – indicating that this was the intellectual student body. Oeri seemed to take out the most. Also, there were few medical students. (Oeri and Vischer were philosophy students)."

A commemorative plaque displayed in the entryway to the courtyard of the Gymnasium lists notable students and faculty. Among them is Jung, alongside figures such as Johann Rudolf Wettstein (Mayor of Basel); Johann, Jakob, and Daniel Bernoulli (mathematicians); Leonhard Euler (mathematician); Johann Peter Hebel (poet); Arnold Böcklin (painter); Alfred Dreyfus (French Army officer); and Hanspeter Tschudi (Federal Councillor). Distinguished faculty members include (chronologically): Thomas Platter (rector), Johann Bernoulli (mathematician), Friedrich Nietzsche (poet and philosopher), Jacob Burckhardt (historian), Christian Friedrich Schönbein (chemist and physician), and Alfred Gasser (historian).

You will search in vain for women's names here. Throughout his education, from grammar school to his advanced studies, Carl was almost exclusively surrounded by boys and men. Under no circumstances were girls and boys taught in the same school building, much less the same classroom. Although there was a secondary school for girls at the time, it was not until 1899 that a grammar school section was introduced to prepare female students for university study.

While Carl was studying at the Gymnasium, his older cousin Louise "Luggy" Preiswerk (Allenspach branch), just a year his senior, was enrolled in the Töchterschule (Daughters' S chool) on Kanonengasse, which opened in 1884. There, she studied English, French, bookkeeping, trade subjects, and fine handicrafts. Upon graduation at age 16, most girls from affluent families attended a pension (a type of boarding school in the French-speaking part of Switzerland) or lived with a French-speaking family to learn the language, gain childcare experience, and acquire household management skills. Luggy, however, had different aspirations. Faced with limited professional options for educated women—teacher, secretary, or office clerk—she decided to pursue bookkeeping and languages. Because courses in the new commercial school would not begin until the fall, Luggy spent the interim working as a *Mägdlein* (maid) in the household of her favorite aunt: Aunt Emilie, Carl's mother.[43]

At the end of each school day, Carl would retrace his steps, walking the same 4 kilometers back home, by whichever path. Unfortunately for Carl, the tram service from Basel to Kronenplatz (in the center of Kleinhüningen) only began operations in 1897—a year after his father's death. By then, the Jung-Preiswerk family had moved to Bottminger Mühle in Binningen. From this new home, Carl would continue his daily walk—again, 4 kilometers each way—to the university and back.

Ad Fontes

Ad fontes (translated as "back to the sources") is a principle rooted in the humanist tradition. Four centuries prior to Jung's birth, the practice of returning to the original wellsprings of classical literature and translating ancient Greek and Roman manuscripts was essential to humanism's basic structure and method. This tradition became deeply embedded in Basel's culture, offering a rigorous pedagogical foundation for Jung's lifelong intellectual inquiries and clinical work.

One of the most celebrated examples of *ad fontes* is provided by Erasmus of Rotterdam, the renowned Basler. In 1516, Erasmus published:
an edition of the Greek text of the New Testament, along with a new Latin translation, which improved and clarified the text of the Vulgate [...] The precious volume, a small folio, was fairly easy to handle, and was printed in two columns: on one side was an edition of the Greek text of the New Testament, and on the other a new Latin translation of the Vulgate, accompanied by the Annotationes that clarified and justified it. Erasmus thus becomes a pioneer in the field of publishing Biblical texts, as the publication of a Greek version of the New Testament was an extraordinary and almost provocative endeavor in 1516.[44]

This "provocative endeavor" of going back to the source to create a new translation that would challenge the conventional reliance on the Latin Vulgate sent shockwaves across Europe. It is now considered a groundbreaking publishing achievement and a key moment in intellectual history that cemented Erasmus's legacy.

Jung's work reflects this same *ad fontes* spirit, as he devoted much of his life to returning to the foundational sources across diverse fields of study. For instance, this methodological approach underpinned his fruitful collaboration with Marie-Louise von Franz, particularly in the study of alchemy. Von Franz, who majored in classical philology (Latin and Greek) with minors in literature and ancient history, translated several significant alchemical texts, including the *Aurora Consurgens* (attributed to Thomas Aquinas). This translation became the third part of Jung's *Mysterium Coniunctionis* (published in 1957).[45]

Over his lifetime, Jung amassed a remarkable collection of rare, antique books, including more than 200 alchemical texts. These texts have since been digitized by ETH Zürich and are now available online.[46] It is unclear, however, whether young Carl knew of the rare alchemical collections housed in the University of Basel Library during his school years.

Table 5
Selection of Books Read by Carl During his Basel Years

* Age given only if documented.
** Full citations included in the references at the end of this volume.

Age*	Author	Title in English
Preschool	Johann Amos Comenius	Orbis Pictus; with pictures from Vaclava Sokol.
Across ages		The Holy Bible
12–13 years	Emanuel Biedermann	Christian Dogma
15 years	Wolfram von Eschenbach	Perceval: The Story of the Grail
	Friedrich Gerstäcker	Unspecified work by Gerstäcker
15–16 years	Johann Wolfgang von Goethe	Faust
	Eduard Mörike	Weylas' Song
	Friedrich Hölderlin	Complete Works Poems
16–20 years	Homer	The Odyssey
	Virgil	The Aeneid; The Eclogues
	Horace	Multiple sources
16–19 years	Pythagoras, Empedocles, Heraclitus	Multiple sources
prior to 20 years	Nicolas Camille Flammarion	One volume in the Flammarion series
16–22 years	Aeschylus, Sophocles, Euripedes, Plato	Multiple sources
16–23 years	Meister Eckardt	Sermons
20 years, 4 May 1896		Minutes of the beyr. Akad 1896 I
20 years, 4 May 1896	Albert Kölliker	Handbook of Human Tissue Science; Elements of the Nervous System
20 years, 4 May 1896	Emil Zuckerkandl	Anatomy of the Oral Cavity; Journal of Scientific Zoology
20 years, 3 & 11 July 1896	Johann Zöllner	Scientific papers
21 years	Carl du Prel	The Philosophy of Mysticism; The Mystery of Humans; Spiritism
21 years, 30 Jan & 7 May 1897	Immanuel Kant	Lectures on Psychology
21 years, 16 Jan 1897	Alfred Russel Wallace	The Scientific Aspect of the Supernatural, 1886 edition
21 years, 15 Feb 1897	Rudolf Wolf (Prof. University of Zürich and ETH Zürich)	Astronomy 1 & 2
21 years, 7 May 1897	Ludwig Friedrich Büchner (Karl Ludwig)	Force and Matter: Principles of the Natural Order of the Universe
21 years, 15 May, 1 July 1897	Friedrich Nietzsche	Complete Works of Nietzsche (Vols 2, 3, 4); Beyond Good and Evil
21 years, 4 May 1897	Arthur Schopenhauer	Appendices and Omissions
22–24 years	Friedrich Nietzsche	Untimely Meditations; Thus Spoke Zarathustra

TOUR 2

Title in German (date of first publication)	Comments	Sources**
Orbis Pictus; with pictures from Vaclava Sokol, 1883	Illustrated children's book read to Carl by his mother	MDR, p. 17
Die Heilige Schrift	With time, Carl knew the Bible inside and out	
Christliche Dogmatik, 1869	He found this on his father's shelf	Ellenberger, p. 65
Parzival, 1200–1215 (likely based on Chrétien de Troyes' *Perceval*)	"It was my favorite book as a child, I thought it was truly wonderful" (Protocols, Oct 4, 1957)	MDR, pp. 27, 165
Nicht näher bezeichnetes Werk von Gersträcker	Travel writing	Shamdasani, p. 12
Faust, 1808	A book Carl's mother encouraged him to read	MDR, p. 27
Gesang Weylas, 1831	"An exquisite poem"	MDR, p. 28; Shamdasani, p. 12
Gesammelte Dichtungen, 1896	Carl found the lyric poem Patmos "insurpasable"	MDR, p. 28
Odyssey	"I loved the Odyssey"	MDR, p. 28
Aeneid; Eclogues	Likely Gymnasium reading	Shamdasani, p. 11
Mehrfache Quellen	Some poems	Shamdasani, p. 11
Mehrfache Quellen	"Heraclitus was my favorite"	MDR, p. 30
Ein Band der Flammarion-Reihe	Rudolf Preiswerk-Allenspach brought a book by Flammarion back from a business trip. Six works were published prior to Rudolf's death (1895). The volume referenced here explored astronomy and the cosmos, and was published by the Academie Française	Zumstein-Preiswerk, C.G. Jung's Medium, p. 73
Mehrfache Quellen	Likely Gymnasium reading	MDR, p. 68; Shamdasani, p. 19
Sermones et Lectiones Super Ecclesiastici (Latin, 1260–1328)	"Only in Meister Eckhart did I feel the breath of life—not that I understood him." His sermons are among the most influential works of medieval Christian mysticism	MDR, p. 68; Shamdasani, p. 20
Sitzungsbericht der beyr. Akad 1896 I		Shamdasani, Folio
Handbuch der Gewebelehre des Menschen (Vol. 5), 1867; *Elemente des Nervensytems* (Vol. 6), 1893		Shamdasani, Folio
Anatomie der Mundhöhle, 1891; *Zeitschrift für wissenschaftliche Zoologie,* XII	Switzerland's first zoo opened 3 July 1874	Shamdasani, Folio
Wissenschaftliche Abhandlungen (Vols 1–4), 1882	Four volumes. Library books borrowed from the University of Basel	Shamdasani, Folio
Die Philosophie des Mystizismus, 1885; *Das Rätsel des Menschen; Der Spiritismus*	Carl gave two books by Du Prel to Luggy on New Year's Day 1897	Zumstein-Preiswerk, C.G. Jung's Medium, p. 142
Vorlesungen über Psychologie		Shamdasani, Folio
Die Wissenschaftliche Ansicht des Übernatürlichen, 1874	First published in English, this book advocates for an open-minded approach to investigating claims of the supernatural.	Shamdasani, Folio
Astronomie 1 & 2 (likely later published as *Handbuch der Astronomie, ihrer Geschichte und Litteratur*)	An overview of astronomical knowledge at the time of publication. Prof. Wolf made significant contributions to astronomy, particularly in the domain of solar physics	Shamdasani, Folio
Kraft und Stoff: Empirisch-naturphilosophische Studien, 1855	An unusual bestseller of the time	Shamdasani, Folio
Nietzsche *Werke* (Vols 2, 3, 4); *Jenseits von Gut und Böse,* 1886		Shamdasani, Folio
Parerga and Parapilomena (Vols 1 & 2), 1851	Essays covering a wide range of subjects, from metaphysics and aesthetics to psychology and social criticism	Shamdasani, Folio
Unzeitgemäße Betrachtungen, 1873–1876; *Also sprach Zarathustra,* 1883	A "powerful experience"	Jung, Nietzsche's Zarathustra, vol. 1, p. 544; Shamdasani, p. 29; Shamdasani, Folio

Table 5 (continued)
Selection of Books Read by Carl During his Basel Years

* Age given only if documented.
** Full citations included in the references at the end of this volume.

Age*	Author	Title in English
22 years, 17 Aug 1897	Justinus Kerner	The Seeress of Prevorst: Being Revelations Concerning the Inner Life of Man and the Inter-Diffusion of a World of Spirits in the One We Inhabit
22 years, 17 Aug 1897	Immanuel Kant	The Critique of Pure Reason
22 years	Arthur Schopenhauer	Will in Nature; The World as Will and Representation; Attempt on Spirit-Seeing and What is Connected with It
22 years, 17 Nov 1897	Felix von Niemeyer	Textbook on Special Pathology and Therapy
22 years, 15 Jan 1898	Eduard von Hartmann	The Philosophy of the Unconscious
22 years, 18 Jan 1898	Emanuel Swedenborg	Secrets of Heaven
22 years, 17 Mar 1898		Archive for Psychiatry
22 years, 16 Mar 1898	Paul Flechsig	Brain and Soul
22 years, 18 Mar 1898	Justinus Kerner	History of Somnambulism
22 years, 23 Mar 1898	Justinus Kerner	History of Modern Possession
23 years	Immanuel Kant	Natural History and the Theory of the Heaven; Dreams of a Spirit Seer; Religion within the Bounds of Reason Alone
23 years, 29 Aug 1898	Karl Kiesewetter	On the History of Modern Occultism
23 years, 13 Sep & 18 Oct 1898	Eduard Hartmann	The Thing-in-Itself and Its Nature; The Self-Destruction of Christianity and the Religion of the Future
23 years, 29 Sep 1898	Joseph Ennemoser	History of Magic
23 years, 16 Sep, 18 Oct 1898	Emanuel Swedenborg	Of Heaven and Its Wonderful Things Therein; The Celestial Bodies in Our Solar System, Which We Call Planets; The Interaction Between Soul and Body; The Interaction Between Soul and Body
23 years, 29 Sep 1898	Wilhelm Wundt	Essays
23 years, 12 Dez 1898	C. A. Ch. Wasianski	About Immanuel Kant in the Last Years of his Life
23 years, 22 Dec, 1898	Albrecht Ritschl	Theologie and Metaphysics; Three Academic Talks
	Carl Gustav Carus	Psyche: The Developmental History of the Soul
25 years	Richard von Kraft-Ebbing	Textbook of Psychiatry
25–26 years	Sigmund Freud	Interpretation of Dreams

Title in German (date of first publication)	Comments	Sources**
Die Seherin von Prevost, 1829	This book documents the experiences of Friederike Hauffe (1801–1829), a woman from Prevost, Germany, who exhibited remarkable psychic abilities. Carl gave this book to Helene Preiswerk on her 15th birthday. Hauffe's visions, presented within, had a profound influence on her	Shamdasani, Folio; Zumstein-Preiswerk, C.G. Jung's Medium, pp. 16, 68, 72
Kritik der reinen Vernunft, 1781	"His philosopher"	Shamdasani, pp. 22–24
Der Wille in der Natur, 1836; *Die Welt als Wille und Vorstellung*, 1818; *Versuch über das Geistersehen und was damit zusammenhängt*, 1851	"His greatest philosophical find"; "enlightened through Schopenhauer and von Hartmann"	MDR, p. 28; Shamdasani, pp. 22, 27
Lehrbuch der speciellen Pathologie und Therapie, 1863		
Die Philosophie des Unbewussten, 1869	Inspired Jung's concept of the unconscious	Shamdasani, pp. 27–28, Folio
Die Himmlischen Geheimnisse (Arcana Cölestia), pub. by Swedenborg, 1750s		Shamdasani, Folio
Archiv für Psychiatrie 23, 1891		Shamdasani, Folio
Gehirn und Seele, 1896	Flechsig was a German neuroanatomist known for his work on brain development and the connection between brain structures and mental functions. This book explores the relationship between the brain and consciousness, contributing to early neuroscience and physiological psychology	Shamdasani, Folio
Geschichte der Somnambulen, 1824	Kerner's work on somnambulism was highly influential in both medical and spiritual circles. His interest in the phenomena of the unconscious, combined with his open-minded approach to exploring cases of altered states of consciousness, marked him as a significant figure in early psychological thought. Somnambulism went on to become the topic of Carl's doctoral dissertation	Shamdasani, Folio
Geschichten Besessener neurer Zeit, 1835		Shamdasani, Folio
Allgemeine Naturgeschichte und Theorie des Himmels, 1755; *Träume eines Geistersehers*, 1766; *Religion innerhalb der Grenzen der bloßen Vernunft*, 1793; *Werke 7,8*	Three books bound together	Shamdasani, p. 24
Zur Geschichte der modernen Occultismus, 1889		Shamdasani, Folio
Das Ding an sich und seine Beschaffenheit, 1871; *Die Selbstzersetzung des Christentums und die Religion der Zukunft*, 1874		Shamdasani, Folio
Geschichte der Magie, 1844	A follower of the new doctrine of animal magnetism, founded by Franz Anton Mesmer	Shamdasani, Folio
Vom Himmel und dem wunderbaren Dingen desselben, 1775; *Die Erdkörper in unserem Sonnensystem, welche wir Planeten heissen*, 1841; *Der Verkehr zwischen Seele u. Leib*, 1830; *Die Wonnen der Weisheit betreff. die eheliche Liebe*, 1845.	Carl read seven volumes	MDR, p. 99; Shamdasani, p. 26; Shamdasani, Folio
Essays 8/3, 1885	Wundt was the founder of experimental psychology	Shamdasani, Folio
Über Immanuel Kant in seinen Letzten Lebensjahren		Shamdasani, Folio
Theologie und Metaphysik, 1881; *Drei Akademische Reden*, 1887	"Its historicism irritated me"	MDR, p. 97; Shamdasani, Folio
Psyche: zur Entwicklungsgeschichte der Seele, 1846, 1851		Shamdasani, p. 27
Lehrbuch der Psychiatrie, 1879	Inspired Carl's decision to specialize in psychiatry	Ellenberger, p. 666; MDR, 108–109
Traumdeutung	Carl read Freud between 1900 and 1903	Brockway, p. 33

39 The Parsonage at Mühlenberg 12 (1935)
Parsonage and home of Carl's uncle, Samuel Gottlob Preiswerk.

ST. ALBAN PFARRHAUS, MÜHLENBERG 12

WHERE ISEMÄNNLI LIVES

Visiting the St. Alban Pfarrhaus (parsonage), an optional stop where Carl spent time each week during his Gymnasium years, will add 15 to 30 minutes to the tour. To get there, pass the main entrance of Basel Münster and proceed onto Rittergasse. Follow Rittergasse to its end at the traffic circle. Cross the circle, angling slightly to the left to continue onto St. Alban-Vorstadt. Turn left at the first intersection onto Mühlenberg. St. Alban Church, where Carl's uncle was pastor, is located a few steps beyond the parsonage.

Every Thursday, Carl was invited to lunch with his uncle, Samuel Gottlob Preiswerk (1825–1912), at the parsonage. The short distance from the Gymnasium made it a convenient walk. Following the death of Carl's father, Samuel became the legal guardian of Johanna Gertrude "Trudi" and Carl (despite Carl being already 18). Carl nicknamed his uncle "Isemännli" (Little Iron Man), due to his strict pietistic morals and unyielding nature.[47] However, Carl was enamored with the intellectual conversations shared at the dining table with his uncle, aunt, and cousins—conversations he did not experience in his own home. His five cousins were 11 to 22 years older than him. All four male cousins would go on to pursue theological study.

TOUR 3

YOUNG ADULTHOOD: FROM THE GYMNASIUM THROUGH UNIVERSITY

Tour 3 explores sites connected to pivotal moments in Carl's young adulthood—a period marked by significant tests of faith, beginning with his "turd vision" at the age of 12. Carl's struggle to reconcile these internal tensions played a crucial role in determining decisions that would profoundly influence the rest of his life and the development of his analytic psychology, including his concepts of individuation and alchemy as a psychological process.

The period also brought deeper encounters with Personality No. 1 and Personality No. 2, which he was beginning to understand as the "spirit of the times" and the "spirit of the depths." As you will learn, Carl was reading the Grail legend at age 15 and engaging with the works of Nietzsche at around age 24.

TOUR 3 OVERVIEW

① **BASLER MÜNSTER, MÜNSTERPLATZ 9**
A Towering Edifice

② **ANTISTITIUM, RITTERGASSE 2**
A Family of Pastors

③ **BISCHOFSHOF, RITTERGASSE 1**
An Opulent Past

④ **MÜNSTER KLOSTERGARTEN, ENTRY OPPOSITE RITTERGASSE 2**
Young Carl's Faith Is Tested

⑤ **HISTORISCHES MUSEUM BASEL, BARFÜSSERPLATZ**
Inspiration: Knights and the Grail Legend

⑥ **LEONHARDSKIRCHPLATZ 1**
At a Threshold: Major Life Choices

⑦ **VESALIANUM, VESALGASSE 1**
Carl Studies Medicine

⑧ **PETERSPLATZ**
The Culmination

⑨ **HAUS ZUM SESSEL, TOTENGÄSSLEIN 3**
Individuation and Alchemy

START
The tour starts at Basel Münster, Münsterplatz 9.

GETTING THERE
Board a tram to Barfüsserplatz and walk up the hill (Münsterberg) to the Münster.

TOUR LENGTH
Allow three hours for this tour located in central Basel.

RETURN
At the Marktplatz tram stop, take in the ornate, red Town Hall. From Marktplatz, trams will take you to multiple places in Basel. For up-to-date tram schedules, visit https://www.sbb.ch/en.

 Scan to follow the tour on Google Maps

This Google Map is also accessible at www.kschaeppi.ch/book

155

1   Basel Münster (1900)

① BASEL MÜNSTER

A TOWERING EDIFICE

Upon arriving at the entrance of Basel Münster (Reformed Protestant Church, Münsterplatz 9), take a moment to pause at its west façade and look diagonally across Münsterplatz toward the Gymnasium. For nine years, Carl passed through the Gymnasium entry, always within sight of the imposing minster. Its mighty presence served as a constant reminder of Basel's religious and intellectual heritage, and for Carl, it was a symbol of not only the city's history, but also his family's personal narrative. Carl's maternal grandparents, Samuel and Augusta Preiswerk-Faber, were married there. Years later, Carl's mother, Emilie Jung-Preiswerk, lived in the Antistitium when her father, Samuel Preiswerk, served as head pastor. On April 8, 1869, during Samuel's tenure, Carl's parents—Paul Jung and Emilie Preiswerk—were also married in the Münster, at the ages of 27 and 21, respectively. Breaking with this family tradition, Jung and his fiancée, Emma Rauschenbach, chose to marry in the Steigkirche in Schaffhausen, Emma's birthplace, on February 14, 1903. During Carl's years at the Gymnasium, Basel Münster was the site of one of the most significant and formative visions of his life.

Basel Münster's thousand-year history has many stories to tell. Some are symbolically rendered in the subtle and overt artistry of its masonry, while others emerge from its origins and the centuries of upheaval that followed. In Carl's time, the church stood for a strict, post-Reformation pietistic morality, emphasizing theology and learning. Originally, however, the Münster was a Roman Catholic cathedral, consecrated in 1019 by its benefactor, Kaiser Heinrich II of Germany (Emperor Henry II), and his wife, Kaiserin Kunigunde (Empress Kunigunde). As it was dedicated to Maria, it was a so-called Marian church.

Despite the Reformation and other transformations throughout its history, remnants of its Marian origin persist. For instance, a band of roses—symbolizing Maria—adorns the façade, and statues of Maria can still be found at the top of the cathedral and in other locations. As a former bishop's church, the Münster holds a legacy tied to the bishops in Basel, who first arrived in the mid-8th century. In addition to its ecclesiastical heritage, it is also a testament to humanitas, evidenced by the tombstone of Erasmus of Rotterdam (1466–1536)— a leading figure of the Renaissance—within the church, behind a pillar on the left.[1]

On the west façade, two pairs of statues flanking the entrance embody a tension of opposites. On the left stand Kaiser Heinrich II, holding a model of the church in his right hand, and Kaiserin Kunigunde.[2] Twelve years after Heinrich II ascended as King of Germany, he and Kunigunde traveled to Rome, where they were crowned Holy Roman Emperor and Empress by the Pope in 1014.[3] Celebrated as an ideal couple, they epitomized the medieval values of piety, sexual restraint, and social engagement,[4] and both were later canonized. Opposite them, to the right of the entrance, stand the Young Seducer, surrounded by threatening snakes and toads crawling from behind, with hellfire at his feet; and the Foolish Virgin, whose flirtatious gaze accompanies her gesture of opening her dress.

Above and between these contrasting pairs once stood a statue of Maria, represented as an intercessor between sacred virtue and worldly temptation. Only the pedestal that once supported her figure remains. From Maria's elevated perspective, the dichotomy (perhaps reflecting compensation) is clear: to her right stand good and piety, while to her left stand evil and folly. For medieval worshippers entering the church (and perhaps even Gymnasium students across the square), these statues served as visual reminders of the eternal struggle between good and evil, the opposition of right and left, and the tension between one's aspirations and the shadows one conceals. As Jung later expressed, the shadow represents "the thing a person has no wish to be."[5] It harbors the repressed, denied, and archetypal darkness within us, contrasting sharply with the religious ideal of light and goodness. The elevation of Maria closer to God, along with the depiction (farther left) of Saint George in heroic combat with a diminutive dragon, mirror and amplify this polarity.

2 Basel Münster Main Portal at the West Façade (1270–1285)
Two couples frame the portal: Kaiser Heinrich II and Kaiserin Kunigunde on the left and the Young Seducer and the Foolish Virgin on the right. Between them, Maria once stood on a pedestal.

Basel's Rich History as a Center of Theology

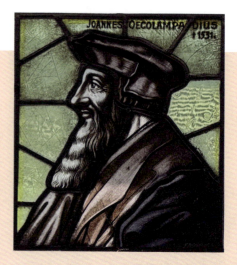

Churches and church spires fill Basel's panorama, bearing testimony to its rich theological past. For seventeen years during the Council of Basel (1431-1448), the Bishop of Basel and clergy of different Catholic orders from across Europe convened in the "Council Room" of the Bischofshof (Bishop's Palace), adjacent to the Basel Münster, to discuss and decide upon matters of faith, doctrine, church administration, and reform. In 1440, their gathering even led to the election of a counter-pope, Felix V. Both the Council and the Reformation left indelible marks on Basel's culture and worldview. In particular, the Council brought significant wealth to the city, as many of the visiting clergy were of noble birth. These clergymen built grand houses around the Münster, supporting local businesses and contributing to Basel's grandeur.

Over the centuries, the city also became home to a variety of religious orders. Basel Münster, originally a Roman Catholic cathedral and seat of the Bishop of Basel, served the broader diocese. Although the Münster had a cloister (a monastic courtyard or walkway), it was not a monastic institution in the strict sense.

By the 14th century, Basel was host to ten convents and monasteries. Among these were several convents for nuns, including the Dominican Convent Klingental on the Kleinbasel Rhine bank, the St. Alban Convent of the Cistercian order along the Grossbasel Rhine bank, the St. Maria Magdalena Convent, the St. Clara Convent (home to the "Klarissen" nuns, followers of Saint Francis), and the Gnadental Convent near the Spalentor gate. During this period, Basel also became a center for the Beguine movement—an informal network of laywomen who sought "to live a religious life in the middle of the world."[6] These women, not formally bound by religious orders, lived independently or in communities, contributing to society through their visionary spirituality, business acumen, and care for the poor and sick. Basel's prominence as a Beguine center at this time is evidenced by the establishment of 22 *beguinages* (houses for Beguine) in the city.

For monks, Basel was home to institutions such as the Predigerkloster (for followers of Saint Dominic), the Barfüsserkloster (home to the "Barefoot Monks," followers of Saint Francis of Assisi), the Augustinerkloster (for followers of Saint Augustus), and the Kartäuserkloster St. Margarethental (Charterhouse of St. Margarethental, for Carthusian monks, followers of Saint Bruno). Additional monastic institutions included St. Peter and St. Leonard.

These institutions played a crucial role in shaping the city's religious and cultural landscape. However, following the Reformation in 1529, many of these convents and monasteries were dissolved or repurposed, as Protestantism took hold in the city.

3   Johannes Oekolampad
(1482-1531), Protestant Reformer
and First Antistes in Basel
Stained glass window in
St. Margaret's Church, where
Carl's uncle, Eduard Preiswerk-
Friedrich, was pastor.

"Spirit of the Times," "Spirit of the Depths"

In Tours 1 and 2, and now in Tour 3, we have repeatedly considered the impact of Basel's intense modernization, juxtaposed against a backdrop of tradition, architecture, and landscapes, as experienced by the Jung family. Long before Carl matriculated at the Gymnasium, he became aware of an inner duality—what he later identified as two distinct personalities: Personality No. 1 and Personality No. 2. Over a lifetime of reckoning with their contradictory natures, he later refined these terms, beginning in his adolescence, into more descriptive characterizations. Personality No. 1 was preoccupied with the driving modern spirit of Carl's contemporary world, which valued science, logic, academic achievement, productivity, and financial success. In contrast, Personality No. 2 was timeless, spiritual, and otherworldly—ephemeral yet deeply compelling. This duality mirrored the opposing influences in Carl's lineage. On one side was his paternal grandfather, a dynamic figure as a medical scientist, public health advocate, and educator. And on the other was his maternal grandfather, a deeply committed theologian and pastor who ultimately rose to the highest ecclesiastical appointment in Basel. Carl's inner conflict between these influences fed into his later wrestle over potential career paths, torn between archeology, science, and—for a time—theology. To better understand how Carl's maternal grandfather's sphere of influence shaped his upbringing, we will now turn our focus to the house in which Carl's mother was raised. Leaving Münsterplatz and the main portal of the Münster behind, head along Rittergasse (Knight Alley) to the house at Rittergasse 2.

4 Basel Münster After a Service (1900)

2 ANTISTITIUM / MÜNSTERHOF, RITTERGASSE 2

A FAMILY OF PASTORS

Carl's lineage included an impressive array of pastors. In addition to his father, Paul Jung, Carl was surrounded by clergy in the Preiswerk family. His great-great-grandfather Alexander Preiswerk (1753–1820), married to Anna Maria Burckhardt—member of a prestigious Basel family—served as pastor in Rümlingen, Bubendorf, and even Kleinhüningen! Samuel Preiswerk, Carl's maternal grandfather, had two sons who also followed in his pastoral footsteps. One son, Samuel Gottlob Preiswerk-Staehelin (1825–1912), became pastor of St. Alban Church, and Carl would regularly join him for lunch during his Gymnasium years. Another son, Eduard Preiswerk-Friedrich (1846–1932), served as pastor of St. Margaret's Church in Binningen-Bottmingen (1870–1879), before succeeding his father as pastor of St. Leonard's Church from 1889 to 1911. Additionally, one of Carl's aunts, Maria Sophia Preiswerk-Faber, married Pastor Edmund Fröhlich (1832–1898), who served in Olten, Brugg, and Zürich. A cousin, Esther Preiswerk-Allenspach, also married a pastor and settled in Malix, Graubünden. Within this family immersed in theology, church attendance was a given, and pastors were highly respected figures in the community, though not always well compensated. Growing up in such an environment, it is no surprise that Carl developed a deep knowledge of the Bible.

Antistes Samuel Preiswerk (1799–1871)
With the Reformation, the title of Antistes was introduced to designate the director and head pastor of churches within a given region. Such a leader was deemed necessary, despite the non-hierarchical structure of the Reformed Church. In addition to his role as Antistes, Samuel Preiswerk also served as the pastor of Basel Münster. He began his career as a vicar in Arisdorf (1820) and later Benken (1821–1824), before assuming pastoral duties at an orphanage (Waisenhaus, 1824–1828) and a church in Muttenz (1830–1833). He subsequently became a professor of languages and exegesis at the Free Academy in Geneva. Upon returning

to Basel, he spent nearly two decades at St. Leonard's Church, first as assistant pastor (1840–1845), then as pastor (1845–1859). In 1859, he was appointed Antistes—a position he held for 12 years until his death in 1871.[7]

A Common Love of Language and a Path Not Taken

A love and talent for languages connected Carl to his father, Paul, and his maternal grandfather, Samuel. This shared passion also created an intellectual bond between Samuel and Paul, long before Paul married Emilie Preiswerk. Samuel's facility with language manifested in various forms: he published the magazine *Morgenland: Old and New for Friends of the Scriptures* (1838–1843), composed hymns, and was a celebrated lecturer of Hebrew and literature at the University of Basel, where he received an honorary doctorate in theology in 1860.[8] During Paul's studies in Hebrew at the University, he became one of Samuel's favored students.

Paul's first academic passion was philology—the study of texts within their historical, literary, cultural, and linguistic contexts. After passing his exams at the University of Basel, he transferred in October 1865 to the University of Georg August in Göttingen, where he specialized in Semitic languages, focusing on Arabic and Hebrew. There, he studied

5 (left) Samuel Preiswerk
Preiswerk served as Antistes from 1859–1871.

6 Paul Jung
Paul was a passionate philologist and favored student of Samuel Preiswerk.

under the renowned Orientalist Heinrich August Ewald (1803–1875), who encouraged him to pursue further research.[9] In 1867, Paul published his dissertation, *Ueber des Karäers Jephet arabische Erklärung des Hohenliedes* (*On the Karaite Jephet's Arabic Explanations of the Song of Songs*), based on a Hebrew manuscript from Syria or Palestine that had been transliterated from Arabic. Protestants such as Paul had been interested "in the Karites from the 17th century onwards, no doubt hoping to find a more *authentic* interpretation of the Scriptures and for missionary purposes."[10]

Paul appears to have become a Reformed pastor primarily for financial reasons—an outcome that was, by some accounts, his personal tragedy.[11] Unable to secure the funds needed to complete his philological studies, he accepted a stipend made available "through a relative who [passed away,] leaving a sum of money for the education of a family member" pursuing the ministry.[12]

Reconfigurations: Establishing the Antistitium

Although the Reformation began in 1529, it was not until the disruptions caused by the French Revolution (1792) that the buildings previously occupied by the bishops were gradually vacated and repurposed for use by Protestant pastors and Antistes. During this transitional period, while the bishops were still residing in the Bischofshof, the newly established Antistitium was located on the corner of Rittergasse 2. This building was originally part of the cloister but separated from it when Rittergasse was created. A small bay window was later added, offering a view onto the new street. To mark the building as the Antistitium, a prominent statue of Johannes Oekolampad (1482–1531), Basel's first Antistes and a significant figure in the Reformation, was placed at the entrance. Oekolampad was an educator, theologian, reformer, and university professor (1522), who frequently engaged in debate with key German and Swiss thinkers and leaders of the Reformation, including Martin Luther, Huldrych Zwingli, Martin Bucer, and Erasmus of Rotterdam.[13]

It was only in 1922 that the Bischofshof and Münsterhof were unified to form the modern headquarters and administrative center of the Evangelical-Reformed Church of Canton Basel-Stadt. During Samuel Preiswerk's tenure as Antistes (1845–1871), he resided at Rittergasse 2, with Oekolampad's statue at the entrance. Later, when Rittergasse was further widened, the statue was relocated to the cloister wall across the road, where it remains today.

The house at Rittergasse 2 was also home to Emilie Preiswerk before her marriage to Paul Jung. Her transition from being the daughter of the Antistes to the wife of a small parish pastor must have been enormous.

Samuel Preiswerk was appointed Antistes following the death of Jakob Burckhardt (the Elder), who had served as Münster pastor and Antistes for 20 years. The patrician family, wealthy through the silk ribbon trade, lived at St. Alban-Vorstadt 64, where their son, Jacob Burckhardt (the

7   Aerial View of Basel Münster (1932)
See the close spatial relationship of the cathedral to Carl's Gymnasium, the Münster cloister, and the Antistitium (Bischofshof and Münsterhof).

Younger, 1818–1897), who would become a renowned cultural historian, grew up. Burckhardt gained recognition for establishing the importance of art in the study of history, especially through his seminal work *The Civilization of the Renaissance in Italy*. Carl regularly encountered him as his history teacher at the Upper Gymnasium, and Burckhardt even signed Carl's report card in 1894. Carl frequently heard witty and serious reflections about Burckhardt passed on through his friend Albert Oeri. Burckhardt's sister was Oeri's grandmother.

Protestant Reformation, Tradespeople, and the Bildersturm (Picture Storm) in Basel

In January 1528, Bern hosted a three-week disputation involving leading reformers, including Ulrich Zwingli of Zürich. Zwingli presented ten theses asserting that the church must be founded solely on biblical revelation, with Christ as its only head. He rejected mass, the veneration of saints, the worship of icons, and clerical celibacy as practices contrary to the Holy Scriptures. He also argued that the flesh and blood of Christ were not materially present at the Last Supper. On January 27, 1528, the Council of Bern abolished the mass and ordered the removal of religious images from churches. A formal mandate to implement reform followed on February 7, 1528.[14]

In Basel, discontent with the external splendor of the city's churches was compounded by resentment among tradespeople, who opposed the wealth held by monasteries and the influence of the Bishop. Seeking a greater role in the city's political regime, they demanded that guild communities elect representatives to the Great Council, which held power in appointing the Small Council (the city's governing body). They also called for the exclusive practice of Reformed doctrine.

When the Council failed to meet these demands, tensions erupted on the night of February 8, 1529. A public assembly in the marketplace gave rise to the Bildersturm (Picture Storm), during which religious images, statues of saints, and crucifixes were torn down and destroyed. The Bishop, along with numerous others, fled the city. In the aftermath, a committee of councils and guilds drafted a new constitution, though it fell short of fully addressing the guilds' demands. On April 1, 1529, church bylaws formally adopting the Reformed faith were implemented. Though Basel's transition to Protestantism came more than a year after Bern's, it was marked by significant pressure and destruction.[15]

Until the formal separation of church and state in 1911, the Basel Protestant Church functioned as a state institution. As a result, the city's churches remained largely devoid of religious imagery.

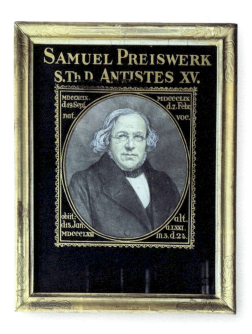

8   Small Gold-Framed Portrait of Antistes Samuel Preiswerk (c. 1859–1871)
Displayed in Rotbergstube, this portrait predates the oil painting (Figure 9) displayed in the Rotbergstube anteroom.

9   Portrait of Antistes Samuel Preiswerk (c. 1859–1871)
This painting hangs in the vestibule of Bischofshof.

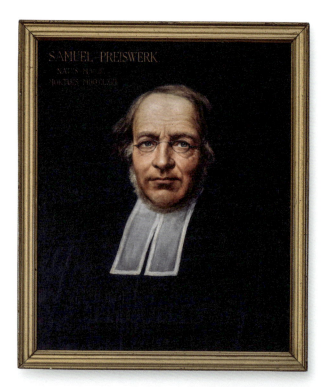

3 BISCHOFSHOF, RITTERGASSE 1

AN OPULENT PAST

Continue to the Bischofshof at Rittergasse 1. As its name ("Bishop's Court" or "Bishop's Palace") suggests, this was once the opulent residence of the Bishop of Basel. Take the small passageway to your left, where a stately arch adorned with delicate wall paintings connects two buildings, one historic and one modern. In earlier times, this double archway served as the entry point for horse-drawn coaches, leading them into the courtyard. Weary travelers could refresh themselves in the bathhouse (dating back to 1266), while their horses were fed in the nearby stalls. A doorway also leads down to the palace's expansive wine cellars.

The Bischofshof boasts many splendid rooms, including the Council Room used during the Council of Basel, the bishops' personal chapel, and the winter and summer reception rooms that hosted social functions and dances. These spaces feature well-preserved medieval wooden ceilings, intricate carvings, frescoes, and ceramic floors, making the Bischofshof a site deserving of its own dedicated tour.

The room crowning the building, above the court door that connects the Bischofshof und Münsterhof, contains the *Rotbergstube*—a small study that resembles a wood-clad jewel box. Built in 1458, it was named after Bishop Arnold von Rotberg (c.1394–1458), who served as Fürstbischof of Basel from 1451 until his death. Rotberg was a participant in the Council of Basel, and his sculptured grave, preserved in the west wing of the Münster, is worth seeking out. At his feet lie two books, symbolizing his dedication to intellectual life. Notably, during his tenure, the first book ever printed—the Gutenberg Bible—was produced in Mainz (1455).

Historically, the Rotbergstube was accessed via a winding tower staircase. Today, it can also be reached from the top-floor vestibule of the Bischofshof. The study, with its birds-eye view of the Rhine, is the oldest preserved room of its kind north of the Alps. Its wood carvings depict both Apollonian and Dionysian lifestyles, while miniature, gold-framed portraits of Basel's Antistes, each inscribed with their name, adorn the walls.

10 Münster Viewed from the Rhine
Bischofshof and the tower of the Rotbergstube (far left).

4 MÜNSTER KLOSTERGARTEN, ENTRY OPPOSITE RITTERGASSE 2

YOUNG CARL'S FAITH IS TESTED

Turning back toward the main portal of the Münster, you will find an entrance to the right of the statue of Oekolampad leading into the tranquil *Klostergarten* (cloister garden). In the Middle Ages, this cloister served as a processional space for bishops and canons. After the Reformation, however, it became a resting place, with artistic gravestones marking the tombs of numerous distinguished figures from Basel's history.

Walk partway down the arcade to enjoy a close-up view of the Münster's colorful, glazed roof tiles, visible across the walled garden. These tiles, characteristic of medieval architecture, lend the cathedral its distinctive appearance. When the sun shines, the green-gold tiles glisten against the blue sky. Imagine that, in its prime, the cathedral's interior and exterior were as vibrant as its roof. However, during restorations in 1883, nearly all of the painted decorations on the cathedral walls and statues were removed.[16] On the west façade, only the original mottled sandstone—ranging in hue from red to white—remains. A small remnant of the original painted decoration can still be seen inside the church, at the arch crossings in the vaulted ceiling.

The Münster's roof tiles gained unexpected significance in Carl's so-called "turd vision." At the age of 12, while studying at the Gymnasium (1887), Carl reflected on the cathedral and experienced a vision that both shocked and deeply unsettled him.[17] Overcome with panic, he dared not complete the thought that had entered his mind. For three agonizing days, Carl was tormented and unable to sleep, trying desperately to suppress the thought. On the third night, in the middle of his sleepless struggle, he reached a turning point. Finally, Carl reached a conclusion: it was permissible for him to think the unthinkable. Reflecting on the moment, he later wrote, "Obviously, God also desires me to show courage. I think, *If that is so and I go through with it, then He will give me His grace and illumination.*"

11 A View of the Distinctive Roof Tiles of the Münster

Carl's Turd Vision

The sky was gloriously blue, the day one of radiant sunshine. The roof of the cathedral glittered, the sun sparkling from the new, brightly glazed tiles. I was overwhelmed by the beauty of the sight, and thought: "the world is beautiful, and the church is beautiful, and God made all this and sits above it far away in the blue sky on a golden throne and..." Here came a great hole in my thoughts, and a choking sensation. I felt numbed, and knew only: "Don't go on thinking now! Something terrible is coming, something I do not want to think, something I dare not even approach."

I gathered all my courage as though I were about to leap forthwith into hell-fire, and let the thought come. I saw before me the cathedral, the blue sky, God sits on His golden throne, high above the world—and from under the throne an enormous turd falls upon the sparkling new roof, shatters it, and breaks the walls of the cathedral asunder. So that was it! I felt an enormous, indescribable relief. Instead of the expected damnation, grace had come upon me.[18]

In Jung's later years, his friend Laurens van der Post offered an interpretation of this vision:
What the vision is telling Jung and us is that whatever the Christian church as represented by the great cathedral on a hill overlooking the Rhine, has given as food to the religious spirit of men in the past, it has exhausted its powers of nourishment. In that shape and form it has served its purpose and ceased to be a source of living religious experience.[19]

Van der Post further explained that, into the 19th and 20th centuries, "such visions were abhorred by the orthodox intellectual establishment and even regarded as highly blasphemous if not a danger to normality and sanity. For this is the means whereby one can realize the inborn courage which allowed the young Jung to admit them to himself and hold on to them."[20]

Experienced at the early age of 12, the turd vision highlights Carl's early disillusionment with religion and the church. To him, the concepts and structures of faith seemed lifeless and oppressive. In later life, Jung connected this perception to his childhood view of his father as dependable yet powerless.

Confirmation

Carl's second major disillusionment with Christianity occurred just months before his 16th birthday. On Good Friday, March 27, 1891, he was confirmed in the church in Kleinhüningen by his own father. Despite high expectations for the ceremony, the experience left him feeling empty and disenchanted.[21]

In his later years, Jung described the lead-up to his confirmation in detail, recalling how his father's preparatory instructions "bored me to death."[22] With his naturally inquisitive mind, Carl longed for meaningful answers to his questions, but found no one willing or able to engage with them. On the day of the ceremony, a member of the church committee, dressed in a frock coat and top hat, arrived to escort Carl from his home. Carl himself wore a new black suit and felt hat, which he felt was already transforming him into an image of lifeless conformity: "It was a kind of lengthened jacket that spread out into two little wings over the seat."[23] He expressed an oppressive fear of the black suit and top hat, which seemed to embody suffocating expectations. This reaction reflected a deep psychological conflict with the black frock and clerical robe—a recurring motif in Jung's memoir, where it appears no fewer than nine times. Carl's complex relationship with these garments, marked by both fear and revulsion, seems to have stemmed from a haunting childhood experience of seeing a drowned man in a black frock after a flood in Kleinhüningen. Carl also hid in the parsonage to avoid a man wearing a black frock, and whittled a mannikin clothed in black, which he kept concealed in a pencil case in the attic.[24]

Paul's Faith

Carl was deeply disappointed by the lack of sacredness in his confirmation ritual. He recognized the bread used for communion as ordinary—purchased from the local bakery—and the wine as sourced from the local tavern. It gradually dawned on him that there was nothing extraordinary about the ceremony, no transformative spiritual experience. He found himself "cut off from the Church and from my father's and everybody else's faith. Insofar as they all represented the Christian religion, I was an outsider. This knowledge filled me with

TOUR 3

sadness which was to overshadow all the years until the time I entered the university."[25] Much of Jung's later work can be interpreted as the result of his lifelong quest to heal this spiritual rift and find or create a replacement for the faith he had lost as a child.

Carl was also acutely aware of and troubled by his father Paul's melancholic demeanor. As a village pastor in a rapidly industrializing town, Paul directly witnessed the harsh realities and struggles of the communities under his pastoral care. Despite these challenges, later generations remembered him with respect for his honorable reputation as a *Seelsorger* (carer of souls).

In 1890, a year before the Jung-Preiswerk family arrived in Kleinhüningen, a group of women associated with the church established the Evangelical Women's Association to shoulder the humanitarian task of

12 Carl's Confirmation Recorded in the Kleinhüningen Church Confirmation Register (27 March 1891) Good Friday, Holy Easter. Paul Jung-Preiswerk also confirmed the Schoren-Institution Girls.

supporting those stricken by poverty as a result of industrialization.[26] A short time later, several upper-class families, including that of Pastor Schwarz (a committed advocate for the lower classes) moved to Kleinhüningen. These pastors were closely associated with Leonhard Ragaz and part of the so-called "religious socialists."[27] Paul's decision to serve in Kleinhüningen may have reflected an alignment with this emerging movement.

On May 10, 1891, two months after confirming his son, Paul officiated the confirmation of 27 "Schoren Girls." He wrote: "Due to a typhoid epidemic in the institution, the confirmation could only take place before Whitsun." These orphaned or "morally neglected" girls had been recruited as cheap labor by the textile industrialist Johann Jakob Richter-Linder from across Switzerland and even France. However, an 1892 survey of "former pupils" reveals that promises made in the institution's prospectus and contracts were not fulfilled. A factory inspector at the time praised the institution for having the "most beautiful workroom" in Switzerland, while also noting that "the girls' working conditions were worse than those of other young female factory workers." Indeed, the girls endured abysmal living conditions and meager, poor-quality meals—mainly watery soups, bread, and potatoes. Despite efforts by the town doctor in the 1890s to calculate proper protein and fat requirements for the girls, only sporadic improvements to the menu were made, with no lasting change. The girls slept two to a straw sack, without proper beds, and received fresh linens only twice a year. Unsurprisingly, bedbug infestations and scabies were rampant. Paul witnessed these abhorrent conditions firsthand.[28]

Carl, like his father, also bore witness to the stark social contrasts in his environment. Both were exposed to the immense wealth surrounding the Münster and the extreme poverty wrought by industrialization. These disparities profoundly influenced their perspectives and values, shaping their attitudes toward life and humanity.

13 Map of Medieval Basel Before 1356
Woodcut depiction of the city of Basel with uncertain dating. The city wall is only indicated in the foreground. The Middle Bridge and the cathedral with its four towers are recognizable.

TOUR 3

5 HISTORISCHES MUSEUM BASEL, BARFÜSSERPLATZ

INSPIRATION: KNIGHTS AND THE GRAIL LEGEND

Pass through the cloister arcade to the broad terrace overlooking the Rhine. Circle around the Münster toward its main entrance, then walk downhill to Barfüsserkirche on Barfüsserplatz—both named after the "Barefoot Monks" (Barfüsser) who once frequented this church. Stay to the right and enter Fasnachtsgasse (Carnival Alley), passing the Neptun Brunnen (another ornate fountain, this one featuring Neptune). Continue around the church until you arrive at the steps in front of the building, now home to the Historisches Museum Basel (Basel Historical Museum), established in 1894. The museum houses notable relics, including fragments of the *Totentanz* (*Dance of Death*) and crests of prominent Basel families, including the Preiswerk family.

If it is a special occasion there may be a market on the space in front of the church, alive with stalls and vendors selling their wares. Pause to take in the bustling scene of Barfüsserplatz, including its many shops and tram stop. From this vantage point, you can also see Kohlenberg (Coal Mountain) and, perched on the hill overlooking the square, the former Chorherrenstift (Canon's Monastery of the Augustinians), now known as Lohnhof (Wage Yard), as well as St. Leonard's Church with its two impressive towers. In Carl's day, Lohnhof served as a prison (1832–1995). However, today, it houses a museum, a hotel, a restaurant, and residential spaces. While monks traditionally retreat from the world, Saint Augustine's rule required canons to engage in duties beyond the monastery enclave. Notably, Carl's mother was born during the two decades when Samuel Preiswerk served as pastor of St. Leonard's Church.

Shortly, we will climb the steep, narrow, winding steps from Barfüsserplatz to Leonhardskirchplatz (Leonard's Church Square). But first, we will explore how these very steps helped Jung recognize the setting of a significant dream he had at the age of 37.

Knight Dream[29]

I was in an Italian City, and it was around noon, between twelve and one o'clock. A fierce sun was beating down upon the narrow streets. The city was built on hills and reminded me of a particular part of Basel, the Kohlenberg. The little streets which lead down into the valley, the Birsigtal, that runs through the city, are partly flights of steps. In the dream, one such stairway descended to Barfüsserplatz. The city was Basel, and yet it was also an Italian city, something like Bergamo. It was summertime; the blazing sun stood at the zenith, and everything was bathed in an intense light. A crowd came streaming toward me, and I knew that the shops were closing and people were on their way home to dinner. In the midst of this stream of people walked a knight in full armor. He mounted the steps toward me. He wore a helmet of the kind that is called a basinet, with eye slits, and chain armor. Over this was a white tunic into which was woven, front and back a large red cross.[30]

Still in the dream, Jung wonders what this apparition means. Someone answers:

Yes, this is a regular apparition, the knight always passes by here between twelve and one o'clock, and has been doing so for a very long time [for centuries, I gathered] and everyone knows about it.

14 Narrow Alleyway and Winding Steps Ascend from Barfüsserplatz up to St. Leonard's Church (1870) The church is on the right, and the large building on the left is the Canon's Monastery of the Augustinian Order that served as a prison called Lohnhof from 1832 to 1995.

The knight's helmet, with its eye slits and chain armor, evokes the statue of St. George at Basel Münster. A red thread (a thread of continuity) ran through Jung's imagination, linking this wandering knight to his youthful fantasies and drawings of castles, knights, and battles with dragons. Certain elements of the dream stand out: a "mysterious figure ... a twelfth century ... knight in full armor ... full of life and completely real," who approaches him in a modern city (perhaps Basel/Bergamo), during the "noonday rush hour." Reflecting on the dream in his memoir, Jung wrote that, after meditating on the dream for a long time, he realized "the knight belonged to the twelfth century. That was the period when alchemy was beginning and also the quest for the Holy Grail.[31] The stories of the grail had been of the greatest importance to me ever since I read them, at the age of fifteen, for the first time."[32]

He continued:

> *I had an inkling that a great secret still lay hidden behind those stories. Therefore it seemed quite natural to me that the dream should conjure up the world of the Knights of the Grail and their quest—for that was, in the deepest sense, my own world ... My whole being was seeking for something still unknown which might confer meaning upon the banality of life.*[33]

Jung's wife Emma dedicated the last three decades of her life to researching and writing about the Grail legend. Her work explored themes of redemption, eternal life, and the importance of seeking and asking the right question. She discovered that the legend reflects not only fundamental human struggles, but also the profound psychic events underpinning Christian culture—precisely the kinds of challenges Carl grappled with during his adolescence.

6 LEONHARDSKIRCHPLATZ 1

AT A THRESHOLD: MAJOR LIFE CHOICES

Walk across Barfüsserplatz and climb the stairs to Leonard's Church Square, the courtyard of the former Augustinian church where Emilie's father, Samuel Preiswerk, served as assistant pastor (1840–1845) and later as pastor (1845–1859), before moving to Basel Münster to assume pastoral duties there. On your left, an archway opens to the Lohnhof. On Leonard's Church Square, itself, a walking labyrinth has been created in recent years. Diagonally across from it stands the parsonage at Leonhardskirchplatz 1, where the Preiswerk family lived when Emilie was born. The large house, with its cream stucco façade and green shutters, exudes historical serenity. Pause here to reflect on the pivotal transition Carl faced at this stage in his life—spanning Gymnasium to university—and his challenge of choosing a future course of study.

Two Dreams Decide Carl's Future

I would go to the University and study–natural science. Then I would know something real. But no sooner had I made this promise than my doubts began. . . . just at the time when No.1 and No. 2 were wrestling for a decision, I had two dreams.[34]

Torn between academic paths, Carl struggled to choose between the sciences and the humanities. He considered history and philosophy, while also feeling a deep draw toward archaeology. Ultimately, two dreams played a decisive role in helping him chart his path forward.

Excavation Dream

I was in a dark wood that stretched along the Rhine. I came to a little hill, a burial mound, and began to dig. After a while I turned up, to my astonishment, some bones of prehistoric animals.[35]

15 Micrograph of a Radiolaria
Exhibited in a permanent exhibition at
the Natural History Museum Basel.

Jung wrote about this dream: "This interested me enormously, and at that moment, I knew: I must get to nature, the world in which we live, and the things around us." Then came a second dream.

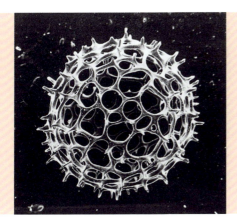

Radiolaria Dream

I was in a wood; it was threaded with watercourses, and in the darkest place I saw a circular pool, surrounded by dense undergrowth. Half immersed in the water lay the strangest and most wonderful creature: a round animal, shimmering in opalescent hues, and consisting of innumerable little cells, or of organs shaped like tentacles. It was a giant radiolarian, measuring about three feet across. It seemed to me indescribably wonderful that this magnificent creature should be lying there undisturbed, in the hidden place, in the clear, deep water. [36]

This dream ignited Carl's desire for knowledge, and the pair of dreams ultimately led him to choose science as a course of study. Radiolaria—protozoa measuring 0.1 to 0.2 millimeters in diameter, characterized by their silica shells and often round forms—played a central role in one of these dreams, appearing in fantastical, 3-feet large forms. Perhaps, Carl was familiar with ongoing research on radiolaria, and particularly the work of Ernst Haeckel (1834–1919), a renowned naturalist and artist. Haeckel, celebrated for his studies of these protozoa, published a monograph on them in 1862. His *Art Forms of Nature*, featuring detailed illustrations of flora and fauna, was released in ten installments between 1899 and 1904, possibly inspiring young Carl's imagination.

16 Pfarrhaus St. Leonhard / Leonhardskirchplatz 1
Samuel and Auguste Preiswerk-Faber, along with their children (including Carl's mother), lived here from 1845 to 1859, when it served as the parsonage of St. Leonard's Church.

Even as Carl committed to science, he remained concerned about his future livelihood. Medicine emerged as a potential career path, though he speculated that his aversion to imitation—perhaps influenced by his grandfather Karl, who had died before Carl was born—may have dissuaded him from fully embracing this choice. He also feared that pursuing medicine, while practical, might prove an inauspicious compromise.

The parsonage stands at the corner of Leonard's Church Square and Heuberg (Hay Hill). From here, turn right onto Heuberg, a tranquil residential street lined today with many attractive, historic homes. In earlier times, this street also housed stores and workshops, including a bookshop and a shoemaker's workshop. Crossing Petersgraben, Heuberg transitions smoothly into Spalenberg and then, after crossing the road, into Spalenvorstadt. Continue along Spalenvorstadt and, at the second right, turn onto Vesalgasse (named after the famous anatomist Vesalius, known as Vesal in German). Take another right to arrive at the Vesalianum (Vesalgasse 1), a significant site in Carl's intellectual journey.

⑦ THE VESALIANUM, VESALGASSE 1

CARL STUDIES MEDICINE

In April 1895, Carl began his studies of natural sciences and medicine at the Vesalianum, a facility built specifically for the study of anatomy and physiology. The Vesalianum replaced the now too small and outdated Anatomisches Institut (Anatomical Institute) at the Old University, which had been in use since the time of Caspar Bauhin (1589–1614) and was later improved by Carl's grandfather, Karl. Notably, a commemorative publication celebrating the opening of the Vesalianum features a photograph of Karl on its front page. Over the preceding six decades, Karl had played an instrumental role in advancing medical education and healthcare in Basel, spearheading initiatives that would shape the academic and clinical landscape that Carl would enter. Over ten semesters (five winter and five summer), Carl studied medicine at several locations throughout Basel before sitting and passing his *Staatsexamen* (federal exams) in March 1900 at the age of 25.[37] During his studies, the cadre of 27 faculty members (including full professors, associate professors, and private lecturers) remained fairly constant (see Table 6).

Carl's medical education unfolded against a backdrop of significant change in medical practice and instruction, driven by the industrialization of Basel during the latter half of the 19th century. Between the 1860s and Carl's graduation in 1900, the field of medicine experienced rapid advancements in knowledge and increasing specialization. These developments, combined with Basel's growing population, led to a rise in medical student enrollment and notable improvements in public health. Earlier models of medical education had relied on personal instruction. Prior to the establishment of teaching clinics and dedicated faculty funding, medical students met with physician instructors in their homes or private practices. For example, in 1826, Dr. J. R. Burckhardt—and, beginning in 1830, Carl's grandfather Karl—held small group discussions for students in their homes.

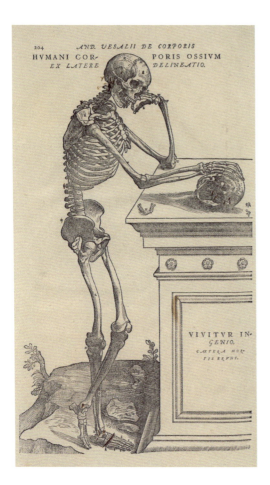

17 Image from *De Corporis Humani Fabrica Libri Septem* (The Fabric of the Human Body) by Andreas Vesalius
Digitized facsimile from the 1543 Basel edition.

18 (right) The Vesalianum (c. 1930)
The Vesalianum was built 1884–1885.

Although a formal department of medicine was created in 1855, it was not until 1865, when student enrollment was sufficiently high, that a teaching clinic was established at the Bürgerspital. This clinic, which offered free healthcare to indigent patients, was staffed by unpaid students and assistant physicians, ensuring that trainees gained hands-on experience while addressing the needs of Basel's underserved populations.

Other signs of modernization in medical education emerged during Carl's studies. One notable example is Emilie Louise Frey, a trailblazer in this era of change. Although Carl and Emilie overlapped at the university for only one year, her presence reflected a shift in attitudes toward women in higher education. Frey was the first woman ever to be admitted to the University of Basel, but her journey was not without obstacles. Initially rejected, she gained admission only after the cantonal government intervened on her behalf. Enrolled in medicine on a trial basis, she passed her *Staatsexamen* in the same year that Carl matriculated, graduating in 1896.[38]

The Modernization of Medical Education at the University of Basel: Resources and Curriculum[39]

By the time Carl began his studies in 1895, the curriculum and resources reflected significant modernization in the facilities and pedagogy. Below is an overview of the key institutions, clinics, and disciplines that defined his medical training. See Table 6 and Map 5, next page.

① Anatomisches Institut (Anatomical Institute)

Established at the Old University in 1865 by Professor Wilhelm His and Carl's grandfather, Karl Jung, the Anatomisches Institut soon outgrew its facilities due to rising enrollment. By the time Carl began his studies, it had already relocated to the ground floor of the Vesalianum (opened in 1885) and featured modern amenities, including a dissection room with 60 workplaces, a demonstration room, a room for anatomical research collections (focusing on embryology and race anatomy), a morgue, and offices for faculty and staff.[40]

② Physiologisches Institut (Physiological Institute)

Established in 1867 within two rooms at the Old University, the Physiologisches Institute gained a dedicated chair and expanded facilities in 1872. By Carl's time, it had been relocated to the upper floors of the Vesalianum.

③ Pathologisch-anatomisches Institut (Pathological-Anatomical Institute)

Initially founded by Karl Jung and Friedrich Miescher (who discovered nucleic acid in 1896), the pathology collection was housed at the Old University. However, its facilities were too small and inconveniently located far from the Bürgerspital (where specimens must have been collected). Thus, in 1880, a new Pathologisch-anatomisches Intitut was established in the hospital's garden, facilitating closer integration with clinical practice. Bacteriology instruction was introduced in 1890, and in 1898, near the end of Carl's studies, the institute underwent significant expansion.

④ Hygienisches Institut (Hygiene Institute)

Opened in 1894 in an Alsatian timber-framed building near the Botanical Garden at Petersplatz, the Hygienisches Institut housed laboratories, specimen collections, and a lecture hall.[41] Teaching (delivered by a single permanent faculty member) covered subjects such as school hygiene, public and private hygiene, balneoclimatology (i.e., environmental cures such as therapeutic baths), and toxicology.

⑤ Medizinische Klinik (Medical Clinic)

Modeled after other contemporary university medical programs, the Medizinische Klinik held 90-minute sessions five times weekly, regularly attended by approximately 50 students. In 1896, shortly after Carl's matriculation, a larger laboratory was added to support student training. Assistants played a crucial role in teaching and clinical practice.

⑥ Chirurgische Klinik (Surgical Clinic)

The Chirurgische Klinik provided hands-on training in cadaver dissection, wound care, surgical instrumentation, and minor surgical procedures. A dedicated facility with specialized staff was established in 1888, and in 1893, the clinic absorbed a bacteriology laboratory and adopted stringent protocols for antisepsis and asepsis. Similar to the Medizinische Klinik, it conducted 90-minute sessions five times weekly, attended by approximately 50 students.

⑦ Geburtshilflich-gynaekologische Klinik (Obstetrics and Gynecology Clinic)

Originally established in 1868 as the Merian'scher Flügal, a private birthing clinic, this facility quickly expanded, increasing its capacity from 22 to 64 beds between 1869 and

1888. In parallel, annual deliveries rose from 86 to 635 over the same period. Initially, practical teaching in obstetrics was limited, but in 1896, during Carl's second year of study, a new chair in obstetrics and gynecology was established, and a large public women's hospital was inaugurated. There, students practiced operations on phantoms (inanimate models) and cadavers while attending clinical sessions for three to four hours weekly.

⑧ **Psychiatrische Klinik (Psychiatry Clinic)**
Psychiatric patients were treated in the "lunatic" ward of the Bürgerspital, where they served as teaching examples for medical students learning psychopathology.

⑨ **Poliklinik im Spital (Polyclinic in the Municipal Hospital)**
In 1874, the University of Basel, the Bürgerspital, and local social services partnered to establish an ambulatory free clinic to support student instruction. In 1890, this clinic was turned into a governmentally-administered general clinic, separate from the hospital. By 1892, the Poliklinik had its own building on Hebelstrasse, complete with lecture rooms and laboratories. Offering daily clinical sessions lasting one to two hours, it attracted many students due to its extensive patient population.

⑩ **Augenklinik (Eye Clinic)**
Founded in 1864 as a privately funded hospital for eye diseases, the Augenklinik relocated twice before settling on Mittlere Strasse in 1877, where it was renamed the New Eye Healing Institute. Regular instruction in ophthalmology began in 1867 with three-hour clinical sessions held weekly at the private hospital. By 1892, training had moved to the Poliklinik on Hebelstrasse, where supervising ophthalmologists maintained independent offices. In 1896, an agreement between the state and social services funded a new inpatient unit at the Bürgerspital, which included twelve beds—five of which were reserved for free care.

⑪ **Ohrenklinik (Ear Clinic)**
Otological instruction began in 1876, with private practice otologists offering consultations at the free Polyklinik. This model persisted until 1892, when a dedicated ear clinic was established at the Poliklinik on Hebelstrasse.

⑫ **Kinderklinik (Clinic for Children's Diseases)**
A children's hospital was established on the Rhine in 1862, and regular pediatric instruction commenced in 1868. Students attended weekly two-hour sessions.

⑬ **Disciplines Without Dedicated Institutes**
Pharmacology was initially taught alongside philosophy, but became a distinct discipline in 1890 with the appointment of a dedicated professor, who also oversaw the General Polyklinik. Early instruction was supported by a donated pharmacological collection, which later formed the basis of the Pharmacology Museum (visited later in this tour). The university's first full professor of pharmacy, Prof. Dr. Karl Heinrich Zönig, was appointed nearly two decades after Carl's graduation. In 1922, Zönig founded the Basel Pharmaceutical Institute at Totengässlein 3, otherwise known as zum Sessel. The institute began modestly with just ten students and a small collection and library. Rooted in the traditions of Galen and Paracelsus, the Pharmacology Museum became a symbol of Basel's historical contributions to pharmacology. Given Switzerland's prominence in the modern pharmaceutical industry, the late establishment of a dedicated pharmaceutical institute in Basel is noteworthy.[42]

Table 6
Where Did Carl Study Medicine in Basel from 1895–1900?
The numbers on Map 5 (right) correspond to the numbers in the table.

Map 5
(right) University of Basel School of Medicine Institutes and Clinics (1895–1900)
The numbered sites correspond to Table 6. Additional points of reference are indicated in black.

	Medizinische Fachrichtungen (German)	Institute Names (English)	Year Established	Director	Year Appointed	Locations Where Carl Jung Most Likely Studied	Year Location Established
①	Anatomisches Institut (initially at the Old University since 1589)	Anatomical Institute	1865	J. Kollmann	1878	Vesalianum, Vesalgasse 1	1885
②	Physiologisches Institut	Physiological Institute	1867	R. Metzner	1895	Vesalianum, Vesalgasse 1	1885
③	Pathologisch-anatomisches Institut	Pathological-Anatomical Institute	1880	E. Kaufmann	1898	Municipal Hospital (Bürgerspital), Merian-Flügel, Petersgraben	1880
④	Hygienisches Institut	Hygiene Institute	1892	A. Burckhardt	1892	Stachelschützenhaus, Petersplatz	1892
⑤	Medizinische Klinik	Medical Clinic	1800	F. Müller	1899	Municipal Hospital (Bürgerspital), Petersgraben	1865
⑥	Chirurgische Klinik	Surgical Clinic	>1888	O. Ildebrand	1899	Municipal Hospital (Bürgerspital), Petersgraben	>1888 / 1893
⑦	Geburtshilflich-gynaekologische Klinik	Obstetrics and Gynecology Clinic	1868	E. Bumm	1894	Frauenspital, Klingelberg	1886
⑧	Psychiatrische Klinik	Psychiatry Clinic	1875	L. Wille	1875	Irrenanstalt Friedmatt, Kantonale Heil- und Pflegeanstalt Friedmatt (1899 name change)	1875
⑨	Poliklinik im Spital	Polyclinic in the Municipal Hospital	1874	R. Massini	1875	Poliklinik, Hebelstrasse	1892
⑩	Augenklinik	Eye Clinic	1864	C. Mellinger	1896	Municipal Hospital (Bürgerspital), Petersgraben	1896
⑪	Ohrenklinik	Ear Clinic	1879	F. Siebenmann	1888	Poliklinik, Hebelstrasse	1892
⑫	Kinderklinik	Clinic for Children's Diseases	1862	E. Hagenbach	1868	Kinderspital am Rhein, Römerstrasse	1868
⑬	Fachbereiche ohne Institut	Disciplines without an Institute	1890	R. Massini	1875	Initially no official institute, then in Haus zum Sessel, Totengässlein 3	1890

TOUR 3

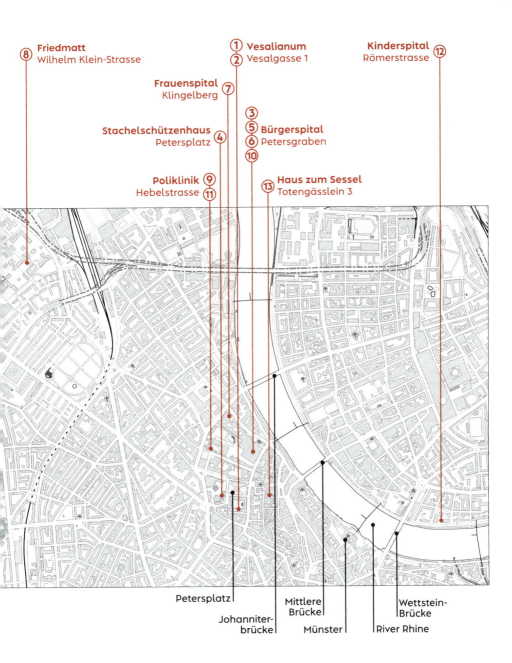

19 Water and Ink Anatomical and Histological Drawings by Jung (c. 1895–1900)
These images are thought to have been drawn by Carl when he was in medical school and working in the anatomy department.

Anatomy and Histology, Detailed Drawings

During his medical studies, Carl developed a fascination with evolutionary theory, comparative anatomy, and morphology. However, he found the practice of vivisection—then a central component of physiological training—inherently distressing, attributing his discomfort to an unconscious identification with the animals being dissected.[43] After completing his introductory courses, Carl secured a paid position as a junior assistant in anatomy.

In the following semester, he assumed responsibility for teaching histology—a role he found deeply fulfilling. Histology required meticulous observation and documentation of microscopic structures, and it is believed that Carl produced detailed histological illustrations as part of this work. These sketches, likely executed in ink and enhanced with watercolor, depicted the intricate cellular organization of tissues.[44]

Years later, cell-like structures would appear in several of Jung's paintings in *The Red Book*. Art historian Jill Mellick has studied these images in detail, describing Jung's artistic process as one of tiling, layering, outlining, and pooling. When tiling, he created small, individual cells (tiles) that he later joined into a cohesive final image. When layering, he applied successive layers of color at various stages of drying to achieve complex chromatic effects. When outlining, he imparted a mosaic-like impression to the images, and when pooling, he allowed different pigments to flow, shift, and concentrate in specific areas, creating a dynamic, organic appearance evocative of living cells or, at times, static and mosaic-like forms.

Mellick's detailed observations of Jung's artistic processes reveal the mind of an experimenter at work. We might speculate whether the strikingly cell-like patterns in his later works were, in part, influenced by his early observations under the microscope—a relatively new scientific instrument during his medical training.[45]

An Epiphany: Carl Chooses to Specialize in Psychiatry

Until the final stages of his medical training, Carl appeared destined for a career in internal medicine. However, to everyone's surprise—including his own—he ultimately chose to specialize in psychiatry. What circumstances in leadership and education were shaping psychiatry at the University of Basel during this pivotal moment?

At the time, the field was led by Ludwig Wille, a German-born psychiatrist who directed the university's psychiatric clinic from 1875 to 1904. Before assuming this role, Wille had gained extensive experience as the director of multiple mental asylums across Switzerland, including the asylum in Münsterlingen (1864, canton Thurgau), the newly established Rheinau asylum (1867, canton Zurich), and the St. Urban asylum (1873, canton Lucerne). In Basel, he served as a senior physician in the psychiatric department of the Bürgerspital and played a key role in the development of psychiatric care in the city. Wille co-founded the Association of Swiss Lunatic Doctors and spearheaded the first Swiss census of the mentally ill. A strong proponent of the no-restraint method, he was highly regarded in the field, even earning the status of honorary citizen of Basel.

In 1886, Wille became the founding director of the state Lunatic Asylum, situated on the outskirts of Basel. This institution held deep personal significance for Carl, as his grandfather Karl had been instrumental in its establishment, and his father had also worked there, providing pastoral care. Under Wille's leadership, the university's psychiatry department aimed to integrate theoretical instruction with clinical training in the treatment of mental illness. However, due to relatively low enrollment compared to other medical specialties, courses at the asylum were held only once a week for two hours. In Carl's final semester, the institution was renamed the Psychiatric Institution, though it would later be known as the Cantonal Sanatorium and Nursing Home Friedmatt (or "Friedmatt," for short).

Carl's initial exposure to psychiatry left him unimpressed. Decades later, he reflected: "The lectures and clinical demonstrations had not made the slightest impression on me. I could not remember a single one of the cases I had seen in the clinic, but only my boredom and disgust."[46] It seems the turning point occurred while Carl was preparing for his *Staatsexamen,* which required a review of psychiatry. While studying, he encountered a preface to an otherwise (according to Carl) unremarkable psychiatry textbook by Krafft-Ebing, which profoundly resonated with him. Two ideas captured his imagination: first, the field's "peculiar" and "incomplete [...] development," which lent psychiatry textbooks a "subjective character"; and second, its description of psychoses as "diseases of personality." Carl's reaction was immediate and visceral. He later described his thinking in that moment: "Here alone the two currents of my interest could flow together and in a united stream dig their own bed. [...] Here at last was the place where the collision of nature and spirit [could become] a reality."[47]

In the winter semester of 1898/99, near the end of Carl's studies, Gustav Wolff joined the faculty as a private lecturer, becoming Wille's assistant. Wolff later succeeded Wille as director of the psychiatry department in 1904 and was promoted to full professor in 1907. However, Carl was frustrated by the prospect of working under Wolff, expressing his

20 Mosaic (1917)
Image from *The Red Book* (p. 79).

dissatisfaction in a letter to his friend A. Vischer on August 22, 1904: "I might just as well be sitting under a millstone as under Wolff, who will remain in his position for the next 30 years until he is as old as Wille." At the time of this letter, he was already working at the Burghölzi Psychiatric Hospital in Zurich. Nevertheless, his comment suggests he harbored desire to return to Basel and assume a leadership position in psychiatry—a prospect that was ultimately realized in the form of an honorary professorship late in life.[48]

Continue on Vesalgasse to Petersplatz. You will pass an Alsatian timber-framed building on your left that, in Carl's time, housed the Hygiene Institute. Follow the diagonal path leading to the center of the park.

21 Jung's Sketch of His Liverpool Dream in the *Black Books* (1927)

Liverpool Dream

I found myself in a dirty, sooty city. It was night, and winter, and dark, and raining. I was in Liverpool. With a number of Swiss—say half a dozen. I walked through the dark streets. I had the feeling that there we were coming from the harbor, and that the real city was actually up above, on the cliffs. We climbed up there. It reminded me of Basel, where the market is down below and then you go up through the Totengässlein (Alley of the Dead), which leads to a plateau above and so to the Petersplatz and the Peterskirche.

When we reached the plateau, we found a broad square dimly illuminated by streetlights, into which many streets converged. The various quarters of the city were arranged radially around the square. In the center was a round pool, and in the middle of it a small island. While everything round about was obscured by rain, fog, smoke and dimly lit darkness, the little island blazed with sunlight. On it stood a single tree, a magnolia, in a shower of reddish blossoms. It was as though the tree stood in the sunlight and were at the same time the source of light. My companions commented on the abominable weather, and obviously did not see the tree. They spoke of another Swiss who was living in Liverpool and expressed surprise that he should have settled here. I was carried away by the beauty of the flowering tree and the sunlit island, and thought, "I know very well why he has settled here."[49]

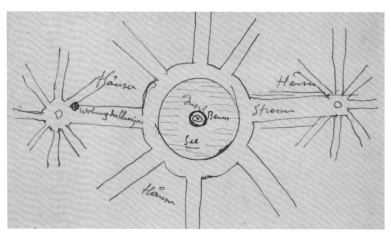

Houses	Island	Houses
House of the Swiss	Tree	Streets
	Lake	

8 PETERSPLATZ

THE CULMINATION

Twenty-seven years after leaving Basel, on January 2, 1927, Jung experienced a significant dream that he later referred to as his "Liverpool dream," despite having never visited the city. This dream held deep importance for Jung, evoking powerful associations with Petersplatz and the nearby Totengässlein (Alley of the Dead).

Jung later commented on this dream:

> *This dream represented my situation at the time. I can still see the grayish-yellow raincoats, glistening with the wetness of the rain. Everything was extremely unpleasant, black and opaque—just as I felt then. But I had a vision of unearthly beauty, and that is why I was able to live at all. Liverpool is the "pool of life." The "liver" according to an old view, is the seat of life—that which "makes to live."*
>
> *This dream brought with it a sense of finality. I saw that here the goal had been revealed. One could not go beyond the center. The center is the goal, and everything is directed towards that center. Through this dream I understood that the self is the principle and archetype of orientation and meaning. Therein lies its healing function. For me, this insight signified an approach to the center and therefore to the goal. Out of it emerged a first inkling of my personal myth. After this dream I gave up drawing or painting mandalas. The dream depicted the climax of the whole process of development of consciousness.*[50]

Jung recounted the significance of the Liverpool dream in various writings over the years, identifying it as a turning point in his psychological development and understanding of his life's purpose. He saw the dream as his first glimpse into his personal myth, providing a guiding narrative that would shape the development of his psychological theories, including his central concept of the Self.[51] Reflecting on the dream, Jung later wrote, "the Self was the goal of the process of individuation.

Progression was not linear but involved a circumambulation of the Self. [...] The task now was one of consolidating these insights into his life and science."[52]

To Jung, the climb up the steep stairway of Totengässlein, ascending from Marktplatz (Marketplace) to St. Peterskirche (St. Peter's Church), was deeply symbolic. Traditionally, this pathway was used for funeral processions, carrying the deceased from the lower city to their final resting place in the cemetery.[53] This association with death and renewal was deeply personal for Jung, as the dream coincided with the loss of several close friends, including Hermann Sigg, who died just seven days later from complications of a spinal puncture.

In the Liverpool dream, the ascent up Totengässlein symbolizes not only death and transformation, but also Jung's commitment to integrating the insights gained from his inner images into his personal life and written works. Thus, for Jung, this dream was of profound value and enduring significance.

This theme of integration and culmination is further reflected in the dream's central setting, as sketched in the *Black Books:* a square featuring a small island at its core, where eight walkways converge like the spokes of a wheel. At the heart of the island stands a single magnolia tree, its branches adorned with reddish blossoms, radiating in a glowing light that seems to both encircle and emanate from it. While Jung recognized the profound beauty and significance of this luminescent magnolia in the dream, the other dream figures remained oblivious (except for, perhaps, the absent Swiss man who, much to the confusion of the others, had chosen to live in Liverpool). The image of the illuminated magnolia bears an uncanny resemblance to a drawing of a spinal cord cross-section in the *Black Books,* perhaps referencing Hermann Sigg and his cause of death. Jung later immortalized this central image in his painting *Window on Eternity,* which was explicitly dedicated to Sigg's memory. This painting would become one of the final mandalas Jung produced.

Standing now at the center of Petersplatz, pause to reflect on whether the point where the pathways converge feels charged with the kind of significance Jung attributed to the hub in his dream.

22 Petersplatz

Setting for Jung's Liverpool dream. In the background, next to St. Peterskirche is Petersgraben 29 where Carl's great-aunt lived.

In close proximity to Petersplatz are two additional sites of interest (mentioned but not included in this tour). The first is the University of Basel Library, located to the west of Petersplatz. This library houses an extensive collection of alchemical texts, as well as books on the history of printing in Basel. The collection spans from the early days of book printing in the 15th century to the end of the 19th century, with a total of 300,000 prints dating before 1850. The second site, situated near the Spalentor medieval city gate, is the Botanical Garden of the University of Basel, which was originally the *hortus medicus* (medicinal herb garden) on the Old University terrace. Over time, the garden moved several times before being permanently established at its current location in 1898. It now rests on the site of the Spalengottesacker (Spalen God's Field), a former cemetery.

23 Window on Eternity (1927)
Image from *The Red Book* (p. 159). The inspiration for this mandala was Jung's Liverpool dream.

9 HAUS ZUM SESSEL, TOTENGÄSSLEIN 3

INDIVIDUATION AND ALCHEMY

From the center of Petersplatz, follow the crooked path that leads across the square. As it crosses Petersgraben, the path becomes Peterskirchplatz, passing between the church on your left and the school on your right. At the end of Peterskirchplatz, turn right onto Nadelberg, then quickly veer left onto Totengässlein. This narrow alleyway, whose name translates to "Alley of the Dead," reflects its historical function as the pathway through which coffins were once carried in solemn procession prior to burial. Now proceed to Totengässlein 3, home to the Pharmacy Museum.

The museum is located in Haus zum Sessel, a building with a long and varied history. Originally a bathhouse known as Badestube unter Krämer, dating back to 1296, the site was subsequently shaped by centuries of academic, medical, and philosophical inquiry that aligned with Jung's lifelong interests.

Enter the courtyard to view the fountain, then ascend the steps leading to the museum's private garden—an ideal setting to reflect on the diverse influences that shaped Jung's psychological theories. Several converging forces helped lay the foundation for his later work: the pressures of modernization, advancements in the natural sciences and medicine, and Basel's deep-rooted ecclesiastical, academic, and philosophical traditions. At the same time, as a young man, Carl had a burgeoning interest in the occult, paranormal phenomena, and synchronicity—themes he later addressed in his university dissertation (addressed in Tour 4).

While there is no evidence that Carl concerned himself with alchemy during his youth, he engaged seriously with the subject roughly 25 years after leaving Basel. Nonetheless, Basel's historical prominence in alchemical traditions makes it relevant to consider the city's role in shaping his later work. In particular, three factors may draw our attention to

24 The Winding Steps of Totengässlein

25 Courtyard of the Haus zum Sessel at Totengässlein 3

this connection. First, Basel was a major hub for alchemists, due to its status as a leading center for the printing of important alchemical texts. Second, from the 1930s onward, Jung increasingly emphasized the psychological significance of alchemy, seeing it as a symbolic representation of inner transformation.[54] And third, Jung came to understand the work of the alchemists as a projection of their inner worlds onto their craft, through an unconscious process akin to what he later termed "active imagination." Thus, he explicitly linked alchemy to his conception of individuation—the transformative process through which an individual integrates the disparate aspects of their psyche into a unified whole.

Hermeticism

A key pedagogical principle in Carl's Gymnasium education was the previously mentioned *ad fontes*, the humanist practice of studying ancient sources. This foundational approach may have influenced the "excavation dream" that guided Carl in selecting his program of study. Over the course of his lifetime, this orientation toward ancient wisdom shaped not only his understanding of his own psyche and that of others, but also his seminal idea of archetypes.

One particularly significant area of Carl's study of ancient sources was his engagement with Hermeticism. The *Hermetica*, a collection of Egyptian-Greek wisdom texts dating from the 2nd century CE or earlier, document dialogues between Hermes Trismegistus (Thrice-Greatest Hermes) and his disciples. These writings explore a wide array of topics, including divinity, cosmology, the mind, nature, alchemy, and astrology. Jung's interdisciplinary approach—deeply informed by these theurgic traditions—is evidenced throughout his Collected Works.[55] For instance, Jung drew extensively upon the Neoplatonist Iamblichus's *On the Mysteries*, a text structured as a series of responses by a priest of the Egyptian god Hermes (likely representing Iamblichus himself) to a skeptical Porphyry. This work addresses complex metaphysical, cosmological, and ethical themes that align closely with Jung's own intellectual explorations. Additionally, Jung's work reflects the influence of Emanuel Swedenborg (1688–1772), whose spiritual hermeneutics left a notable imprint on his ideas.[56]

Table 7
Lives Intersecting Through Haus zum Sessel

Name	Connection to Haus zum Sessel	Historical significance
Johann Amerbach (1440-1513)	Printer who resided at Haus zum Sessel from 1480 to 1513.	Renowned early printer who established one of Basel's most important printing workshops.
Johann Froben (1460-1527)	Amerbach's son-in-law and owner of the printing workshop at Haus zum Sessel (1507).	Leading printer of his time. Published the first edition of Erasmus's *Adagia* in 1513, forging a significant friendship and collaborative relationship with the author.
Urs Graf (1485-1527)	Worked in Froben's printing shop.	Engraver and artist who collaborated on numerous printed works with Froben.
Erasmus of Rotterdam (1467-1536)	Resided at Haus zum Sessel (1415-1416) while having numerous manuscripts printed there.	Influential scholar of the Northern Renaissance. More than 100 of his manuscripts were printed by Froben, cementing a lasting friendship between them.
Theophrastus von Hohenheim (Paracelsus) (1493-1541)	Lived at Haus zum Sessel	Known as Paracelsus, he studied medicine at the University of Basel (starting at age 16 in 1509) and later returned to the city in 1526 to care for Froben during his illness (remaining in Basel for only one year).
Hans Holbein the Younger (1497-1543)	Lived at Haus zum Sessel.	Renowned Renaissance artist who illustrated and painted several portraits of Erasmus during his time at Basel.
Johannes Oporinus (Oporin) (1507-1568)	Worked as a proofreader for Froben and an assistant to Paracelsus, before becoming a printer.	Established a significant printing house in Basel. Published the first Koran in Latin and Vesalius's *De humani corporis fabrica* (On the Structure of the Human Body).
Andreas Vesalius (Vesal) (1514-1564)	His first textbook of anatomy was printed at Haus zum Sessel in 1543.	Author of *De humani corporis fabrica* (On the Structure of the Human Body), a landmark text in anatomical studies. Conducted public dissections in Basel while awaiting publication.
Josef Anton Häfliger (1873-1954)	Founder of the Pharmacy Museum at Haus zum Sessel in 1925.	His correspondence with Jung in 1941 contributed background knowledge for Jung's alchemical research.
Tadeus Reichstein (1897-1996)	Commemorated with a plaque in the Pharmaceutical Museum.	Nobel laureate and director of Basel's Pharmaceutical Institute. Shared a scholarly interest in alchemy with Jung.

Erasmus of Rotterdam

At the age of 19, Carl purchased a copy of the 1563 edition of *Adagia (Collectaneas adagiorum)*—a compilation of Greek and Latin proverbs by Erasmus of Rotterdam—from an antiquarian bookstore in Basel.[57] This work, renowned for its timeless, classical wisdom, was integral to both scholarly and political discourse, making it immensely popular. Initially published in 1513 with 800 Latin aphorisms, *Adagia* expanded to an extraordinary 4,151 entries by 1536.[58] Many scholars believe that such a monumental collection could only have emerged from an intellectual environment like that of Basel, where the study of classical texts was highly valued. *Adagia* remains one of the most comprehensive anthologies of proverbs from classical antiquity ever assembled.

One particularly enigmatic entry, *"Vocatus atque non vocatus Deus aderit"* ("Called or not called, God will be there"), attributed to the Oracle of Delphi, had a profound impact on Jung,[59] who had this phrase engraved in stone above the threshold to his home in Küsnacht, and later inscribed on his tombstone. His friend Laurens van der Post recalled: "[Carl] was still reading the book with its worn leather covers when I saw him last just before he died."[60]

It is unclear whether Carl, at the time of acquiring the book, was aware of the fascinating history of the 1513 edition: it had been pirated in Basel, prompting Erasmus to visit the city and address the matter personally. This incident eventually led to his forming a lasting friendship with the printers and, for a time, residing at Haus zum Sessel. Hans Holbein the Younger also resided there at various points, during which time he painted several portraits of Erasmus.

Basel Printing Legacy at Haus zum Sessel

As the story goes, the first manuscript of Erasmus's *Adagia* was en route to a Parisian printer when it was either intentionally or accidentally pirated and leaked to Johann Froben, the renowned printer operating the workshop at Haus zum Sessel. Froben wasted no time in producing the print edition, which featured a title page designed by the celebrated artist Urs Graf and set in the then-modern Antiqua typeface. The result delighted Erasmus, who was so impressed with the quality of Froben's work that he forged a lifelong friendship with the printer. Eventually, Froben became Erasmus's primary publisher, producing 148 of his works.[61] His reputation as one of the foremost printers of his time helped elevate Basel to a preeminent position in the global book trade.

Prior to Froben, Johann Amerbach had established Basel's first printing workshop at Haus zum Sessel. Nearly 40 years after the initial publication of *Adagia*, another eminent Basel printer, Johannes Oporinus, produced Andreas Vesalius's groundbreaking *De humani corporis fabrica* (*On the Structure of the Human Body*) in 1543. This seminal work on human anatomy featured over 400 woodcuts and ornate initials, illustrated by artists from the workshop of Titian, making it not only a scientific milestone but also an artistic masterpiece.[62] Spanning more than 600 pages, the book was regarded as one of the most visually stunning publications of its time.

Basel's printing industry was remarkably prolific. The Bible was printed in thirteen languages, and handwritten alchemical manuscripts were reproduced in printed form, making esoteric knowledge more widely accessible. During the 16th century, Basel became a magnet for intellectuals and alchemists, who sought access to its wealth of printed knowledge or wished to have their own works printed. Wherever books were printed, intellectuals gathered, and Basel thrived as a hub for scholarship, art, and innovation.

Paracelsus

Paracelsus (1493–1541),[63] a healer, visionary, and unorthodox thinker critical of the medical establishment, resided at Haus zum Sessel at various points in his life. At the age of 16, he began studying medicine at the University of Basel. After completing his education, he was summoned back to Basel to treat the ailing printer Johann Froben, whom he reportedly cured. Erasmus, who was also in Basel at the time, witnessed Paracelsus's medical skills, leading the two scholars

26 Paracelsus (D. Theophrast, Paracelsus Brombast) (1550/1650)
Copper engraving.

to exchange correspondence on medical and theological subjects. In 1527, as a licensed physician in Basel, Paracelsus was granted the privilege of lecturing at the University of Basel. In a departure from academic convention, he delivered his lectures in German, rather than Latin, making his teachings accessible to a broader audience. During this time, he became a close friend of Erasmus.

Jung may have seen a reflection of himself in Paracelsus, as evidenced by his two lectures on the polymath, "Paracelsus as a Spiritual Phenomenon,"[64] and "Paracelsus the Physician," with the latter exploring the scholar's psychology. The first lecture was delivered in June 1929 at the Literary Club of Zurich in the house in Einsiedeln where Paracelsus was born. The second was presented in Basel in 1941, commemorating the 400th anniversary of Paracelsus's death, for the Swiss Society for the History of Medicine and Natural Sciences.[65] During his tenure at the University of Basel, Paracelsus emphasized practical experience over formal education, inviting barber-surgeons, alchemists, apothecaries, and others lacking in academic training to contribute to his lectures. He famously declared: "The patients are your textbook, the sickbed is your study." This philosophy resonates with analytical psychology, where practitioners must undergo their own analysis before treating patients, ensuring that experiential understanding informs their work.

Alchemy

As early as September 1919, Jung referred to one of his mandala images (*The Red Book,* image 121) as the *Lapis Philosophorum* (Philosopher's Stone)—a central concept in alchemy. This reference predated his formal psychological engagement with alchemical symbolism.[66] By the time his writings in the *Black Books* concluded around 1932, Jung had become an avid collector of alchemical and rare books, and he began transcribing extensive excerpts from the texts—a project in which he collaborated with Marie-Louise von Franz. This effort culminated in a series of eight copybooks, accompanied by an index volume titled *Index Omnium Rerum Achymicarum* (*Index of All Things Alchemical*). It was later noted by the editor of the *Black Books* that these copybooks reflect Jung's detailed engagement with alchemical sources, as library call slips pasted within the volumes indicate his extensive research at the University of Basel Library during the winter of 1935.[67]

In *Psychology and Alchemy,* written toward the end of World War II and published in 1944, Jung wrote:

> The real nature of matter was unknown to the alchemist: he knew it only in hints. In seeking to explore it he projected the unconscious into the darkness of matter in order to illuminate it. In order to explain the mystery of matter he projected yet another mystery—his own psychic background—into what was to be explained: Obscurum per obscurius, ignotum per ignotius! This procedure was not, of course, intentional; it was an involuntary occurrence.[68]

He continued:

> *I am therefore inclined to assume that the real root of alchemy is to be sought less in philosophical doctrines than in the projections of individual investigators. I mean by this that while working on his chemical experiments the operator had certain psychic experiences which appeared to him as the particular behavior of the chemical process. Since it was a question of projection, he was naturally unconscious of the fact that the experience had nothing to do with matter itself (that is, with matter as we know it today). He experienced his projection as a property of matter; but what he was in reality experiencing was his own unconscious. In this way he recapitulated the whole history of mankind's knowledge of nature. [...] Such projections repeat themselves whenever man tries to explore an empty darkness and involuntarily fills it with living form.*[69]

Jung did not perceive alchemy as merely the precursor to modern chemistry, but as an essential part of the history of psychology, concluding that there is a direct relationship between alchemical symbols and the psychoanalytical process.[70] He argued that the alchemical transformation of base materials (such as lead) into gold symbolized the psychological process of individuation, and he further contended that alchemy was, in a broader sense, "a part of the history of psychology as the history of the discovery of the deep structures of the psyche and unconscious."[71] Jung's extensive engagement with alchemical texts stemmed from his belief that their symbolic structure offered insights into the workings of the unconscious mind.

The Pharmacy Museum of the University of Basel

The Pharmacy Museum is located in the historic Haus zum Sessel. A commemorative plaque at the entrance highlights the building's storied past:

> *From 1507–1527 this property housed the printing shop of Johannes Froben. Erasmus of Rotterdam and Paracelsus lived here as guests. Urs Graf and Hans Holbein the younger worked with Froben as illustrators. In 1516 Johannes Froben printed Erasmus' Greek translation of the New Testament here.*

Founded in 1925, the museum originated from a donation by the pharmacist and medical historian Josef Anton Häfliger (1873–1954), who contributed his private collection of historical pharmacy vessels, obsolete medicines, prescriptions, woodcuts, and books. Today, it boasts one of the world's largest collections on the history of pharmacy.[72] Jung and Häfliger may have crossed paths as students at the University of Basel, where Häfliger began his studies in philology and history during the winter semester of 1895/96—shortly after Carl's matriculation. Although they pursued different fields—Jung focusing on medicine and Häfliger transitioning to pharmacy—they shared an enduring interest in historical and scientific scholarship. Häfliger went on to direct the St. Johann Pharmacy for more than 40 years, gaining renown as an expert in galenics (the preparation of medicines according to the principles of Galen).[73] In 1932, he was appointed Associate Professor of the History of Pharmacy and Galenics at the University of Basel.

On September 11, 1941, Jung initiated a correspondence with Häfliger, sending him images from alchemical texts that he believed may be of interest. These included illustrations from the *Lambsprinck'schen* and *Basil Valentinischen* woodcut series, depicting stages of the alchemical process,[74] as well as the title page of *Tripus Aureus* (*The Golden Tripod*), published in 1618. Jung wrote again on October 21, 1941, seeking clarification about *muscus pomambra,* a term he had encountered in relation to Paracelsus. Häfliger responded:

Herrn Prof. Dr C.G. Jung, Küsnacht – Zürich
Dear Colleague!
Pomambra is an abbreviation of Pomum Ambrae. These were plague balls to carry around or place in sickrooms. The strong smelling ingredients: nutmeg, musk, essential oil containing drugs are said to "improve the air."
At your service with pleasure with the highest esteem
Yours sincerely, J. A. Häfliger

27 Letter from Häfliger to Jung

Notated as 22.X.1 (likely indicating October 22, 1941).
Transcription by the author.

Schweizer. Sammlung
Für Histo. Apothekenwesen
an der
Pharmazeutischen Anstalt
der Universität
Basel
Totengässlein 3
Telephon 456.70

Basel, den 22.X.1

Herrn Prof. Dr C.G. Jung
Küsnacht - Zürich

Sehr geehrter Herr Kollege!
Pomambra ist eine Abkürzung von Pomum Ambrae. Das waren Pestkugeln zum Mittragen oder Aufstellen in den Krankenstuben. Die stark riechenden Bestandteile: Muskatnuss, Moschus, aether. Öl haltige Drogen sollen die Luft "verbessern."

Sehr gerne zu Ihren Diensten
mit vorzüglicher Hochachtung

Ihr ergebener

J.A. Häfliger.

Jung also wrote on July 16, 1942, to inquire whether Häfliger could provide him with an image of the *Einhorn Becher* (*Unicorn Mug*) for use in an upcoming publication.

Today, the Pharmacy Museum houses a large collection of historical pharmaceutical artifacts and features an herbal remedy shop called the Herbarium. Among its highlights is a reconstructed alchemical laboratory, offering visitors insight into the working methods of the historical alchemists.

28 An Alchemy Laboratory
Display in the Pharmacy Museum, University of Basel.

The museum also shares a significant connection with Tadeus Reichstein, a Polish-born researcher, Nobel Prize laureate, and former director of the University of Basel Pharmaceutical Institute. Reichstein's contributions to pharmaceutical and organic chemistry, including his synthesis of vitamin C (ascorbic acid) and his Nobel Prize–winning research on adrenocortical hormones, are commemorated with a plaque in the museum's courtyard. Born into a Polish Jewish family, Reichstein emigrated to Switzerland during the 1905 Pogroms. As a youth, he worked in his uncle's apothecary, where he learned to make pills, cook syrups, and spread plasters. He later earned a doctorate in chemistry from ETH Zürich. His early research led to a commercially viable synthesis of vitamin C—the patent for which was sold to Hoffmann-La Roche, securing long-term funding for his laboratory.

Reichstein had a deep interest in Jung's work and alchemy. Between 1934 and 1939, he attended Jung's lectures on Nietzsche's *Thus Spoke Zarathustra* and alchemy. Moreover, at his inaugural lecture at ETH Zürich in 1931,[75] he spoke about alchemy—a topic he revisited decades later in a lecture titled "Über Alchemie" ("On Alchemy"), delivered on April 3, 1968 at the Psychology Club Zurich (founded by Jung). During this talk, Reichstein remarked: "The secret of alchemy is from projected psychology, and it is no accident that the concept 'analysis' plays such a great role in chemistry as in modern psychology." He further emphasized that alchemical texts should be interpreted symbolically, rather than literally, stating, "the alchemical process is the process of individuation."[76]

The Pharmacy Museum and its shop are open to the public, offering visitors a fascinating journey through the history of pharmacy and its intersections with alchemy and Jung's intellectual legacy. After taking time to explore the museum, proceed to the Marktplatz tram stop, situated in front of the remarkable Basel Town Hall.

TOUR 4

BOTTMINGER MÜHLE: SÉANCES AND ENCOUNTERS WITH THE FEMININE

This tour retraces Carl's steps between the University of Basel and his new home at Bottminger Mühle (Bottminger Mill) in Binningen. The Jung family relocated to Bottminger Mühle following the death of Carl's father, which necessitated their departure from the Kleinhüningen parsonage. At the time, Carl was just 21 years old and in his first year of medical studies. You will learn about the many séances he attended and the feminine influences that shaped his life during this period.

Similar to Kleinhüningen, Binningen is situated approximately 4 kilometers outside of Basel. To enhance your visit, consider reserving a table for lunch at the Bottminger Mühle restaurant (bottmingermuehle.ch), conveniently located next to the tram stop. Please note that this restaurant, while sharing the same name, is not the site of Carl's home.

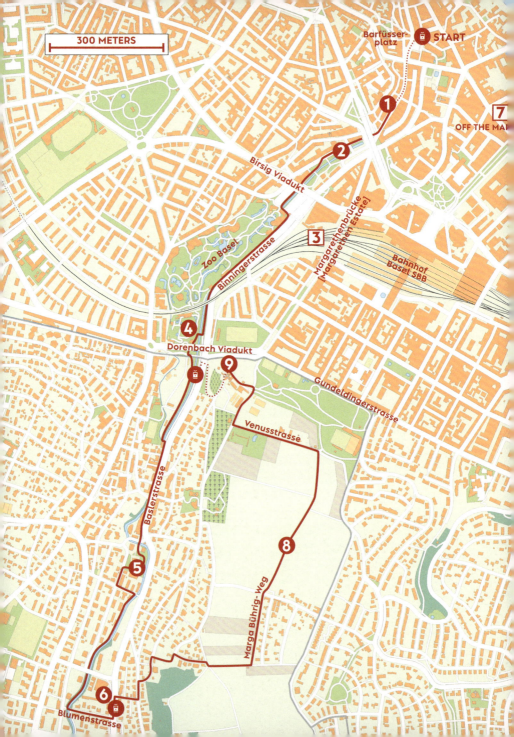

TOUR 4 OVERVIEW

① **ZOFINGIA STUDENT FRATERNITY, STEINENVORSTADT 36 (HISTORIC SITE)**
Carl Finds His Voice and Place in a Community of Peers

② **NACHTIGALLENWÄLDELI**
Spooky Nights in the Forest Along the Birsig

③ **MARGARETHENSTRASSE 19 (HISTORIC SITE)**
A Bustling and Loved Extended Family Home

④ **MARGARETHEN-BRÜCKLEIN**
Family Ties Between Church and Mill

⑤ **BINNINGER SCHLOSS, SCHLOSSGASSE 5**
Castle Near the Woods

⑥ **BOTTMINGER MÜHLE, BOTTMINGERSTRASSE 68, BINNINGEN**
The Mill's Many Incarnations

⑦ **THE PREISWERK SISTERS' DRESS SHOP, ST. ALBAN-ANLAGE 5 (HISTORIC SITE)**
Les Demoiselles Helene & Valerie Preiswerk: *Robes et Manteaux*

⑧ **BRUDERHOLZ, MARGA BÜHRIG-WEG**
Broader Horizons: The Colorful Hills of Binningen

⑨ **ST. MARGARETHENKIRCHE, FRIEDHOFSTRASSE, BINNINGEN**
Leaving Basel for Zürich

START
The tour starts at Barfüsserplatz in Basel.

GETTING THERE
Barfüsserplatz is easily accessible via multiple tram lines.

TOUR LENGTH
Allow two to five hours, including your return to central Basel by tram. The walk covers a flat 4 kilometers from Barfüsserplatz to Carl's home at Bottminger Mühle, and the return walk spans a hilly 4 kilometers. For a shorter journey, take tram line 10 between Barfüsserplatz and the Bottminger Mühle tram stop in either or both directions.

RETURN
Returning to Basel involves retracing the cousins' path via St. Margaret's Church and over the Bruderholz. Begin by climbing the steep Mühlesteig (mill path), located directly across from the mill. Turn left onto Waldeckweg, then right onto Schweissbergstrasse, and ascend the 120 steps of Himmelsleiterli (Stairway to Heaven), which lead up to Bruderholz. At the top of the stairs, turn right onto Binzenweg and follow David Joris-Strasse, then turn left onto Marga Bührig-Weg.
Straight ahead, you will see the round roof of the Observatory. Turn left onto Venusstrasse to pass by the Observatory, then right onto Friedhofsweg. From this vantage point, you can enjoy a bird's-eye view of Basel from St. Margaret's Church. Descend via Kastanienweg, then walk along the Birsig River, past the Zoo, and back to Nachtigallenwäldeli.

By Tram
Alternatively, you can catch tram line 10 back to Basel from one of several locations: Bottminger Mühle; the tram stop at the bottom of Kastanienweg, where it intersects with Baslerstrasse; or farther along at the Heuwaage stop, where the Birsig River flows under the city.

 Scan to follow the tour on Google Maps

This Google Map is also accessible at www.kschaeppi.ch/book

215

1 Bierbrauerei zum Löwenfels (Lion Rock Beer Brewery) (1892)
Once located at Steinenvorstadt 36. During Carl's time as a member of "Breo," the Basel section of the Zofingia Association met here.

ZOFINGIA STUDENT FRATERNITY, STEINENVORSTADT 36 (HISTORIC SITE)

CARL FINDS HIS VOICE AND PLACE IN A COMMUNITY OF PEERS

Lifelong Friends

From Barfüsserplatz, walk along Steinenvorstadt to number 36. Although the building that once housed the student fraternity Zofingia was demolished in 1928—several years after Carl's medical school years—the site was occupied by the Bierbrauerei zum Löwenfels (Lion Rock brewery), which served as the home of the Basel chapter of Zofingia, known as Breo (derived from the family name Brändlin). The fraternity's insignia adorned the building. Carl Jung joined Zofingia on May 18, 1895, just one month after being admitted to medical school. Today, this pedestrian zone is lined with numerous bars and restaurants, as well as the terminal stretch of the Birsig river, which now runs underground. However, in Carl's time, it was a poor neighborhood, and the open river posed a significant public health hazard. Human waste was routinely discarded from houses directly into the water, and further downstream, a slaughterhouse contributed additional refuse. The river often carried insufficient water to wash away the accumulating waste. Despite a devastating cholera outbreak in 1855 that claimed over 200 lives, followed by a typhoid epidemic in 1865 that resulted in 400 deaths and 4,000 infections, it was not until 1898—more than 30 years later—that the Grosser Rat (Great Council) voted to cover the river.

Despite the hardship of his father's passing, Carl's university years appear to have offered him newfound freedom and rich experiences, including the formation of lasting friendships through his involvement in Zofingia. Founded in 1819, Zofingia is a color-bearing Swiss student fraternity, with Breo as one of its twelve branches. The fraternity boasts a long and distinguished list of members who have influenced history and culture.[1] Among the notable Basel members are: Johan Konrad Kern (Editor of the Swiss Federal Constitution and co-founder of ETH

TOUR 4

2 Zofingia Brothers Wearing Their Cerevises (Caps) and Sashes (1895–1900)
Jung is on the far left.

Zürich), Jacob Burckhardt (historian), Wilhelm His (medical doctor and anatomist), Friedrich Miescher (first scientist to isolate nucleic acid), and Paul Sarasin (co-founder of the Swiss National Park).

In Carl's time, Zofingia members adopted special nicknames known as "cerevis names" (see Table 8), in reference to the ceremonial caps or "chapeau" they wore (and continue to wear) as part of their student uniforms. These caps featured red and white silk ribbons and gold embroidery.[2] The term "cerevis" also relates to the Latin word for a yeast used to brew beer.

Carl's own cerevis name was Walze (Barrel). His friend Albert Oeri later unraveled the origins of this moniker, linking it to Carl's habit of "barreling thoughts." He recounted:

Table 8
Cerevis Names of Carl's Zofingia Friends[3]
Though not included in this table, Carl's close friend Gustav Steiner was also a member of Zofingia.

Carl Jung	Walze (Barrel)	1875–1961
Andreas Vischer	Ei (Egg)	1877–1930
Albert Oeri	ES (IT)	1875–1950
Georg Walter	Paris	
Rudolf Burckhardt	Oberst (Colonel)	
Achilles Müller	Elsy	
Paul Preiswerk	Boris	
Ernst Preiswerk	?	
Gustav Preiswerk	?	

Once, when we couldn't find a speaker, Jung suggested that we might hold a discussion without specifying the topic. The minutes read, "Jung vulgo Barrel," the pure spirit having gone to his head, urged that we debate hitherto unresolved philosophical questions. This was agreeable to all, more agreeable than might have been expected under our usual "prevailing circumstances." But "Barrel" blithered endlessly, and that was dumb. Oeri, vulgo "IT," likewise spiritually oiled, distorted, in so far as such was possible, these barreling thoughts.[4]

Carl's closest university friends were Albert Oeri (1875–1950), Andreas Vischer (1877–1930), and Gustav Steiner (1878–1967). Oeri and Carl first met in early childhood through their fathers, who were acquainted. Their friendship deepened during their shared participation in Zofingia, and continued throughout their lives.[5] Oeri's father, Johann Jakob Oeri (1844–1908), was a teacher at the Gymnasium in Basel. Reflecting on their early years, Oeri recalled: "I got somewhat better acquainted with Jung behind his back by secretly reading his school compositions awaiting correction in my father's study."[6] A group photograph of the 1889 Oberes Gymnasium faculty includes Oeri's father,[7] as well as several other educators who, only a couple years later, taught Carl.

After university, Oeri married Hanna Preiswerk (Vetter branch), with whom he had six children.[8] He was also an ancestor of the Hoffmann-Oeri family, who would later become majority stakeholders in the Basel pharmaceutical company. As an adult, Oeri played a significant role in Swiss journalism and politics. Serving as Chief Editor of the *Basler Nachrichten* and a member of both the Basler Grosser Rat (Great Council) and National Parliament, his voice carried considerable influence, particularly during World War II. In 1935, on the occasion of Jung's 60th birthday, Oeri wrote about aspects of Jung's early Zofingia lectures, noting, among other things, Jung's difficulty with mathematics.

Another of Carl's close university friends, Gustav Steiner (1878–1967), who once participated in Carl's séances, provided a more detailed account of their Zofingia years in his memoir.[9] After graduating from the Gymnasium, Steiner studied German and history at the University of Basel. He began his teaching career at the Knabensekundarschule Basel and, after earning his doctorate, taught German and history at the Obere Realschule and Mathematisch-naturwissenschaftliches Gymnasium Basel. As a historian and literary scholar, he authored several academic texts and served as Editor of the *Basler Stadtbuch*. He also held the title of Master of the Zunft zum Goldenen Stern (Guild of the Golden Star), which historically comprised shearers, surgeons, and wound specialists—areas about which he wrote extensively.[10] The guild's heraldic flag features a single golden star, set against a blue background. Notably, when Jung later designed his personal *ex libris* (bookplate), he incorporated a star at the center of the shield, possibly a nod to Steiner's guild.[11]

Carl's friend Andreas Vischer (1877–1930) became the brother-in-law of Albert Oeri through his marriage to Gertrud Oeri (née Jakob). Gertrud's father, Johann Jakob, was a teacher at the Gymnasium. Vischer studied medicine at the University of Basel, specializing in surgery, and earned his doctorate in 1904. He later achieved his Habilitation in 1918, marking his qualification to teach at the university level. Vischer was appointed as the successor to Hermann Christ as Head of the Mission Hospital of the German Orient Mission in Urfa (Turkey), which had been founded in 1897. In 1912, the governor of Urfa named him surgical director of the city's state hospital. The outbreak of World War I prevented Vischer and his wife from returning to Urfa until 1919, when they witnessed the Franco-Turkish conflict over the city. Afterward, he set up a medical practice in Basel but remained deeply involved in humanitarian efforts, particularly those aimed at aiding stateless Armenian refugees. From 1928 until his death, he served as President of the Swiss Aid for Blind Armenian Orphans in Lebanon. His experiences as a surgeon in Turkey were documented in his 1921 writings, including has "Diaries from Urfa 1919/1920" and "Experiences of a Swiss Doctor with the Turkish Nationalists, 1921."[12]

Carl served as the Chairman of Zofingia from 1897 to 1898. A notable event in the fraternity's history occurred on August 1, 1897, when a fire broke out in the attic of the building adjacent to Löwenfels. The incident was recorded in the fraternity chronicle: "The chestnut tree in the courtyard, well known in Zofingia circles, is badly scorched; but it does not seem to have been fatally hit. The larger half of its crown is still a lush green."[13] However, the gothic ocular window overlooking the courtyard was destroyed.

Zofingia Lectures

Between 1896 and 1899, Carl delivered five lectures on theological and philosophical topics at Zofingia meetings—one each year.[14] These lectures were later published posthumously in 1983 as *The Zofingia Lectures,* accompanied by an extensive introduction by Marie-Louise von Franz. In this introduction, von Franz noted that Jung, himself, would not have wished for these essays to be published in their original form, as he later expressed a desire to rewrite all of his works. It is important, therefore, to read these lectures with an awareness of their context— he was addressing his peers at university, between the ages of 21 and 24, in a setting quite different from a formal academic environment. The fraternity gathered at the pub zum Löwenfels, drinking beer while listening to their friend's impassioned talks. As von Franz observed, "The lectures were supposed to meet a high scientific standard and at the same time to express political and other opinions in an outspoken manner befitting a closed circle whose members felt free of academic and social conventions."[15] In his introduction to the first lecture, Carl petitioned his audience to indulge him, sarcastically apologizing in advance for any offense his words might cause. He acknowledged that his language may include elements of "rudeness, incivility, impropriety, insolence, cheekiness, [and] unmannerliness." Oeri later recalled that Carl was "a merry member of the student club, always prepared to revolt against the 'League of Virtue', as he called the organized fraternity

The Five Zofingia Lectures

Lecture 1: The Border Zones of Exact Science (November 1896)
Carl's first lecture explored the limitations of traditional scientific methods when addressing phenomena such as consciousness, psychology, and the psyche's less tangible dimensions. While advocating for empirical rigor, he argued that science must also acknowledge its "border zones"—areas where its tools are insufficient. These reflections reveal his belief that science should remain open to the metaphysical and symbolic aspects of human experience, foreshadowing his later work on the unconscious.

Lecture 2: Some Thoughts on Psychology (May 1897)
In his second lecture, Carl articulated his early vision of psychology as a discipline distinct from the natural sciences, emphasizing the importance of understanding subjective experience, symbolic meaning, and the inner life. Rejecting purely mechanistic interpretations of the psyche, he called for a psychology integrating empirical inquiry with an appreciation for the complexities of human consciousness. These ideas laid the groundwork for his later development of depth psychology.

Lecture 3: Inaugural Address upon Assuming Chairmanship
Delivered upon becoming the fraternity's chairman, this lecture set forth Carl's ideals of intellectual rigor, ethical responsibility, and personal authenticity. He challenged his peers to pursue knowledge not for personal gain, but for the greater purpose of intellectual and moral development. His emphasis on self-discovery and purpose reflects values he would later integrate into his psychological theories, particularly in his concepts of individuation and the pursuit of meaning.

Lecture 4: Thoughts on the Nature and Value of Speculative Inquiry (Summer 1898)
In this lecture, Carl championed speculative inquiry as a method for exploring profound questions that lay beyond empirical analysis, stressing the importance of imagination, intuition, and openness to the unknown in advancing understanding. His defense of speculative thought anticipated his later work on the unconscious, archetypes, and symbolic life, through which he sought to bridge rational and intuitive modes of inquiry.

Lecture 5: Thoughts on the Interpretation of Christianity, with Reference to the Theory of Albrecht Ritschl (January 1899)
In this lecture, Carl examined Christianity's psychological and ethical dimensions, describing its role as a moral framework capable of fostering personal transformation via community. Rejecting rigid theological doctrines, Carl focused on Christianity's capacity to inspire ethical behavior and individual growth, anticipating his later exploration of religious symbols and myths as psychological expressions of the universal human experience.

Throughout his Zofingia lectures, Carl repeatedly referenced Friedrich Nietzsche, engaging with him as both an inspiration and a cautionary figure. In particular, he admired Nietzsche's bold critique of societal norms and his emphasis on the potential for human self-overcoming, but was wary of the nihilistic implications of rejecting traditional values entirely. This early engagement with Nietzsche foreshadowed his later, more comprehensive examination of *Thus Spoke Zarathustra* and its implications for the psyche, individuation, and the human search for meaning.

3 Carl's Song Folder (1895)
Featuring the Zofingia insignia and Basel skyline.

brothers."[16] In retrospect, Carl's lectures were described as strongly worded, "saucy," and "beery"—a tone fitting for the lively, informal setting in which they were delivered.[17] However, beneath their irreverent style, these lectures reflected core values and convictions that would be refined and developed in Jung's later work.

When Carl delivered his first Zofingia lecture, he was still living in Kleinhüningen, and his father had not yet died. Having grown up in a household steeped in theological discourse, he was undoubtedly influenced by the sermons he had heard from an early age and the séances taking place in the parsonage. Oeri later referred to Carl's lectures not simply as talks, but as orations—emphasizing their impassioned and provocative nature.

After passing the *Staatsexamen* in July 1900, Jung began working as an assistant psychiatrist at the Burghölzli Psychiatric Clinic in Zürich by December of the same year. Carefully storing and preserving his Zofingia lectures, he appears to have considered them significant artifacts of his early intellectual development. Another cherished memento from this period was his song folder, adorned with the Zofingia insignia and featuring his own painting of a panoramic Basel cityscape, reflecting his deep connection to the fraternity and the formative experiences of his university years.

4 Nachtigallenwäldeli Today with the Birsig-Viadukt
Built 1857–1858 initially for steam trains.

② NACHTIGALLENWÄLDELI

SPOOKY NIGHTS IN THE FOREST ALONG THE BIRSIG

Continuing along Steinenvorstadt toward its terminus, pass under the highway overpass and arrive at the point where the Birsig emerges from beneath the city. Take the path that keeps the river to your left and look for the sign marking the entrance to the Nachtigallenwäldeli (Forest of the Nightingale), named for the bird whose melodious song is typically heard at night. While today's path is illuminated after dark, this was not the case in Carl's time. Carl found it unsettling to walk through the dense forest at night, when he would frequently encounter nocturnal animals. To avoid going alone, he would entice friends to accompany him by spinning compelling stories. Otherwise, as he recounted in his memoir, he carried a gun in his pocket for protection.

As you continue along the path, you will pass beneath the stone arch of the Birsig-Viadukt. Below, the Birsig flows, while above, the first trains once crossed, their whistles echoing through the area. Today, the road atop the viaduct, Viaduktstrasse, connects Basel's central train station to Pauluskirche.

The Nachtigallenwäldeli path leads to the entrance gate of Basel Zoo. Established in 1874, the zoo was still relatively new when Carl walked this route. In recent years (2015–2017), the forest was revitalized with the planting of 45 young trees. A network of paths now includes three newly constructed footbridges leading to the zoo entrance. To continue, turn left at the zoo entrance and follow the path between the tram tracks and the zoo wall. Here, the Birsig disappears into the zoo grounds before reemerging downstream.

5 Artisanal Ironwork of Rudolf Preiswerk and Son
This gate was awarded a prize at the National Exhibit in Geneva, 1896.

3 MARGARETHENSTRASSE 19 (HISTORIC SITE)

A BUSTLING AND LOVED EXTENDED FAMILY HOME

You will soon pass under a railway bridge that supports the train connecting France to Basel. The expansion of this railway line eventually necessitated the demolition of the Preiswerk-Allenspach home, which occurred after the death of Carl's Uncle Rudolf in 1895. The development of Basel's train station, which included a connection to the French East Railway, had already begun as early as 1860.

The home at Margarethenstrasse 19 was a stately baroque residence purchased by Carl's Aunt Célestine and Uncle Rudolf Preiswerk-Allenspach. Célestine was a country girl of 18 when she married Rudolf, who was also Carl's godfather. Together, they raised fifteen children. Affectionately known as "d'Margarete," the house became a beloved gathering place for Carl and his sister Trudi.

Two of the Antistes's sons, Lucas and Rudolf, were skilled ironworkers. Lucas initially ran a mechanical workshop and foundry in Kleinhüningen, while Rudolf established an iron casting shop at Münsterberg 8 in Basel. Later, Rudolf moved both his home and workshop to Margarethenstrasse 19, where Carl got to see the artisan at work.

Rudolf's exceptional craftsmanship was posthumously honored with first prize at the 1896 National Exhibition for a hand-forged gate featuring a central Swiss cross (image left). His impressive and diverse artistic work is preserved in three photographic pattern books.[18] After Rudolf's death in 1895, his eldest son and Carl's cousin, also named Rudolf, took over the iron construction and wrought iron workshop.

As you wander through Basel, you may notice exquisite examples of ornamental ironwork. These intricate gates stand as enduring testaments to the city's artisanal heritage and charm.

6   Path Along the Birsig River
The nostalgic Margarethen-Brücklein is in the foreground.

MARGARETHEN-BRÜCKLEIN

FAMILY TIES BETWEEN CHURCH AND MILL

At the small footbridge known as Margarethen-Brücklein, where the Dorenbach River—originating in the Allschwiler Wald (forest)—joins the Birsig, take a moment to pause. From this idyllic bridge, look up through the surrounding foliage to your left. If it is not too dense, you may catch a glimpse of St. Margarethenkirche (St. Margaret's Church) perched quaintly yet proudly on the hill.

St. Margaret's Church held special significance for the Jung family, as another of Carl's uncles, Eduard Preiswerk-Friedrich (1846–1932), served as the church's pastor from 1870 to 1879. Although Eduard was no longer the pastor during Carl's years in the area, the church remained an important family landmark. During Eduard's tenure, St. Margaret's Church was the sole place of worship in the parish. Eduard also owned Bottminger Mühle, and it seems likely that he, his wife Emma Maria Preiswerk-Friedrich, and their four children (Margaretha (1873–1949), Eduard (1874–1949), Heinrich (1876–1940), and Dorothea (1881–1940)) lived there during his nine years as pastor. By the time Carl's father, Paul Jung, passed away in 1896, Eduard had moved on, following in the footsteps of his father, Samuel Preiswerk, to become the pastor at St. Leonard's Church in Basel. However, the close ties between the families continued. Eduard's children, who were similar in age to Carl, lived in the parsonage at Leonhardskirchplatz 1 during Carl's own years at Bottminger Mühle.

7 Binninger Schloss South View
Another tower motif, the castle, is two tram stops away from the Bottminger Mühle.

5 BINNINGER SCHLOSS, SCHLOSSGASSE 5

CASTLE NEAR THE WOODS

After crossing the Margarethen-Brücklein footbridge, the Birsig now runs on your left. Continue along the path until a second small footbridge brings into view the tower of Binninger Schloss, a castle originally with a moat dating back to 1299.[19] As a youth, Carl would have first encountered the lower mill at Baslerstrasse 54, located at the entrance to Binningen, before this castle. This "lower" mill is believed to have predated the castle. However, it suffered a turbulent history, having burned down in 1446, only to be rebuilt in 1817, before burning down again roughly a century later.

Historically, Bottmingen and Binningen were a single municipality until 1837. The lower mill near the Binninger castle is referred to as Binninger Mühle, while the upper mill, closer to the Bottminger castle (although now in the town of Binningen), is known as the Bottminger Mühle. Between 1889 and 1900, Binningen had an average population of 4,663.[20]

The castle, itself, has long been a gathering place. Its restaurant has been in operation since 1871 and continues to serve visitors to this day. Feel free to explore the castle garden. The Birsig meanders to the left of the castle. Leave the castle turning left onto Parkstrasse and take the next left onto Brückenstrasse to rejoin the path along the Birsig. The Birsig again runs on your left.

To return to Basel, turn left at Blumenstrasse and backtrack toward the Bottminger Mühle tram stop. Just a few meters further along Bottmingerstrasse, you will arrive at Bottmingerstrasse 68, the last surviving building of the original Bottminger Mühle complex.

8 Bottminger Mühle (1887)
This is where the Jung family lived as of 1896. In the foreground are the tracks of the train already powered by a steam locomotive beginning in 1887.

BOTTMINGER MÜHLE, BOTTMINGERSTRASSE 68, BINNINGEN

THE MILL'S MANY INCARNATIONS

Story of the Mill

Bottminger Mühle was built in 1796–1799 as a large milling complex designed to serve the residents of both Bottmingen and Binningen. The mill's buildings were arranged at right angles, forming a central courtyard around a well,[21] and local farmers would bring their grain there to be ground. In 1836, a fire partially destroyed the complex, but it was promptly rebuilt by the owner. After 1850, additional mill canals and ponds were added to expand its functionality. The mill remained operational until 1863, when the emergence of new steam-powered mills made business less profitable. To adapt, the mill was transformed into a recreational space, with a pond constructed for ice skating in the winter and small boating in the summer. Over time, five additional ponds were constructed to harvest ice, which was transported to Basel and the surrounding areas for food preservation.

When the Jung-Preiswerk family moved there in 1896, they resided at Bottmingerstrasse 68, in a building owned by Eduard Preiswerk-Friedrich.[22] Photographs taken between 1887 and 1900 depict the building as a large, two-story Alsatian-style house set in a picturesque park with tall trees.[23] The house had seven rooms, two kitchens, and three attic rooms (*Mansarden*) on the second floor. The first floor included a woodshed and workshop. Another house on the property, built by Gustav Preiswerk-Vetter, featured two towers. This residence had five rooms and a kitchen on the second floor, along with two attic rooms, a tower room, a balcony, and a washroom.

The Birsigtalbahn (BTB), a steam-powered tramway inaugurated on October 4, 1887, brought new accessibility to Bottminger Mühle. Running from Heuwaage Bahnhof in Basel to Therwil, the BTB stopped directly in front of the mill. This was the first tramway in Basel and the first "secondary tramway" (a tramway serving a community outside of a city center) in Switzerland.[24]

The improved transport connections spurred development around the mill, with new buildings appearing around 1900. On February 9, 1904, a second fire broke out. By this time, Carl's mother and sister had moved to Küsnacht, and it appears that Gustav Preiswerk-Vetter and his family had relocated to Bottmingerstrasse 50.[25] Following the fire, the mill began to give way to urban development, with residential expansion in the surrounding area.[26] Over the following decades, much of the mill complex was dismantled, with a significant portion torn down around 1956.

Restaurant Bottminger Mühle
After the 1904 fire, the building closest to the road was converted into an inn, now known as Restaurant Bottminger Mühle. If you stop for lunch, you can enjoy the historical ambiance, complete with some original pictures of the mill.

9 (left) Restaurant Bottminger Mühle

10 Water Healing Institution
Cover of a six-page brochure advertising the water healing institution in Bottmingen, a sanatorium for nerve illnesses, which opened in 1888.

Sanatorium in Schloss Bottmingen

Just two stops beyond the Bottminger Mühle tram stop lies Schloss Bottmingen, a castle owned during the late 19th century by Wilhelm Ritter. Ritter transformed the castle into a hotel and restaurant, frequently hosting large weddings and celebrations. To further expand his business, in 1888 he opened a *Wasserheilanstalt* (Water Healing Institute) and a *Sanatorium für Nervenkranke* (Sanatorium for Nerve Illnesses). A new building was constructed above the castle's moat to house the institute, though it was later demolished due to its lack of aesthetic appeal.

The water used for therapies was channeled from the Birsig via the Chänelbach (Channel Stream), which at the time was celebrated for its purported miraculous healing properties. The treatments offered at the sanatorium followed the hydrotherapy principles of the holistic priest Sébastian Kneipp, with patients immersing themselves in tubs of (presumably) cold water to alleviate ailments such as rheumatism and digestion problems.[27] Villagers often observed patients walking barefoot through outdoor water baths as part of their treatment regimen. The Birsigtal (Birsig Valley) and its healing institute gained a reputation far beyond the local area, attracting visitors from Paris, America, and England. Wealthy guests arrived by horse-drawn coach or the BTB, which operated hourly.[28] One can imagine the Jung-Preiswerk family, living at Bottminger Mühle, watching these affluent foreign travelers pass by their home on their way to the sanatorium—only a short tram ride from the mill.

11 Three Preiswerk Women at Bottminger Mühle (September 1901)
From left to right: Auguste Weiss-Preiswerk (Carl's Aunt Gusteli), Emilie Jung-Preiswerk (Carl's mother), Sophie Fröhlich-Preiswerk (Carl's aunt, also called Maria Sophia).

Deaths of Two Fathers

The Preiswerk-Allenspach and Jung-Preiswerk cousins shared a similar fate when their fathers died within a year of each other. Carl's Uncle Rudolf passed away in 1895, and his father, Paul, succumbed in January 1896. As was customary, the cousins wore black mourning attire for six months following their respective losses.[29] Carl's sister, Trudi, was just 11 years old and finishing her fourth year of secondary school when their father died. Their uncle, Samuel Gottlob Preiswerk, became Trudi's legal guardian and, seemingly, Carl's as well—though he was legally an adult at the time.[30]

Uncles Samuel Gottlob, Johannes "Hans" Preiswerk-Gerber, Gustav Preiswerk-Vetter, and Eduard Preiswerk-Friedrich convened to discuss the family's future. One suggestion was for Carl to withdraw from medical school and take a paying job as a bank clerk or merchant at the Preiswerk's colonial goods store on Spalenberg. However, after much deliberation, another solution emerged, when Carl's uncle, Eduard Preiswerk-Friedrich, invited Emilie, Carl, and Trudi to move into the upper floor of the mill, providing them with a new home.[31] The Preiswerk-Allenspach cousins, who lived nearby on Margarethenstrasse 19, helped Emilie, Carl, and Trudi with the move.

Carl was undoubtedly relieved to receive financial support in the form of a 3,000 Swiss franc interest-free loan, complete with a generous repayment period, which allowed him to complete his medical studies without interruption.[32] Alongside his academic pursuits, Carl took on new responsibilities, such as managing the household finances.[33] His Aunt Gusteli, who had cared for him during his early childhood when his mother Emilie was periodically hospitalized in Basel, was also living at Bottminger Mühle. Later in life, Gusteli married a widower named Weiss, and the couple resided on the ground floor. After her husband's passing, Carl found a way to assist his aunt financially by helping her sell her inherited antiques—an endeavor that proved profitable for them both.[34]

Carl's Encounters with the Feminine: Cousins, Mother, and the Occult

Even at age 82, as Jung completed the first three chapters of his memoir, he reflected on his early years as a predominantly solitary experience. He wrote sparingly about the women in his youth, including family members and time spent with them. Yet in 1897, just a year after the Jung-Preiswerks moved to Bottminger Mühle, Emilie's brother, Gustav Preiswerk-Vetter, completed construction on a new house situated on the same property. Adolf lived in the house with his wife and eleven children,[35] bringing Carl and Trudi into close proximity with a total of 26 cousins. Map 6, "Who Lived Where", illustrates just how many extended family members surrounded Carl during his Basel years.

In *MDR*, Jung reflected on his awkwardness when encountering an attractive young woman while traveling as a Gymnasium student. He remarked, "Since I knew no other girls except my cousins, I felt rather embarrassed and did not know how to talk to her."[36] What a surprise,

then, to discover that Carl grew up amidst a large network of female cousins, many of whom were active participants in his explorations of spiritualism and séances. One cousin in particular, Helene "Helly" Preiswerk (Allenspach branch), exhibited mediumistic abilities and became the thinly veiled subject of Jung's dissertation, "On the Psychology and Pathology of So-Called Occult Phenomena."[37] Written during his early years at the Burghölzli, this academic treatise marked an important step in Jung's explorations of consciousness. However, his clumsy efforts to conceal Helly's identity had unintended consequences, damaging her reputation. Additionally, Jung's unauthorized and objectifying treatment of the Medium S. W. (Helly) in the text—quite typical of the time—strained his relationship with his maternal relatives. This tension between Jung and the feminine extended even beyond his family. Years later, an active imagination described in *The Red Book*—containing vivid symbolic imagery drawn from his walks between the university and Bottminger Mühle—suggested that he had internalized this conflict with the feminine.[38]

12 Carl's Close Cousins: Five Preiswerk-Allenspach Sisters, of Whom Three Remained Unmarried (c. 1906)
From left to right, Esther (1878–1948), Ottilie (1886–1971), Helly (1881–1911), Sophie (1889–1967), Vally (1883–1948).

In the new environment of Bottminger Mühle, with numerous family members nearby, Carl's mother, Emilie, embraced a more active role. For the first time, she was not living in a parsonage! Born into the parsonage of St. Leonard's Church, Emile later lived at the house at Rittergasse 2 when her father became Antistes. After marrying, she moved with her husband, Paul Jung-Preiswerk, to the parsonage in Kleinhüningen, where Paul served as pastor. It was only at Bottminger Mühle that Emilie had her first secular home to manage independently. In this new setting, her spiritual skills seemed to unfold. Even as a youth, Emilie kept a journal in which she recorded "all kinds of inexplicable, parapsychological" phenomena.[39] At the mill, such occurrences continued. In the summer of 1898, strange incidents took place, such as a nutwood tabletop inexplicably cracking from "rim to beyond the center," and a bread knife breaking explosively into four pieces.[40] Both objects were part of Emilie's dowry, once owned by her father, the Antistes.[41] These eerie events led the family to regard the mill as haunted.

During this period, spiritism and occult phenomena were highly fashionable. Activities such as *Tischrücken* (table-turning), seeing ghosts, entering trance states, automatic writing, and communicating with spirits were common pastimes. Guided by spiritual interests, artists across various countries sought to visualize the spiritual and supernatural realms, contributing to a broader interest in the paranormal. Today, this widespread fascination with spiritualism during Carl's Basel years is an area of growing historical research, and artworks created in these spiritist settings are being increasingly recognized and acquired by museums.[42]

Many of Carl's nearby family members shared an interest in spiritualism. Though Aunt Gusteli did not actively participate, she had no objections, especially when her father, the Antistes, was said to materialize during séances. She saw nothing forbidden in these activities.

Emmy Zinsstag (1882–1962), a school friend of Helly and later her sister-in-law (through marriage to Helly's favorite brother, Wilhelm), contributed to preserving the family stories, as her colorful and poignant memories of Carl's aunts, cousins, and friends were later compiled into a book by her daughter, Stephanie Zumstein-Preiswerk, offering rich details about the family's paranormal interests.[43] Emmy, along with cousins Luggy and Helly, attended the newly established Basler Töchterschule (School for Daughters) on Kanonengasse, which opened in 1884.

It remains unclear which school Carl's sister Trudi attended after the family's move to Binningen when she was only 13. Two possibilities include the Secondary and Realschule, established in 1897 and located in the old town center between Baslerstrasse and Hauptstrasse, which had recently opened its doors to girls; and the Handarbeitsschule (handicraft school), founded in 1828, which offered practical education for young women.[44]

Family séances began in 1895 at the parsonage in Kleinhüningen, while Carl's father, Paul, was gravely ill. These gatherings, attended by Carl, his mother Emilie, his cousins Helly and Luggy, and Helly's friend Emmy

13 (left) From left to right:
Emma (Emmy) Zinsstag (1882–1962) and
Cousins Luggy Preiswerk (1874–1957)
and Helly Preiswerk (1881–1911) (undated)
An inscription by Stephanie Zumstein-
Preiswerk on the back of the original
photograph reads: "All three participated
in the spiritual meetings that C.G. Jung
organized."

14 Helly Preiswerk (1881–1911) (1902)
This picture was taken in the year that
Jung's dissertation was published.

Zinsstag, had to be kept secret from Paul, as well as from Rudolf and Célestine, parents of the Preiswerk-Allenspach cousins. Helly was only 13 years old when she first served as medium.

By 1898, séances were being held regularly every Saturday at Bottminger Mühle, enticing the Preiswerk-Allenspach cousins to walk approximately 40 minutes from Basel to participate.[45] Their route may have followed Margarethenstrasse, climbing the steep Margarethenhügel (Margaret's Hill) before reconnecting with the main road, or they may have crossed the Birsig at the Margarethen-Brücklein and followed the river to the mill, as Carl often did. In addition to the Preiswerk-Allenspach cousins, Rudolf and occasionally Gustav's children—Bertha, Martha, Hanna, and Hedwig—also joined the séances.

Once settled in Binningen, Trudi was deemed old enough to participate and at times took on the role of medium. However, her efforts were less convincing than those of Helly, who was the centerpiece of the family's occult phenomena. Helly took her role seriously, hiding spells around the house to ward off ghosts and banishing the spirit of an Italian murderer, believed to be the cause of the strange occurrences at the mill. Helly's mediumship was deeply collaborative with Carl.

She dictated her revelations to him, which were recorded and illustrated in mandala-like forms. In her trances, she channeled voices, including that of her late grandfather, Samuel Preiswerk: "The (deceased) pious Antistes, revered by all, spoke from the medium's mouth and accompanied her to the other world and to distant celestial bodies. That he took part in the fate of his descendants and advised them seemed quite natural to them."[46]

Despite her children's enthusiasim, Carl's Aunt Célestine, recently widowed, disapproved of the occult activities. When her children wished to attend the séances, they claimed they were going to help in the garden at the mill. However, by the fall of 1899, Aunt Célestine became aware that Helly was returning home from the mill utterly exhausted. Concerned, she alerted the family's guardian, Samuel Gottlob Preiswerk, who put an end to the séances. Helly was soon sent to Montpellier, France, where two of her best friends' aunts ran a prestigious fashion boutique, to train in the fashion industry and dressmaking.[47]

Carl formed close relationships with his cousins Luggy and Helly, partly through their shared interest in spiritualism. For Helly's 15th birthday, Carl gifted her two popular books by Justinus Kerner: *The Seeress of Prevorst: Being Revelations Concerning the Inner-Life of Man* and *Inter-Diffusion of a World of Spirits in the One We Inhabit*.[48] Additionally, on New Year's Day 1897, Carl presented Luggy with two volumes by Carl du Prel: *The Mystery of Humans* (*Das Rätsel des Menschen*) and *Spiritism* (*Der Spiritismus*).[49] At the same time, Helly was deeply engrossed in a vividly illustrated book on astronomy and the cosmos by Nicolas Camille Flammarion, written in French. This book—a cherished possession brought home years earlier by Helly's now-deceased father from a business trip—had become a favorite among the cousins. Flammarion's work speculated that Mars was inhabited and featured artificially constructed channels through which water flowed. Notably, some of the imagery Helly recounted in her trance states—such as visions of flying to Mars—appears to have originated from this book.[50]

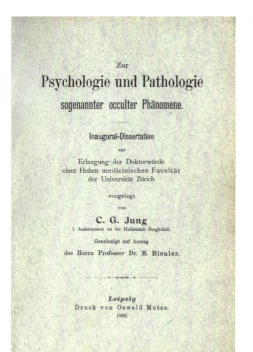

15 Cover of Jung's Dissertation, *The Psychology and Pathology of so-called Occult Phenomena* (1902)

Between Empiricism and Spiritualism

While Carl pursued study of the empirical sciences, he became increasingly drawn to the occult and séances, likely influenced by his father's death and recurring dreams of his father returning. His intellectual curiosity and sensitivity to the cultural and intellectual currents of his time are reflected in the topics of his Zofingia lectures. Although intellectual forums of the period were largely male-dominated, séances offered rare spaces where women could exercise authority and express their voices. Thus, the occult provided an avenue for creative expression that did not overtly challenge the gendered norms of the era. In her 1993 analysis, author Claire Douglas described a recurring dynamic in the early development of depth psychology: the relationship between female occultists and male scientists. She described this as a "common phenomenon... deriving from the link between repressed aspects of the feminine in both women and in her male observer."[51]

16 Letter from Valerie Preiswerk to her Sister Esther Preiswerk (1916)
Although the letter is dated five years after Helly's death, Vally still used the stationery bearing both their names: Mlles. H. and V. Preiswerk.

17 Emma Jung-Rauschenbach Wearing a Dress Possibly Made by Helly Preiswerk (1905)

7 THE PREISWERK SISTERS' DRESS SHOP, ST. ALBAN-ANLAGE 5 (HISTORIC SITE)

LES DEMOISELLES HELENE & VALERIE PREISWERK: *ROBES ET MANTEAUX*

Helly suffered greatly due to the end of the séances and the wounds inflicted by Carl's involvement and dissertation. However, after completing her education in haute couture in Paris, she returned to Basel. In 1903, she and her sister Valerie "Vally" established a thriving dressmaking business specializing in fashionable dresses and coats. Both sisters earned the professional title of *Schneiderin* (seamstress), and their names appeared in the Basel address book under *Damenkonfektion* (women's clothing). Their dress shop, located near the St. Alban Church where their uncle, Samuel Gottlob, had served as pastor, was a short distance from the Gymnasium Carl attended during his youth. The sisters' letterhead read *Mlles. H. & V. Preiswerk, Robes et Manteaux* (dresses and coats) and featured a drawing of a confident woman in high fashion, wearing a hat and carrying a case.

By this time, Carl and Emma Jung-Rauschenbach had married. In the spring of 1905, Helly received a brief letter from Emma:

> *Dear Cousin,*
> *May I get to know you? Carl has told me a lot about you. I've also heard that you make ladies' costumes with real Parisian chic. Unless you tell me otherwise, I'll come and try them on.*
> *Emma Jung-Rauschenbach*[52]

Emma soon visited the shop, where Helly, just 21 years old, created a beautiful dress for her.

The sisters' dressmaking business prospered, and they lived together with their mother, Célestine, in a now-demolished Gothic home at St. Alban-Vorstadt 3. Tragically, Helly contracted tuberculosis and passed away at the young age of 30. After Helly's death, Vally continued to manage the shop independently until 1925. It remained at its original location for 20 years.

18 A View of Binninger Hills (2024)
The area still retains its pastoral character.

19 (below) Landscape by Jung (c. 1900)
Pastel on paper.

TOUR 4

8 BRUDERHOLZ, MARGA BÜHRIG-WEG

BROADER HORIZONS: THE COLORFUL HILLS OF BINNINGEN

During Carl's time in Binningen, his artistic focus shifted from drawings of dragons and fortresses to pastels and painted landscapes. These works often depicted expansive fields and broad skies, evoking the openness of the farmland surrounding the mill. This pastoral landscape was a bright contrast to the industrial neighborhoods he traversed on his way to the Gymnasium.

Climbing Mühlesteig (Mill Path) directly across from the mill reveals a breathtaking 360-degree panoramic view of the Gempen, Blauen, and Ballon D'Alsace in the French Vosges, as well as the Belchen in Germany.[53]

The pastoral landscape in Figure 19 stands in bright contrast to the industrial neighborhoods Carl traversed on his way to the Gymnasium. Among the several landscapes he painted between 1889 and 1900, one is inscribed *Kennst du das Land?* (Do You Know the Country?). Another shows patches of ploughed land against a backdrop of snowy mountains. Carl also painted *Castle Ruin* (c. 1900), *Farmers' Houses and Clouds* (c. 1900), and *Landscape with Castle* (c. 1900), working with gouache and pastel. Perhaps this is one way Carl passed the few months between his *Staatsexamen* in March and his professional appointment at the Burghölzli, which began in December of the same year.

At the end of Marga Bührig-Weg, the dome of the Observatory comes into view. The original observatory, located at the Bernoullianum—an institute for physics, chemistry, and astronomy—was established in 1874 near Petersplatz and funded by citizens of Basel. Carl's uncle, Hans Preiswerk-Gerber, worked there as a technical assistant for 35 years. His son Matthias was the same age as Carl. In 1928, the Observatory was relocated to Venusstrasse.

20 St. Margarethen Kirche
Built in 1673 on the foundations of an earlier church (dating between the 9th and the 11th centuries), the so-called angle hook floor plan is the result of two rectangular sections intersecting at nearly a right angle. This configuration is unusual; only one other church in Switzerland features this design.

ST. MARGARETHEN KIRCHE, FRIEDHOFSTRASSE, BINNINGEN

LEAVING BASEL FOR ZÜRICH

The modern St. Margaret's Church, where Carl's Uncle Eduard once served as pastor, is a picturesque site with extensive holdings, including a working dairy farm, a vineyard, public event spaces, and a cemetery. From its vantage point, the church offers sweeping views of Basel and Kleinhuningen, providing a reflective glimpse over the region that shaped Carl's life from childhood to early adulthood.

When Carl completed his medical studies and passed his *Staatsexamen,* he departed Basel to begin his psychiatric training at the Burghölzli Psychiatric Hospital in Zürich under the renowned Professor Eugen Bleuler. This pivotal phase of his career began on December 10, 1900. Bottminger Mühle marked his last home in the Basel region, but his connection to Basel did not end there. On October 15, 1943, Jung was appointed Extraordinary Professor of Medical Psychology at the University of Basel. Unfortunately, due to health issues, he delivered only a few lectures in this role. Nevertheless, Basel's recognition of Jung's contributions endured. In 1955, on the occasion of his 80th birthday, the university presented him with a letter of congratulations signed by the university president and faculty. This acknowledgment honored not only Carl's late-career appointment, but also his grandfather's significant role in establishing the university's medical faculty in the 19th century.[54]

TOUR 5

INTERLOCKING SPHERES: JUNG, HESSE, AND NIETZSCHE

Three extraordinary figures—Carl Jung, Hermann Hesse, and Friedrich Nietzsche—each made profound contributions to their respective fields: Jung in psychology, Hesse in literature, and Nietzsche in philosophy. Their lives and intellectual trajectories intersected in time, space, and meaning—sometimes near the Spalentor, one of the three remaining ancient gateways to Basel. Much like Haus zum Sessel in Tour 3, the Spalentor may have held symbolic significance in the individuation journeys of these three men. Each spent substantial time in Basel, with Jung and Hesse overlapping as contemporaries.

In addition to their shared ties to Basel, these figures had at least three key experiences in common:
- fathers who were heavily engaged in Protestant theology (Jung and Nietzsche's fathers were pastors, while Hesse's was a missionary);
- unique spiritual journeys rooted in a critique of Christianity, aimed at addressing psychological and existential questions; and
- deep engagement with Eastern religions.

The religious upbringings of these three men reflected distinct Protestant traditions: Jung's in the Evangelical Swiss-Reformed Church, Nietzsche's in Lutheranism, and Hesse's in Pietism.

TOUR 5 OVERVIEW

① **BASLER MISSION, MISSIONSSTRASSE 21**
Hesse's Basel and Path to Individuation

② **RESTAURANT ZUM TELL, SPALENVORSTADT 38**
Hesse's Analysis and Creative Outpouring

③ **NIETZSCHE FOUNTAIN**

④ **NIETZSCHE'S BASEL HOMES: SCHÜTZENGRABEN 47 (HISTORIC SITE)**

⑤ **SPALENTORWEG 48**

⑥ **SPALENTORWEG 5**

⑦ **SPALENTORWEG 2**
The Baumannhöhle on Schützengraben and Other Homes

START
The tour starts at Barfüsserplatz in Basel.

GETTING THERE
Board tram 3 heading to St. Louis Grenze. Exit at the Pilgerstrasse stop.

TOUR LENGTH
Allow 90 minutes, including your return to central Basel.

RETURN
From the Spalentor tram stop, board tram 3 to Barfüsserplatz (central Basel).

 Scan to follow the tour on Google Maps

This Google Map is also accessible at www.kschaeppi.ch/book

1 Photograph of Hermann Hesse
This photograph was taken by Hesse's wife, Maria Hesse (née Bernoulli), who, with her sister Mathilde, opened a photographic studio on Bäumleingasse 14 in 1902.

2 Basel Mission (1861)
Hesse lived in the Knabenhaus (Boys' House) whenever his parents were away on a mission.

1 BASEL MISSION, MISSIONSSTRASSE 21

HESSE'S BASEL AND PATH TO INDIVIDUATION

The life and career of Hermann Hesse (1877–1962), the Nobel laureate in literature, were deeply intertwined with the city of Basel and, later, the psychological insights of Jung. Hesse's connection to Basel began early: at the age of 4, his missionary parents relocated to the city. During the decade he spent in Basel—with only one interruption—he resided in ten different locations. When his parents traveled for their missionary work, he stayed at the Knabenhaus (Boys' House) of the Basel Mission at Missionsstrasse 21. This Mission—a prominent Protestant institution founded around 1800—was dedicated to spreading Christianity to Africa, Latin America, and Asia. However, when Hesse's parents were in town, the family resided nearby on Müllerweg, close to Schützenmatt Park.

Hesse's strict, Pietist upbringing underpinned his lifelong struggles with mental health. Raised with the expectation that he would follow in his father's footsteps as a Pietist minister, Hesse faced a profound inner conflict. Rejecting this path, he attempted suicide at the age of 15. However, he eventually charted his own course, finding independence as a bookkeeping assistant at the Reich'schen Bookstore, situated a mere 200 meters from Basel Münster and Carl's Gymnasium on the (for Hesse) propitiously named Freie Strasse (Free Street).[1] Reflecting on his time in Basel, he wrote:

> *You know that I'm comfortable here. You also know that Basel has, if not its own style, then at least its own peculiar atmosphere. In the city and the people there is a delicious treasure of solid tradition, partly in the form of money, partly in terms of outward appearance, partly and above all in terms of education.*[2]

3 Restaurant zum Tell
Hesse spent time at this restaurant, and part of his novel *Steppenwolf* takes place in this setting.

2 RESTAURANT ZUM TELL, SPALENVORSTADT 38

HESSE'S ANALYSIS AND CREATIVE OUTPOURING

Restaurant zum Tell, located on Spalenvorstadt, is believed to be one of the real-life inspirations for the settings in Hesse's novel, *Steppenwolf*. This work, which explores the existential struggles and inner turmoil of its protagonist, Harry Haller, is deeply rooted in Hesse's observations and personal experiences in Basel. The Restaurant itself is named after William Tell, the Swiss folk hero who embodied the Swiss values of both respect for authority and courage to challenge injustice. Tell's legacy, closely tied to the founding myth of the Swiss Confederacy more than 700 years ago, imbues the location with historical and cultural significance.[3] Hesse explicitly referenced this restaurant in *Steppenwolf*, the novel for which he received the Nobel Prize in Literature in 1946.

Although Hesse's literary output began as early as the 1890s, his creative energy surged following his engagement with psychoanalysis under Dr. Josef Bernhard Lang, a student of Jung. By the spring of 1916, Hesse had undergone more than 70 analytic sessions with Dr. Lang, immersing himself deeply in Jungian psychology.[4] During this period, Hesse penned *The Difficult Path* (1916), a fairytale likening psychoanalysis to a grueling mountain ascent, as well as *A Dream Sequence,* which reflected on his analytic explorations.[5] That same year, Dr. Lang introduced Hesse to Jung, whose influence is evident in Hesse's subsequent works, most notably *Demian* (1919). This novel, hailed by Jung as a portrayal of the individuation process, was profoundly shaped by Jungian ideas.[6] Specifically, Jung's "Seven Sermons to the Dead," privately printed in 1916, introduced the figure of Abraxas, which resonated throughout *Demian*.

Hesse's psychoanalysis appears to have sparked a profound shift in his creative expression, leading him to take up watercolor painting at the age of 42. This newfound passion coincided with his 1919 relocation to Montagnola, Tessin, in the Italian-speaking region of Switzerland. Over the years, Hesse produced approximately 3,500 watercolors, most of them small in format and frequently accompanied with poetic illustrations. In 1930, he wrote to a female student, "even in the midst of a difficult and problematic life [painting and drawing are] able to stir belief and freedom in us." For Hesse, painting was not only a creative outlet, but also a therapeutic endeavor integral to his psychoanalysis, supporting his exploration of soul, libido, and purpose.[7]

In 1921, unable to continue writing *Siddhartha*—his story set in India—Hesse accepted an invitation to the Psychology Club Zurich. There, he reunited with Jung and requested analysis, which Jung subsequently provided from his office in Küsnacht.[8] Following this experience, Hermann returned to *Siddhartha* and completed the novel. Though he expressed admiration for Jung's work in several letters, Hesse ultimately resumed therapy with Dr. Josef Bernhard Lang.

A few years later, as Hesse was working on the novel *Steppenwolf* in Basel, he became increasingly distressed by his tumultuous marriage to the Basler singer Ruth Wenger (née Haussmann), to whom he was married from 1924 to 1927. It is perhaps no coincidence, then, that the novel explores the psychological theme of an individual's struggle with both a divided society and a divided self. Its protagonist, Harry Haller, embarks on an existential journey that begins with a nighttime walk through an old part of the city. There, he encounters a mysterious portal bearing the inscription: "MAGIC THEATER—ENTRANCE NOT FOR EVERYBODY." This door (or threshold) motif likely reflects Hesse's personal confrontation with the multiple facets of his own psyche at the time.

In 1930, Hesse published *Narcissus and Goldmund,* which became his most commercially successful novel. The work explores the Jungian archetypes of anima and animus (*Eros* and *Logos*), presenting them as complementary aspects within a single person. Through this dynamic, his novel was able to illustrate yet another facet of the individuation process so central to Jung's theories.

3 NIETZSCHE FOUNTAIN

4 NIETZSCHE'S BASEL HOMES:
SCHÜTZENGRABEN 47 (HISTORIC SITE)

5 SPALENTORWEG 48

6 SPALENTORWEG 5

7 SPALENTORWEG 2

THE BAUMANNHÖHLE AND OTHER HOMES

The proximity and overlaps of the daily paths of Carl, Hesse, and Nietzsche in Basel is striking—Nietzsche's residences and his route to the university, Hesse's Restaurant zum Tell and its imagined "magic gate," and Carl's Vesalianum, where he studied and worked during medical school, all lie within a small radius. To trace these connections, begin by walking toward the Spalentor. Before we consider Nietzsche's influence on Carl and Hesse, let us first explore the four houses that Nietzsche inhabited during his decade in Basel.

From Spalentor, cross the street to the Nietzsche Fountain. From 1873 to 1875, Nietzsche rented a room at Schützengraben 47 (in a house which no longer exists), directly above Franz Overbeck, his close friend and fellow professor. The two playfully referred to their shared space as the *"Baumannhöhle"* (Baumann's cave), in a reference to a scene in Goethe's *Faust* involving a den of bears, as well as a nod to their landlady, Anna Baumann.[9] In 1869, both Nietzsche and Overbeck were appointed professors at the University of Basel—Nietzsche in classical philology and Overbeck in theology. Their friendship was marked by intellectual discussion, shared meals, and music-making. Overbeck, a prominent figure in liberal Protestant theology, spent his entire career in Basel.

To further explore Nietzsche's time in Basel, continue down Spalentorweg (Spalentor Gate Way) to view Spalentorweg 48, 5, and 2. Above the threshold of No. 48, where Nietzsche lived from 1875 to 1876, a commemorative plaque honors his memory.

Nietzsche: A Wellspring for Carl and Hermann

The works of Friedrich Nietzsche (1844–1900) had a profound influence on both Jung and Hesse, albeit in distinct ways. Nietzsche's exploration of the self—establishing a dichotomy between the little-s "self" and the big-S "Self"—helped shape Jung's conception of individuation, a cornerstone of his psychological theory. Likewise, Nietzsche's philosophy permeated Hesse's analytic process and creative works.

Hesse's final novel, *The Glass Bead Game* (also published as *Magister Ludi* or *Master of the Game*) pitted art historian Jacob Burckhardt (1818–1897) and Friedrich Nietzsche "against one another as the two most significant inspirational forces which helped to form Hesse's outlook." Hesse himself acknowledged, "[No] other writer except Nietzsche ever engrossed, attracted, tormented me to the same degree, forced me to reflect to the same degree." For Hesse, Nietzsche's nihilism represented a daunting intellectual challenge and source of despair, yet one he countered with creativity and personal mysticism.[10] Nietzsche's connection to Basel began in 1869, when, at the age of 24, he embarked on a decade-long tenure as a professor of classical philology

4 Fountain Dedicated to Friedrich Nietzsche
Nietzsche passed this fountain daily on his
walk to work, and it was later dedicated to him.

at the University of Basel. His office was located in the Old University on Rheinsprung, where he worked alongside Jacob Burckhardt, who was teaching history with a focus on art during the years of overlap. Nietzsche attended some of Burckhardt's lectures, and they shared a lively exchange.[11]

Between the ages of 22 and 24, Carl read Nietzsche's *Untimely Meditations* (four short works published between 1873 and 1876) and the recently released *Thus Spoke Zarathustra* (1883). These provocative texts on God and morality stirred intense discussion among Carl and his cousins, including Helene "Helly" Preiswerk (Allenspach branch). While in a trance state, Helly allegedly issued warnings about Nietzsche's flawed theological ideas, seemingly directed at Carl.[12] Though Nietzsche had left Basel more than a decade prior, his presence lingered. His university appointment had been at the Pädagogium, the predecessor of Carl's Gymnasium at Münsterplatz. Later, in 1889, Nietzsche suffered a psychological breakdown at the age of 44 and was briefly admitted to Friedmatt Asylum.[13] At the time, Carl was completing his medical studies and on the cusp of choosing psychiatry as his specialty.

Throughout his life, Jung frequently returned to Nietzsche's work. His early Zofingia lectures referenced Nietzsche's philosophy extensively, particularly in the 1898 lecture, "Thoughts on the Nature and Value of Speculative Inquiry," which explored the psychological implications of Nietzsche's ideas. Later, Jung reflected:

> When I read Zarathustra for the first time as a student of twenty-three, of course I did not understand it all, but I got a tremendous impression. I could not say it was this or that, though the poetical beauty of some of the chapters impressed me, but particularly the strange thought got hold of me. He helped me in many respects, as many other people have been helped by him.[14]

After his break with Freud in 1914, Jung engaged deeply with Nietzsche's *Thus Spoke Zarathustra* while working on his *Black Books* and *The Red Book*.[15] Jung's annotations in *Zarathustra* reflect

5   Artbook Edition of Nietzsche's
Thus Spoke Zarathustra

a sustained engagement with Nietzsche's ideas, with the editor of the *Black Books* identifying 27 instances in which Jung referenced Nietzsche, either generally or specifically.[16] Between 1934 and 1939, Jung delivered 86 seminars on *Thus Spoke Zarathustra*. These lectures, later compiled into the two-volume *Nietzsche's Zarathustra*,[17] suggest that Jung approached Nietzsche's work through the lens of his own psychological self-experimentation, reading Nietzsche's work as if it were analogous to his process of active imagination presented in *The Red Book*.[18] Additionally, Jung wrote about Nietzsche extensively in his Collected Works and, in his memoir, reflected on Nietzsche's influence on his life and work.

Given the influence of Nietzsche on many of Jung's foundational concepts, many scholars claim that a deep engagement with Nietzsche is essential for a full understanding of Jung's psychological theories.[19] For example, Jung adapted and expanded on Nietzsche's articulation of the Dionysian and Apollonian duality in his work, and referred to Nietzsche when illustrating the difference between the "I" and the "self": "In unconscious fantasy the self often appears as the super-ordinated or ideal personality, as Faust is in relation to Goethe and Zarathustra to Nietzsche."[20] Jung's *The Red Book* also mirrors *Thus Spoke Zarathustra* in structure, organized into multiple books comprised of short chapters.

6 Page Spread in Jung's Original Handcrafted Edition of *The Red Book*

However, the two works diverge significantly in their conclusions. While Nietzsche's work famously proclaims the death of God, *The Red Book* depicts the "rebirth of God in the soul."[21]

Is it a coincidence that the format of Jung's *The Red Book* resembles the exclusive artbook edition of Nietzsche's *Thus Spoke Zarathustra*? Nietzsche's seminal text was released in 1908 as a luxury edition with art design by Henry van de Velde, a leading artist and head of the School of Applied Arts in Weimar. Published by Leipziger Insel Verlag, the first 100 copies were bound in leather, while the subsequent 430 copies were bound in parchment. Jung's *The Red Book* (created between 1914 and 1930) represents an equally remarkable artistic endeavor. Created during a transformative period in Jung's life, it was based on entries transcribed from his *Black Books.* Though it remained unpublished for more than 60 years after his death, *The Red Book* garnered considerable attention upon its release, not only for its profound psychological insights but also as a unique and priceless work of art.[22]

Spanning the psychospiritual dimensions of Jung's journeys to the depths and the material, physical production of visual art, *The Red Book* vividly captures the integration toward wholeness that defines Jung's approach to psychic well-being and his way of life.

END MATTER

CONTENTS

266 FAMILY TREES

272 WHO LIVED WHERE IN BASEL AND BASELLAND?

274 ABBREVIATIONS

274 LIST OF MAPS

274 LIST OF TABLES

275 IMAGE CREDITS

277 ENDNOTES

283 REFERENCES

285 MAIN INDEX

292 FAMILY NAME INDEX

294 ABOUT THE AUTHOR

295 ACKNOWLEDGMENTS

FAMILY TREES

Carl Jung once wrote, "while I was working on my genealogical tree, I understood the strange community of destiny that linked me to my ancestors."[1] Indeed, an examination of the Jung-Frey and Preiswerk-Faber family lines reveals some interesting parallels and intergenerational influences that extend beyond their shared status as prominent Basel citizens. The Jung family, though relatively new to Basel, rapidly established significant influence within Basler society. Carl's grandfather, Karl Jung, was a transformative figure in the city's medical and academic spheres. Residing at Elisabethenstrasse 9—the home where Carl's father was raised—Karl was instrumental in shaping the University of Basel's medical faculty. Known as Doctor Med. et Chir. and later as Professor of Anatomy, Surgery, and *Entbindungskunst* (the art of delivery), Karl founded the Museum Anatomicum, established a home for children, and served as Dean of the University of Basel. His contributions extended beyond medicine to politics, making him a prominent and multifaceted figure.

Remarkably, Karl Jung, Samuel Preiswerk, and later Carl Jung, himself, all lectured at the University of Basel and were accorded great respect, each receiving honorary titles. Samuel Preiswerk, a minister and theologian, received an honorary doctorate from the University of Basel in 1860. Decades later, Carl Jung was appointed Professor in Medical Psychology at the university at the age of 70 (1945), following a long and distinguished career as a medical doctor and psychiatrist.[2]

Both family lines demonstrated strong vocational stability, with medicine and psychiatry serving as the primary professions on the Jung side, and ministry defining the Preiswerk family contributions.

In addition to his professional achievements, Karl was a poet and Freemason.[3,4] Similarly, his grandson, Carl, was prolific in his creative output, producing thousands of pages of writing in his *Black Books, The Red Book,* Collected Works, lectures, and papers.

As Carl Jung himself observed, there was a clear intergenerational transmission of values, professions, and intellectual pursuits within these family lines, with themes of healing, spirituality, language, and prestige that seem to have consciously or unconsciously shaped his identity and work.

Table 9
The Jung-Frey Branch: Carl's Aunt, Uncles, and Cousins

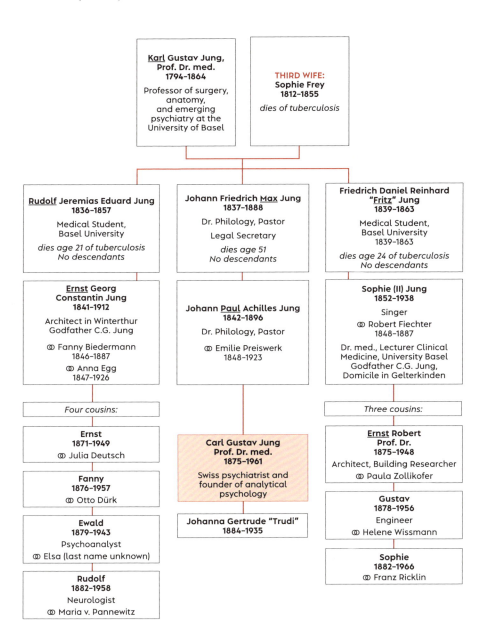

Table 10
Jung Family Tree

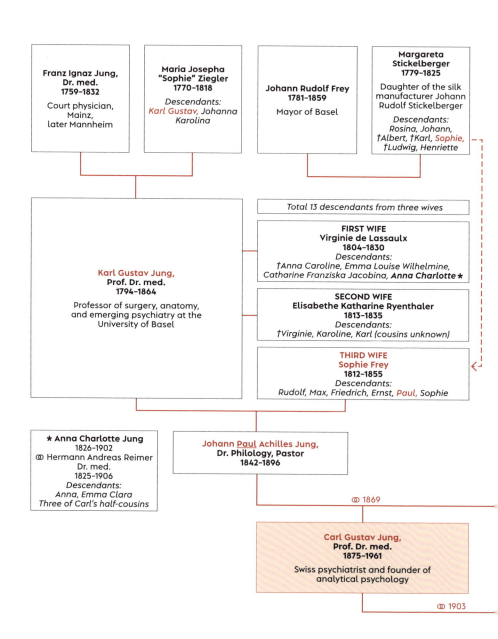

268

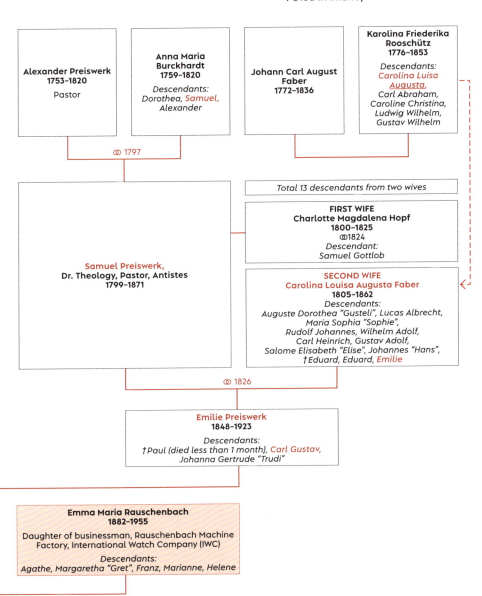

269

Table 11
Preiswerk-Hopf and Preiswerk-Faber Branches: Carl's Aunts, Uncles, and Cousins
41 cousins from 5 of 13 family branches. Some participated in séances, their names are marked with an asterisk.

All Children of Samuel Preiswerk (1799–1871)
Ø not shown in Table 11

Hopf Branch:
1. Samuel Gottlob, 1825–1912

Faber Branch:
2. Ø Auguste Dorothea "Gusteli", 1828–1904
   (⚭ Emanuel Weiss, 1829–1900, Chemist; no descendants)
3. Ø Lucas Albrecht, 1829–1908, Mechanic, Constructor
   (⚭ Rosina Oser, 1834–1911; six cousins of which one † in infancy, who lived in Kleinhüningen, Basel, and Geneva. Lucas emigrated to Argentina)
4. Ø Maria Sophia, 1831–1914
   (⚭ Edmund Fröhlich, 1832–1898, Pastor; six cousins who lived in Brugg)
5. Rudolf Johannes, 1832–1895
6. Ø Wilhelm Adolf †, 1835–1836
7. Ø Carl Heinrich, 1836–1856
8. Gustav Adolf, 1837–1913
9. Ø Salome Elisabeth "Elise", 1839–1899
   (⚭ Albrecht Carl Paul Manuel, 1835–1908, Banker; seven cousins who lived in Bern)
10. Johannes "Hans", 1842–1909
11. Ø Eduard †, 1843–1844
12. Eduard, 1846–1932
13. Ø Emilie, 1848–1923
    (⚭ Paul Jung, 1842–1896)

FIRST WIFE ⚭ 1824 **Magdalena Hopf** 1800–1825	**Samuel Preiswerk** 1799–1871 Dr. Theology, Pastor, Antistes
Samuel Gottlob Preiswerk 1825–1912 only child Pastor St. Alban Church "Isemännli" ⚭ 1850 **Maria Charlotte Staehelin** 1826–1908	**Rudolf Johannes Preiswerk** 1832–1895 fifth child Iron Worker ⚭ 1865 **Célestine Allenspach** 1845–1923
Six half-cousins who lived at Mühlenberg 12 **Samuel**, 1853–1923 **Richard**, 1855–1934 **Charlotte**, 1858–1931 **Adolf**, 1861–1936 **Heinrich**, 1864–1950 † **Theodora**, 1870–1870	*Fifteen cousins who lived at Margarethenstr. 19 ("d'Margarete")* * **Rudolf**, 1866–1923 **Celestine**, 1867–1917 **Bertha**, 1868–1944 **Clara**, 1870–1938 **Emilie**, 1871–1956 **Friedrich**, 1872–1898 * **Louise "Luggy"**, 1874–1957 **Wilhelm**, 1876–1946 **Ernst**, 1878–1948 **Mathilde**, 1880–1952 * **Helene "Helly"**, 1881–1911 * **Valerie "Vally"**, 1883–1948 * **Ottilie**, 1886–1971 **Esther**, 1887–1974 **Sophie**, 1889–1967

Carl's 64 Cousins and Half-Cousins

During his youth, Carl had a remarkable 64 cousins and half-cousins from the Preiswerk and Jung families (excluding 5 who died in infancy). Both grandfathers—Samuel Preiswerk and Karl Gustav Jung—had 13 children. Carl's mother, Emilie Preiswerk, was the youngest of 13; his father, Paul Jung-Preiswerk, the twelfth.

On the Jung side, Carl had ten cousins: four from the Jung (Biedermann branch—Ernst, Fanny, Ewald and Rudolf); three from the Fiechter (Jung branch—Ernst, Gustav and Sophie); and three half-cousins from

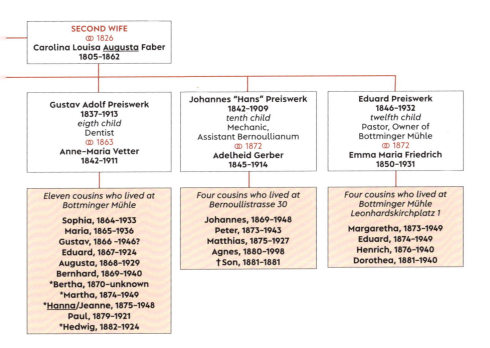

the Reimer (Jung branch—Anna, Emma and Clara). These half-cousins lived in Görlitz and Stuttgart. Their father, Dr. Hermann Andreas Reimer (1825–1906), founded the world's first epilepsy sanatorium in Görlitz in 1855, linking the family to this emerging field of medicine.

On the Preiswerk side, Carl had 59 cousins and half-cousins, 54 of whom survived into his youth. Five died in infancy, and two more passed in 1898. Notably, Ernst Fiechter, Hanna Preiswerk (Vetter branch), and Matthias Preiswerk (Gerber branch) were all born in Carl's birth year. The cousins who participated in the family séances are noted with an asterisk.

Map 6
Who lived where in Basel and Baselland?
This map shows that many relatives lived in close proximity to the places where Carl lived and studied.

① **Jung-Preiswerk, Paul & Emilie**
Dorfstrasse 16, Kleinhüningen

② **Jung-Frey, Karl Gustav & Sophie**
Elisabethenstrasse 9

③ **Jung-Preiswerk, Emilie and family following Paul's death**
Bottmingerstrasse 68, Binningen

④ **Preiswerk-Faber, Samuel & Auguste**
Leonhardskirchplatz 1

⑤ **Preiswerk-Faber, Samuel & Auguste**
Rittergasse 2

⑥ **Preiswerk-Allenspach, Rudolf & Célestine**
Margarethenstrasse 19
(historical site)

⑦ **Preiswerk-Allenspach, Célestine (widowed) with daughters Helly and Vally**
St. Alban-Vorstadt 3
(historical site)

⑧ **Preiswerk-Friedrich, Eduard & Emma Maria**
Bottmingerstrasse 68, Binningen

⑨ **Preiswerk-Friedrich, Eduard & Emma Maria**
Leonhardskirchplatz 1

⑩ **Preiswerk-Staehlin, Samuel Gottlob & Maria Charlotte**
Mühlenberg 12

⑪ **Preiswerk-Vetter, Gustav Adolf & Anna Maria**
Bottmingerstrasse 68, Binningen

⑫ **Preiswerk, Helly & Vally, Fashion Store**
St. Alban-Anlage 5

⑬ **Socin-Frey, Eduard & Henriette, Carl's great-aunt**
Petersgraben 29

⑭ **Stückelberg, Ernst**
Petersgraben 1 / Blumenrain

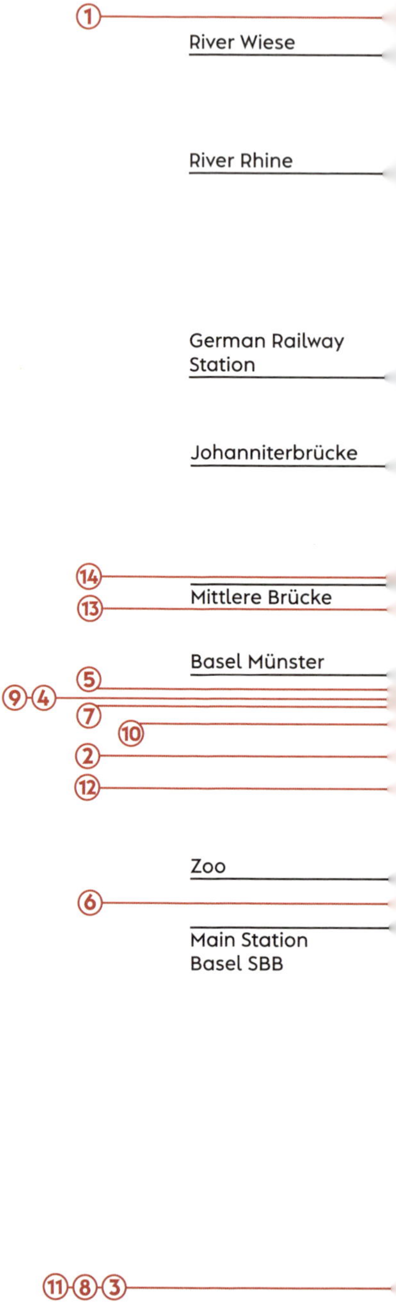

River Wiese

River Rhine

German Railway Station

Johanniterbrücke

Mittlere Brücke

Basel Münster

Zoo

Main Station
Basel SBB

ABBREVIATIONS

AMB	Anatomical Museum Basel
BMA	Archives, Mission 21
DE	Photographer: Donata Ettlin
ERK BS	Evangelical-reformed Church Basel-Stadt
ETHLibUA	ETH Library, University Archives Private Collections and Autographs (Hs)
FWCGJ	Foundation of the Works of C.G. Jung, Zürich
HafMuBa	Harbour Museum Basel
HMB	Historical Museum Basel
JFA	Jung Family Archive
JFA, Courtesy of	Courtesy of the Jung Family Archive
KS	Photographer: Kathrin Schaeppi
KuMuBa	Art Museum Basel (Kunstmuseum Basel)
NatLibBe	National Library Bern
NHMB	Natural History Museum Basel
PD	Public Domain
PM UB	Pharmacy Museum University Basel
SIK-ISEA	Swiss Art Archive Zürich (Schweizerisches Kunstarchiv Zürich)
StABS	Cantonal Archive Basel-Stadt
UB	University Library Basel
UZLib MC	University Zürich Library – Medizin Careum

LIST OF MAPS

Tour Overview, p. 12 / Tour 1, p. 22 / Tour 2, p. 84 /
Maps Tour 3, p. 154 / Tour 4, p. 214 / Tour 5, p. 252: Geodata Canton Basel-Stadt

1 Kleinhüningen in 1882, p. 24, © swisstopo, 1882
2 Trades and Places Along Young Carl's Dorfstrasse, p. 30, © swisstopo, 1882
3 Kleinhüningen in 1918, p. 76, © swisstopo
4 Kleinhüningen in 1932, p. 77, © swisstopo
5 University of Basel School of Medicine Institutes and Clinics (1895–1900), p. 189, Geodata Canton Basel-Stadt
6 Who lived where in Basel and Baselland?, pp. 272–273, Geodata Canton Basel-Stadt

Tour details and additional information on maps: Sibylle Ryser

LIST OF TABLES

1 A Brief Chronology, p. 18–19
2 Population of Canton Basel-Stadt, p. 70, Source: Jenny, Oscar (1924). The population of the canton of Basel-Stadt on 1.12.1910: Statistics communicated by Basel-Stadt
3 Carl's Classmates in the Unteres Gymnasium (1886–1891), p. 140
4 Carl's Classmates in the Oberes Gymnasium (1891–1895), p. 141, Transcription: Vreni Jung
5 Selection of Books Read by Carl During his Basel Years, pp. 146–147
6 Where Did Carl Study Medicine in Basel from 1895–1900, p. 188
7 Lives Intersecting Through Haus zum Sessel, p. 202
8 Cerevis Names of Carl's Zofingia Friends, p. 219, Transcription of a letter from Jung to Andreas Vischer, April 29, 1902; ETH Lib UA, Hs 1269: 17a
9 The Jung-Frey Branch: Carl's Aunt, Uncles, and Cousins, p. 267
10 Jung Family Tree, pp. 268–269
11 Preiswerk-Hopf and Preiswerk-Faber Branches, pp. 270–271

IMAGE CREDITS

TOUR 1

1 StABS, NEG Hi C 42193
2 JFA, Courtesy of, Photographic Archive: Willi Bürgin
3 © Kantonale Denkmalpflege Basel-Stadt, Photographer: Jakob Höflinger
4 StABS, Neg Hi C 42347
5 HafMuBa, Source: NatLibBe, 2025, Photographer: Ernst Bürgin
6 © HafMuBa, Source: NatLibBe, 2025
7 © HafMuBa, Source: NatLibBe, 2025
8 © HafMuBa, Source: NatLibBe, 2025
9 © HafMuBa, Source: NatLibBe, 2025
10 JFA, Courtesy of
11 KS, 2022
12 KS, 2023
13 © FWCGJ, Photographer: C.G. Jung House, 2023
14 PD, WGA19209
15 JFA, Photographer: Andreas Jung
16 JFA, Photographer: Jakob Höflinger
17 JFA, Courtesy of, Photographer: Bulacher & Kling
18 ETHLibUA, Hs 1269 118F
19 JFA, Courtesy of
20 KS, 2021
21 KS, 2021
22 DE, 2025
23 NatLibBe, 2025, Photographer: Ernst Lauer
24 JFA, Courtesy of
25 StABS, Neg 05850, Photographer: Bernhard Wolf
26 KS, 2015
27 NatLibBe, 2025
28 KS, 2017
29 KS, 2020
30 JFA, Courtesy of
31 © HafMuBa
32 JFA, Courtesy of
33 © 2007 FWCGJ, First published by W.W. Norton & Co. The damned dragon has eaten the sun..., (1914–1930). C.G. Jung, The Red Book, Liber Secundus, page 119
34 JFA, © FWCGJ, C.G. Jung, Sketchbook, pupil number booklet, 3rd and 4th grade students in Kleinhüningen (ca. 1884). Inscription K. Jung fec[it].
35 KS, 2023
36 © HafMuBa
37 KS, 2022
38 StABS, AL 17 1 / Bild 4, 772
39 StABS, AL 17 2
40 DE, 2025
41 © 2007 FWCGJ, First published by W.W. Norton & Co. Quadrated Circle in the Sky (1919/1920). C.G. Jung, The Red Book, Liber Secundus, page 125
42 Company Archive of Novartis AG, Publ MI 000.334_010
43 StABS, BILD Falk. D 15, 1, Engraving: Emanuel Büchel, c. 1749

44 GNU Free Documentation License; Balloon pilot and Photographer: Norbert Blau, Neuf-Brisach, 2003
45 © 2007 FWCGJ. First published by W.W. Norton & Co. The Well-Fortified Golden Castle (1928). C.G. Jung, The Red Book, Liber Secundus, page 163
46 PD, Plan de Belfort 1780, Source: Bibliothèque nationale de France https://timelessmoon.getarchive.net/amp/media/plan-de-belfort-1780-71086e

TOUR 2

1 StABS, BILD Schn. 11, Artist: Johann Jakob Schneider
2 Public domain, via Wikimedia Commons, Engraving: Matthäus Merian (the Elder)
3 StABS, BILD WACK E 58
4 JFA, © FWCGJ, C.G. Jung, Castle and Town II (ca. 1898)
5 StABS, Neg A 1464, Photographer: Brothers Metz
6 StABS, Neg 01190, Photographer: Bernhard Wolf
7 StABS, Neg 01241 b
8 StABS, AL 45 6 081 01
9 StABS, BILD 3, 104 b, Drawing: H. Maurer, Lithography: P. Christen
10 StABS, NEG 01480 b, Photographer: Bernhard Wolf
11 StABS, BALAIR 2479W, Photographer: BALAIR
12 StABS, NEG 3744, Photographer: Bernhard Wolf
13 SIK-ISEA, HNA 1.4.34.1, 2210260002CFF1
14 SIK-ISEA, HNA 1.4.34.1, 200804001DS1
15 KuMuBa, Kupferstichkabinett, 49, kw51_0025745_20220623_001
16 DE, 2025
17 StABS, SMM Inv.2016.1.31.4, Photography Studio: A. Varady & Company
18 StABS, BILD Falk. A90, Lithography (Detail): Anton Winterlin
19 PD, 10.3931/e-rara-14012
20 HMB, Inv. 1870.1262, Photographer: Andreas Niemz
21 STABS, Schifflände und Eisengasse, Neg 6585, Photography Studio: A. Varady & Company
22 KS, 2021
23 AMB, Courtesy of, Iron Plaque
24 AMB, Courtesy of, Wax Model 1
25 AMB, Courtesy of, Wax Model 2
26 DE, 2025
27 DE, 2025
28 StABS, NEG B 93 1
29 StABS, BILD Visch. C 29, Lithographer: Frédéric Emile Simone, Publisher: Christian Friedrich Beck (1818–1893), Basel
30 NHMB, Photographer: Gregor Brändli
31 KuMuBa, Photographer: Serge Hasenböhler, 2025, Reproduction rights and requests KS
32 StABS, SMM Inv 2016.1.6.2, Photography Studio: A. Varady & Company
33 StABS, NEG 6, Photographer: Rudolf Fechter
34 StABS, AL 45, 1-96-4

35	KS, 2023
36	KS, 2023
37	JFA, Courtesy of
38	StABS, S17A
39	StABS, NEG 5122 b, Photographer: Bernhard Wolf

TOUR 3

1	StABS, Neg A 0096, Photographer: Fritz Burckhardt
2	DE, 2025
3	KS, 2024, Created by Binninger Ferdinand Aeberli (c. 1933)
4	StABS, Neg A 103, Photographer: Fritz Burckhardt
5	StABS, PA 663b V 3 (1)
6	JFA, Courtesy of, section of a photograph
7	StABS, BALAIR 327W
8	KS, 2024
9	ERK BS, Photographer: Peter Schultess, 2019
10	StABS, AL 45, 1-6-2
11	Courtesy Münsterbau Hütte, Photographer: Peter Schultess, 2019
12	ERK BS, C.G. Jung, Confirmation Register 1891, Photographer: KS, 2024
13	HMB, Photographer: Peter Portner
14	StABS, AL 45, 2-88-5
15	NHMB, Radiolaria (Rhizopoda), Photographer: KS, 2024
16	KS, 2024
17	E-rara, Andreas Vesalius, https://www.e-rara.ch/nev_r/doi/10.3931/e-rara-7521
18	StABS, BILD 32, 155, Photographer: Ochs-Walde Basel
19	JFA, © FWCGJ. Photographer: Susanne Eggenberger-Jung
20	© 2007 FWCGJ. First published by W.W. Norton & Co., Mosaic (1917). C.G. Jung, The Red Book, Liber Secundus, page 79
21	© 2020 FWCGJ, First published by W.W. Norton & Co. C.G. Jung, The Black Books, Vol. 7, page 134 [7 . 124b]
22	KS, 2025
23	© 2007 FWCGJ, First published by W.W. Norton & Co., Window on Eternity (1927). C.G. Jung, The Red Book, Liber Secundus, page 159
24	KS, 2021
25	KS, 2024
26	PD, 12976700 /e-rara
27	ETHLibUA, Hs 1056 31 152 0001
28	PM UB, Photographer: Daniel Spehr, 2019

TOUR 4

1	StABS, NEG B 1002
2	JFA, Courtesy of
3	JFA, © FWCGJ, C.G. Jung, Song Folder with the Student Association Zofingia Insignia (1895)
4	DE, 2025
5	Courtesy of E. and N. Preiswerk
6	DE, 2025

7	Creative Commons, ShareAlike 3.0 Germany, WP 20171119 10 10 42 Pro, Photographer: Andreas Kraneis, 2017
8	Courtesy of Margrit Gutzwiller and Gianni Jauslin, Binningen
9	KS, 2024
10	UZLib MC, Khist Scan 20251001
11	ETHLibUA, Hs 1269 123F 0001, Photographer: Hans Preiswerk, Bernoullianum, Basel (stamp on back)
12	ETHLibUA, Hs 1269 127F 0001
13	ETHLibUA, Hs 1269 120F 0001
14	ETHLibUA, Hs 1269 125F 0001, Photographer: C. Kling-Jenny
15	UZLib MC, Source: C.G. Jung Dissertation, Zur Psychologie und Pathologie sogenannter occulter Phänomene, Univ. Zürich, 1902
16	StABS, PA 523 3 1
17	Courtesy of JFA, Emma Jung-Rauschenbach in Black Dress (1905), Photographer: C. Ruf, Zürich
18	KS, 2024
19	© 2009 FWCGJ, Landscape (c. 1900), *Art of C.G. Jung*, p. 68
20	StABS, NEG 3203, Photographer: Bernhard Wolf

TOUR 5

1	UBH, Port DE Hesse H 1877, 1, Courtesy of H. Siegenthaler-Hesse, Photographers: Maria and Mathilde Bernoulli
2	BMA, QS-30.018.0008, Inscription: J.J. Stehlin, Architect
3	DE, 2025
4	DE, 2025
5	Nietzsche's Art Book, Writer: Friedrich Nietzsche, Art Design: Henry van de Velde, Photographer: KS, 2020
6	© 2007 FWCGJ. First published by W.W. Norton & Co. Double Page. C.G. Jung, The Red Book, Liber Secundus, pages 64–65. Photographer: KS, 2025

IMAGE CREDITS

ENDNOTES

FOREWORD

1 C. G. Jung, and Aniela Jaffé, *Memories, Dreams, Reflections, recorded and edited by Aniela Jaffé,* trans. Richard and Clara Winston (New York: Vintage Books, 1963/1989).
2 C. G. Jung and Aniela Jaffé, *Jung's Life and Work: Interviews for Memories, Dreams, Reflections with Aniela Jaffé,* edited by Sonu Shamdasani, with Thomas Fischer as Consulting Editor, trans. Heather McCartney and John Peck (Princeton NJ: Philemon Series, Princeton University Press, 2025), 4 May 1957.
3 Ibid.
4 Ibid.
5 Bändeliherren (literally, "ribbon men") organized networks of rural home silk weavers around Basel, whose work they financed and sold. Ibid., 1 October 1957.
6 Ibid., 4 May 1957.
7 Ibid., 1 October 1957. The Birs is a river that flows through Laufen and ends as a tributary to the Rhine between Basel and Birsfelden.
8 *C. G. Jung Letters,* selected and edited by Gerhard Adler in collaboration with Aniela Jaffé, trans. R. F. C. Hull, 1975, (Princeton NJ: Bollingen Series, Princeton University Press), vol. 2., pp. 270–271.
9 In Count Hermann Keyserling ed., *Mensch und Erde,* (Darmstadt: Otto Reichl Verlag, 1927). This was later split into two essays, which appear (unhelpfully) in different volumes of the Collected Works: "The Structure of the Psyche" (CW 8), and "Mind and Earth" (CW 10).

INTRODUCTION

1 See the explorations by key figures in the study of the mind, including Theodor Flournoy, Pierre Janet, Jean-Martin Charcot, and Sigmund Freud. Jung emerged as part of this tradition, contributing to the field through curiosity and dedication, giving rise to new insights.
2 "International Association for Analytical Psychology." Available at: https://iaap.org (retrieved January 10, 2023).

TOUR 1

1 *Memories, Dreams, Reflections* (hereafter *MDR*), p. 7.
2 This territory was ceded by France to Germany in 1871 following the Franco-German War. It was retroceded to France in 1919 after World War I, ceded again to Germany in 1940 during World War II, and finally returned to France in 1945.
3 Lüem, p. 116. Eventually, an iron construction replaced the old bridge.
4 *MDR,* p. 15. In *The Red Book,* Jung described blood and drowning bodies.
5 One wonders if, in later years, Jung's encounter with *The Mercurial Fountain,* the first image of the alchemical sequence *Rosarium Philosophorum,* resonated—consciously or unconsciously—with his childhood experiences.
6 Feldges, 2003.
7 A house was typically provided to pastors as part of their compensation for their service.
8 https://Programmzeitung_ETdD_2015_Web.pdf (retrieved August 17, 2022).
9 *Signpost Rundgang 2. Das Dorfzentrum,* Signpost 2 Kronenplatz, Bürger Korporation Kleinhüningen.
10 Zumstein-Preiswerk, p. 36.
11 *MDR,* p. 20.
12 Jung, *Visions Seminars,* vol. 1, lecture 7, p. 122. This particular aunt has not been identified. There is a slight possibility that she was the sister of Carl's grandmother who lived on Petersgraben.
13 *MDR,* pp. 21–23.
14 Personal communication with Franziska Kuhn, July 2023.
15 Hoerni et al., pp. 148–153.
16 *MDR,* p. 16.
17 *MDR,* p. 16.
18 Sherry, pp. 2–9. As first noted by Franz Jung.
19 *MDR,* p. 8.
20 *MDR,* p. 9. Personal communication with Thomas Fischer.
21 On the back of a photograph of three Preiswerk women (ETH Library, University Archive, Hs 1269:123F), S. Zumstein-Preiswerk noted: "Emilie suffered from depressions, then Aunt Gusteli helped out." The photograph is dated 1901, 23 years after the hospital stays.
22 *MDR,* p. 8. In the "Krankengeschichten: Medizinischen Abteilung Frauen 1878" ("Medical History: Medical Department Women 1878") of the Bürgerspital Basel, opened in 1842, Emilie Jung is not listed as a patient. However, 25 cases of "Hysterie" are documented in that year. Of these, four refer to "Dolores Hysterie" (grief or sorrow hysteria) and one refers to "Melancholia." Staatsarchive Basel-Stadt, Spital V 32.20–22. See also Tour 2, Route A, station 6 (Bürgerspital).
23 *Reflections,* p. 34, entry May 4, 1957.
24 *MDR,* p. 20; Zumstein-Preiswerk, p. 59.
25 *MDR,* pp. 26–27.
26 Oeri, p. 183.

277

27 *Freud-Jung Letters*, pp. 94–95. Stated in a letter to Freud dated October 28, 1907. See also the 1968 interview of Gene Nameche with Jolande Jacobi for the C.G. Jung Biographical Archive at the Countway Library of Medicine, Boston.
28 The Huns were a nomadic people who lived in Central Asia, the Caucasus, and Eastern Europe between the 4th and 6th centuries AD. There may be some truth to the legend. See the chapter on this legend prepared by the Bürger-Korporation Kleinhüningen, p. 13.
29 *MDR*, pp. 9 (Laufen) and 15 (Kleinhüningen, River Wiese).
30 Hugger, pp. 86–89.
31 In Basel, the cemeteries at the time included Kannenfeld, Horburg, and Wolfgottesacker, of which only Wolfgottesacker—where the family grave of Karl Jung is located—remains. The cemetery near the Hiltalingerbrücke was repurposed in 1932 to make way for a tank storage facility, creating an irreverent and uncomfortable resting place.
32 Hugger, p. 89.
33 Oeri, p. 185.
34 Death dates: Karl Jung (grandfather), 1864; Samuel Preiswerk (grandfather), 1871; Rudolf (paternal uncle), 1857; Max (paternal uncle), 1888; and Fritz (paternal uncle), 1863.
35 According to Ulrich Hoerni.
36 *MDR*, p. 96.
37 *MDR*, p. 306.
38 "Seven Sermons to the Dead." Available at: http://Carl.gnosis.org/library/7Sermons.htm.
39 Jung, in discussion with Aniela Jaffé, *The Red Book*, p. 346, n. 78. See also, "Seven Sermons to the Dead," ibid.
40 Koellreuter, pp. 268–270.
41 Lüem, pp. 18–19.
42 "Basel-Kleinhüningen." Available at: https://de.wikipedia.org/wiki/Basel-Kleinhüningen.
43 Lüem, pp. 18–19.
44 Available at: https://Carl.statistik.bs.ch/haeufig-gefragt/wohnviertel/19-kleinhueningen.html (retrieved August 22, 2022).
45 On May 21–22, 1892, Paul Jung was elected as member of the synod in Kleinhüningen, Basel. See Jung Family Archive.
46 A document in the Jung Family Archive, dated Kleinhüningen, September 4, 1888, from the School Commission, requests Paul Jung to withdraw his resignation as president of the school commission.
47 See Jung Family Archive, document dated October 22, 1892. The University of Basel established Friedmatt Asylum in 1865 when it created a chair for psychiatry. German psychiatrist Ludwig Wille was the first to be appointed to this position. Available at: https://blog.zhdk.ch/bewahrenbesondererkulturgueter/en/3-3-basel/.
48 *Confirmation-Register der Gemeinde Klein Hüningen 1885–*.
49 German names of professions: *Schmid, Fabrikarbeiter, Gärtner, Mechaniker, Pfarrer, Taglöhner, Schwimmlehrer, Gemeinde-Präsident, Schuhmacher, Siegrist, Wäscherin*.

50 Spycher, Ernst. *Bauten für die Bildung: Basler Schulhausbauten von 1845 bis 2015 im Schweizerischen und internationalen Kontext*, Schwabe Verlag, 2018, pp. 292–293.
51 Spycher, ibid. The first town school was located at Dorfstrasse 35, at the corner of Schulgasse (1823).
52 *MDR*, p. 17.
53 *MDR*, p. 18. Following an earthquake in 1356 with an estimated magnitude of 6.7–7.1, the most destructive known for central Europe, key structural elements, including parts of the towers of Basel Münster, collapsed. The original Romanesque towers were subsequently rebuilt in the Gothic style.
54 Foundation C.G. Jung Küsnacht. Many of these drawings were shown at a special exhibition (2020–2021) at the House of C.G. Jung in Küsnacht and printed in the accompanying *Exhibition Guide 2020/21*.
55 Hoerni et al, p. 153.
56 Jung, *Black Books*, vol. 1, p. 14.
57 Nancy Krieger was able to succinctly translate the complex.
58 Jung, *Nietzsche's Zarathustra*, pp. 259–262.
59 Jung, *Black Books*, vol. 1, p. 14.
60 Jung, *Nietzsche's Zarathustra*, vol 1, pp. 259–262.
61 König, *Chemie und Pharma*, pp. 21–22, 30–31. This publication is an important resource for not only the history of the Clavel family but also the broader history of chemistry and pharmaceuticals.
62 "Ecstasy of Colors." Available at: https://live.novartis.com/article/ecstasy-of-colors/ecstasy-of-colors-1--.
63 A relevant article on the Clavel family is available at: https://Carl.zrieche.ch/jahrbuch/alexander-clavel-und-der-wenkenhof/.
64 *Protocols of the Kleinhüninger Council Meetings, 1887–1893* (Staatsarchiv Basel-Stadt).
65 Hugger, pp. 21–23. See p. 23 for a description of the unification negotiations held on March 12, 1905.
66 See also Sherry, pp. 8–9, for an interpretation relating this image to Basel and its environs.
67 Personal communication with Ulrich Hoerni, December 15, 2023.
68 As cited in *MDR*, p. 82; and Hoerni et al, p. 65.
69 An image by Vauban is available at: https://Carl.akg-images.de/CS.aspx?VP3=SearchResult&ITEMID=2UMEBMYU1Y5JP&LANGSWI=1&LANG=English (retrieved January 14, 2023). A still-existing fortification by Vauban, designated as a UNESCO World Heritage Site, is located in Neuf-Brisach in the Upper Rhine Valley. This later fort closely resembles the image depicted in *The Red Book*, p. 163.
70 Lüem, p. 28. A relative on Jung's mother's side, Colonel Lucas Preiswerk-Forcart, helped seal the destiny of the fortress of Hüningen through a mortar battery.
71 As mentioned in Hoerni et al, n. 11. See also *Reflections*, entry dated May 4, 1959.
72 See Hoerni et al., p. 65; *The Red Book*, image 163.
73 In his essay "Concerning Mandala Symbolism," CW9i, para 691, ill. 36.

TOUR 2

1. *MDR*, p. 82.
2. Lüem, p. 39. The castle was located at Klybeckstrasse 248. See also Meyer, who described the castle as a *Weiherhaus* (moat house), first mentioned in 1438. Available at: https://altBasel.ch/haushof/klybeck_schloesschen.html (retrieved August 6, 2022).
3. For further images, see Hoerni et al, pp. 54, 56–58; and *C.G. Jung: Early Visual and Creative Works*, p. 13.
4. Koellreuter, p. 294.
5. Koellreuter, pp. 299–300.
6. See "Markgräflerhof," available at: https://de.wikipedia.org/wiki/Markgr%C3%A4flerhof; and "Universitätsspital Basel," available at: https://de.wikipedia.org/wikiUniversit%C3%A4tsspital_Basel.
7. "History of Wenkenstrasse School." Available at: https://www.lexikon-riehen.ch/organisationen/schul-und-forderzentrum-wenkenstrasse/.
8. "History of the Seidenhof." Available at: https://altbasel.ch/haushof/seidenhof.html.
9. The building was a representative Swiss court, designed by Johann Conrad Rapp-Wick (1800–1868), constructed around 1830 and demolished in 1937.
10. Exhibit brochure: *Stückelbergs wiederentdeckte Wandbilder: Fragmente aus einem Basler Künstlersalon*. Exhibition at the Museum Kleines Klingental, March 13, 2023 to March 10, 2024. Copyright 2023, Kantonale Denkmalpflege Basel-Stadt and Museum Kleines Klingental.
11. The bridge was reconstructed in stone between 1903 and 1905.
12. See also "Karl Gustav Jung," available at: https://en.wikipedia.org/wiki/Karl_Gustav_Jung (retrieved April 7, 2023). As an aside, his brother, Sigismund von Jung (1745–1824), married the youngest daughter of Friedrich Schleiermacher, the theologian and German philosopher.
13. Fischer, "C.G. Jung and the University of Basel."
14. Kurz, p. 21.
15. Kurz, p. 32.
16. Anatomical Museum of the University of Basel. Original preparations of human body parts, organs, and tissue are displayed in the museum, arranged in systematic and topographic order to illustrate the structure of the human body. Exhibits on prenatal development are also included.
17. Hannah, pp. 19–20. Jung described that his grandfather kept a pig and walked it through Heidelberg like a dog, much to the amusement of onlookers.
18. "Freimaurerei." Available at: https://freimaurerei.ch/beruhmte-freimaurer/?menu=open (retrieved April 10, 2023).
19. "Grand Lodge Alpina of Switzerland." Available at: https://en.wikipedia.org/wiki/Grand_Lodge_Alpina_of_Switzerland.
20. Shortly after the first Swiss Freemason lodge was established in 1736 in Geneva, 30 branches of Freemasonry emerged in Switzerland. Today, a museum in Bern is dedicated to the Freemasons. See "Freimaurerei Museum," available at: https://freimaurermuseum.ch (accessed January 9, 2023).
21. Hofmeier, pp. 47–49.
22. Evans, p. 708.
23. Hofmeier, p. 54. The case was reported in the *Basler Chroniken*.
24. Hofmeier, pp. 28–29.
25. *MDR*, p. 16.
26. This site was previously home to an Augustinian cloister. In 1849, Basel architect Melchior Berri constructed the museum, which was then known as the Berri Building.
27. Hoerni et al, p. 24.
28. Gossman, p. 423.
29. This phenomena was examined by the ethnologist Paul Hugger; see Hugger.
30. *MDR*, p. 24.
31. *MDR*, p 102.
32. Personal communication with Ulrich Hoerni. Above the entrance to Jung's tower in Bollingen are the words *Philemonis sacrum – Fausti poenitentia* ("The sacred offering of Philemon – the repentance of Faust"). This juxtaposition contrasts Philemon's sacred offering with Faust's repentance for his pact with the devil. The reference ties to Jung's inner character and guide, Philemon (with whom he dialogued during his active imaginations), and Goethe's Faust.
33. *MDR*, p. 24.
34. Jung recalled that his father applied for the stipend on his behalf, and when Carl received it, he felt ashamed, having not expected such kindness. See *MDR*, p. 86.
35. *MDR*, p. 24.
36. *MDR*, p. 30.
37. *MDR*, p. 30.
38. See images reproduced in *The Art of C.G. Jung* and *C.G. Jung: Early Visual and Creative Works*.
39. *MDR*, p. 31.
40. Report cards were viewed at the Jung House Museum Archive in Küsnacht.
41. *MDR*, p. 43.
42. A psychoanalytic perspective might interpret *The Red Book* as Jung's late attempt to compensate for these emotional wounds.
43. Zumstein-Preiswerk, p. 35.
44. See European History Network of Excellence. *New Testament of Erasmus* (1516). Available at: https://ehne.fr/en/encyclopedia/themes/european-humanism/cultural-heritage/new-testament-erasmus-1516.
45. Marie-Louise von Franz translated another alchemical text, *Musaeum Hermeticum*, and later provided commentary on *Hal ar-Rumuz* (*Explanation of Symbols*) by the Arabic alchemist Muhammad Ibn Umail. Available at: https://Carl.marie-louisevonfranz.com/en/biography (accessed December 21, 2022).
46. E-rara is a rare books platform on which rare books, including Jung's alchemical collection, may be accessed in digital form via ETH Zürich. Available at: https://e-rara.ch/.
47. Zumstein-Preiswerk, p. 125, n. 56.

TOUR 3

1 In this tour, only the points that connect with Jung are emphasized.
2 *Humanitas* refers to the development of human virtue in all its forms, to the fullest extent. The term thus implies qualities such as understanding, benevolence, compassion, and mercy, as well as fortitude, judgment, prudence, eloquence, and even a love of honor.
3 See "Henry II, Holy Roman Emperor and German King," available at: https://www.encyclopedia.com/reference/encyclopedias-almanacs-transcripts-and-maps/henry-ii-holy-roman-emperor-and-german-king.
4 Liebendörfer, 2003, pp. 12-13.
5 CW16, para 470. See also Samuels, pp. 138-139.
6 Degler.
7 Basilea Reformata 2002, p. 263.
8 Translation of *Das Morgenland. Altes und Neues für Freunde der Heiligen Schrift*.
9 He was also in contact with two other important figures, Lotze and Ehrenfeuchter. Personal communication with S. Eggenberger-Jung.
10 Almbladh, pp. 31-37.
11 Personal communication with Ulrich Hoerni.
12 Wehr, p. 20.
13 Schwinn Schürmann, p. 403.
14 *Chronik der Schweiz*, p. 227. Available at: https://de.wikipedia.org/wiki/Reformatorischer_Bildersturm (retrieved December 21, 2022).
15 In Zürich, the process took a more peaceful turn. See *Chronik der Schweiz*, p. 226.
16 Burckhardt, A.
17 *MDR*, pp. 30, 36.
18 *MDR*, pp. 36-40.
19 Van der Post, p. 104. Indeed, Reformed Protestantism emphasized the work ethic—particularly hard work, frugality, and discipline—which were associated more with Calvin than with Zwingli. Religious dogma, such as the concept of the immaculate conception, often conflicted with common sense. The hoped-for "illumination" appeared intangible to the individual.
20 Van der Post, p. 101.
21 *MDR*, pp. 52-56, specifically p. 55.
22 *MDR*, p. 52.
23 *MDR*, p. 54.
24 It has been suggested that fear of the black robes may relate to the Catholic priests and Jesuits as the shadow of the Swiss Reformed Church. See the play *ERANOS*, written by Murray Stein and Henry Abramovitch.
25 *MDR*, p. 56.
26 Lüem, p. 115.
27 Schürch and Koellreuter, pp. 51-57.
28 Bitter, pp. 16-18. *"Wegen einer in der Anstalt errschwerten Typhus Epidemie könnte die Confirmation erst vor Pfingsten stattfinden."*
29 Various references to this knight dream exist: it is documented in *Black Books*, vol. 1, p. 16; commented upon in *Black Books*, vol. 2, p. 160; and presented in a more descriptive version in *MDR*, p. 164.
30 *MDR*, p. 164.
31 Carl's future wife, Emma Rauschenberg, shared this enthusiasm for the Grail legend, which she was researching and writing about at the time of her death.
32 *MDR*, p. 165.
33 *MDR*, p. 165.
34 *MDR*, pp. 84-85.
35 *MDR*, p. 85.
36 *MDR*, p. 85.
37 Consulted documents from the Basel City State Archive (1895-1900) include the *Directory of University Teachers, Directory of Personnel* (including students), the *Semester Program,* and the *Directory of Fees*. Interestingly, Carl Jung is not listed in the latter, likely due to a stipend covering his university studies. Collections listed in the 1895 Summer Semester Program include the Public Library, Art Collection, and Ethnographic Collection at the Museum (Augustinergasse); the Sculpture Gallery (Klostergasse); and the Historical Museum (Barfüsserkirche). The Anatomical Institute was in the Vesalianum, while the Comparative-Anatomical Collection was housed in the university building.
38 "Emilie Louise Frey." Available at: https://hls-dhs-dss.ch/de/articles/042121/2003-05-02/. See also Eggmann, pp. 76-83.
39 Burckhardt, A., pp. 299-320.
40 Burckhardt, A., p. 313.
41 The author, Dr. Albrecht Burckhardt, director of the Hygienic Institute, wrote the sourcebook on the University of Basel School of Medicine.
42 "History of the Department of Pharmaceutical Sciences Basel." Available at: https://pharma.unibas.ch/en/about-us/departmental-history/#:-:text=In%20 1917%20Prof.,a%20collection%20and%20a%20library.
43 *MDR*, pp. 100-101.
44 Foundation C.G. Jung Küsnacht, p. 13.
45 Carl Jung was apparently influenced by the mosaics in the Mausoleum of Galla Placidia in Ravenna, Italy, which he viewed in 1914 and 1932. See Hoerni et al, p. 41; and "Dr. Jill Mellick – The Red Book Hours," available at: https://www.youtube.com/watch?v=Vd3EdxR43dg.
46 *MDR*, p. 108.
47 *MDR*, p. 109.
48 ETH Library, University Archive, Hs 1269: 21a-23a.
49 *MDR*, pp. 197-198.
50 *MDR*, pp. 98-100, 198-199. See also "The Psychology of the Unconscious Processes," CW7, paras. 114-115.
51 For an overview, see Jung, *Black Books*, vol. 7, pp. 98-104.
52 Jung, *Black Books*, vol. 1, p. 99.
53 Kessler et al., caption p. 6.
54 Jung, "Editorial Note to the First Edition," CW12.
55 Jung, *Black Books*, p. 26, fn. Jung also cites Iamblichus's *On the Mysteries* (1497) in CW9i, para. 573.
56 Jung, *The Red Book*, p. 27.
57 Jaffé, p. 136.
58 "Adagia." Available at: https://en.wikipedia.org/wiki/Adagia (retrieved December 21, 2022).
59 The inscription above the threshold of the house in Küsnacht, *Gerufen und nicht gerufen wird Gott da sein* ("Bidden or not, God is present"), means that, invited or not, God (spirituality) is present in everyday life. As interpreted in Shamdasani, p. 47: "the god will be on the spot, but in what form and to what purpose?"
60 Van der Post, p. 95.
61 Kessler, pp. 27-28.

ENDNOTES

62 Kurz, p. 15. Johann Stephan von Calcar (1499–1546), a student of Titian, worked in Venice.
63 Michaleas et al.
64 Jung, CW13, para. 109–188.
65 Jung, CW15, para. 3, n. 1; para. 13, n. 1.
66 Jung, *The Red Book*, p. 169.
67 *Black Books*, p. 188. See "Card Catalogue," October 26, 1935, *Tractatus Aureus and Tabula Smaragdina*.
68 Jung, CW12, para. 345–346. See also "Psychology and Alchemy," available at: https://en.wikipedia.org/wiki/Psychology_and_Alchemy (retrieved December 25, 2022). The Latin phrase *obscurum per obscurius, ignotum per ignotius means* "an explanation that is less clear than the thing to be explained."
69 Jung, CW12, para. 346.
70 Calian, pp. 167–168.
71 "Carl Jung." Available at: https://en.wikipedia.org/wiki/Carl_Jung#cite_note-jungbio1-45 (retrieved December, 25 2022).
72 "Häfliger von Luzern, Familie (Provenienz)." Available at: https://query-staatsarchiv.lu.ch/detail.aspx?ID=1814579.
73 For more information on the Galenic humoral system of medicine, see "The Cabinet of Curiosities," available at: https://www.cabinet.ox.ac.uk/four-humours-galenic-medicine.
74 See "Lambsprinck," available at: https://www.e-rara.ch/zut/content/zoom/11665948?query=lambsprinck; and "Tripus Aureus," available at: https://www.e-rara.ch/cgj/content/zoom/2044768?query=tripus%20aureus.
75 Reichstein, "The Meaning of Alchemy."
76 Reichstein, "Über Alchemy," pp. 2, 5. See also Shamdasani, p. 6. Reichstein was a chemist, full professor of pharmaceutical chemistry, chair of pharmacy, and head of the Pharmaceutical Institute. In 1934, he was appointed titular professor; in 1937, associate professor; and in 1938, professor of pharmaceutical chemistry and director of the Pharmaceutical Institute at the University of Basel. In 1946, he also became chair of organic chemistry. He held both appointments until 1950.

TOUR 4

1 "[Partial] List of Members of the Swiss Zofingia Association," Available at: https://de.wikipedia.org/wiki/Liste_von_Mitgliedern_des_Schweizerischen_Zofingervereins.
2 Zumstein-Preiswerk (ETH Library, University Archive, Hs 1269: 15–23a).
3 Letter transcript, April 29, 1902, from Jung to his friend Andreas Vischer (ETH Library, University Archive, Hs 1269: 17A). Translation of nicknames added where appropriate.
4 Oeri, p. 186.
5 Hannah, p. 41.
6 Oeri, p. 183.
7 *Basler Zeitschrift*, 1882–1883, p. 159. See also Staatsarchiv Bild 41, 47. Dr. Oeri is in the first row, first on the left, with a hat and cane.
8 Hanna Preiswerk (1876–1966) was the daughter of Eduard Preiswerk (1829–1858) and Maria Groben (1839–1917). Albert and Hanna's fourth daughter, Sibylle, married Peter Birkhäuser (1911–1976), a trained graphic artist. During a personal crisis and encouraged by his wife, Birkhäuser undertook Jungian analysis. Beginning in 1953, he developed his own style of painting psychological reality guided by his dreams, creating an extensive body of dream paintings.
9 Ellenberger, pp. 665–666, 687–688; Steiner, 1965; Zumstein-Preiswerk, p. 86.
10 Steiner, 1935, pp. 69–109.
11 The star is a recurring symbol in Jung's drawings, such as the mandala sketches created during World War I when he was stationed as a medical doctor in Chateaux-D'Oex. It also appears in the center of the *Ex Libris* he designed in 1925. See Hoerni et al, p. 98.
12 Kieser, *Historisches Lexikon der Schweiz*.
13 Develey, pp. 90, 163.
14 The lectures were later published as *The Zofingia Lectures* (Jung, 1983/1896/1899).
15 *The Zofingia Lectures*, pp. xiii, 3.
16 Psychologischer Club Zürich.
17 *The Zofingia Lectures*, pp. xiii, 3; Brockway, p. 139.
18 Zumstein-Preiswerk, *NZZ*.
19 Von Scarpatetti, pp. 76–78.
20 Von Scarpatetti, p. 158.
21 Stoecklin, *Basler Zeitung*, 1988.
22 A change of ownership is recorded for Bottmingerstrasse "No 69" in the fire records of the municipality of Binningen for 1896. "Preiswerk Ed., pastor" is named as the new owner of the property, and "Preiswerk-Vetter Gustav" is also entered here as the owner of a building. The respective homes are estimated at 11,300 and 19,000 Swiss francs.
23 Zumstein-Preiswerk, p. 62; Zumstein, *NZZ*, Sundgau, Riegelbau.
24 After the nostalgic tram stop at Heuwaage (Heuwaage-Bahnhöfli) was dismantled, it was carefully rebuilt in Rheinfelden in 1989. Available at: https://wp.tram-bus-basel.ch/2024/03/23/der-heuwaage-bahnhof/.
25 The Preiswerk brothers owned a property at Bottmingerstrasse 50, where Preiswerk-Vetter was registered as a resident in 1906.
26 Von Scarpatetti, p. 291.
27 Kreis-Schäppi, pp. 106–109. The Kneipp method was developed by the priest Sebastian Kneipp (1821–1897).
28 Strub, p. 617.
29 Zumstein-Preiswerk, pp. 55, 61.
30 Zumstein-Preiswerk, n. 56.
31 Zumstein-Preiswerk, pp. 125, n. 60. See Zumstein-Preiswerk, pp. 62, 132, family tree.
32 According to Zumstein-Preiswerk (p. 133, family tree), the 3,000 Swiss francs came from Eduard Preiswerk (1846–1932), while Jung (*MDR*, p. 97) suggested that it came from his uncle Ernst Jung (1841–1912), his only surviving living paternal uncle.
33 *MDR*, p. 96.
34 *MDR*, p. 97.
35 Zumstein-Preiswerk, p. 63.
36 *MDR*, p. 79.
37 Jung, "On the Psychology and Pathology of So-Called Occult Phenomena," CW1.

38 Jung, *The Red Book: Reader's Edition*, pp. 220–224.
39 Zumstein-Preiswerk, p. 7.
40 *MDR*, pp. 104–105.
41 Zumstein-Preiswerk, n. 44.
42 Lenbachhaus Munich.
43 Zumstein-Preiswerk, *C.G. Jung's Medium*.
44 Gertrude is not listed as a student at the Töchterschule in Basel between 1897 and 1901 (Staatsarchiv, Signature. Erziehung W24), nor in the Sekundarschule Binningen (1897–1915) and the Arbeitsschule Binningen (1834–1947).
45 Zumstein-Preiswerk, p. 75. The séances stopped while Helly prepared for her confirmation but resumed thereafter. This book details the content and process of the séances.
46 Zumstein-Preiswerk, *NZZ*.
47 Bair, p. 52; Zumstein-Preiswerk, *NZZ*.
48 Zumstein-Preiswerk, pp. 16, 68, 72.
49 Zumstein-Preiswerk, p. 142.
50 Zumstein-Preiswerk, p. 73.
51 Douglas, pp. 12, 322 n. Examples provided include Franz Anton Mesmer (1734–1815), Fräulein Oesterlin, and Maria Theresa Paradis; Justinus Kerner (1786–1862) and the Seer of Prevorst (Friederiche Hauffe); J. M. Charcot and Blanche Wittman (1882); Pierre Janet and Leonie (1886–1888); Josef Breuer and Anna O. (1895); Théodore Flournoy and Hélène Smith (1899); and finally Jung and Helene Preiswerk, Miss Miller (1911–1912), Kristine Mann (1921–1922), Christiana Morgen (Miss X, 1934–1939), Sabina Spielrein, and Toni Wolff.
52 Zumstein, p. 106: *"Liebe Cousine, darf ich Sie kennenlernen? Carl erzählte mir viel von Ihnen. Ich habe auch gehört, dass Sie Damen-Costüme mit echtem pariserischem Chic anfertigen. Wenn Sie mir nichts Gegenteiliges berichten, komme ich zur Anprobe vorbei. Emma Jung-Rauschenbach."* The original letter has not been located.
53 Hoerni et al, pp. 66–69; *C.G. Jung: Early Visual and Creative Works*, pp. 20–21.
54 This letter and Jung's reply were discovered in the ETH Library, University Archive by Jung's great-grandson Thomas Fischer. See Fischer, "C.G. Jung and the University of Basel."

TOUR 5

1 Liebendörfer, 2012, pp. 10–21.
2 Hesse, *Basler Erinnerungen*, p. 438. Letter, January 16, 1900.
3 "William Tell." Available at: https://houseofswitzerland.org/swissstories/history/william-tell-symbol-switzerland-known-throughout-world.
4 Brought to Sonnmatt, Lucerne. Baumann, p. 13.
5 Hesse, *Gesammelte Werke*, vol. 6, p. 67.
6 Baumann, p. 17.
7 From a letter to a female student in Duisburg, 1930. The full quote reads: "In response to your greetings, I am sending you a little picture I painted these past few days – for painting and drawing are my way of relaxing. The picture is designed to show you that the innocence of nature, the vibrancy of a few colours, are at any one given moment – even in the midst of a difficult and problematic life - able to stir belief and freedom in us." See "Hermann Hesse," available at: https://www.anthologialitt.com/post/hermann-hesse-on-painting.
8 Baumann, p. 18. The analysis took place February 19 to 20, May 19 to 25, and June 17 to July 2. See Hesse, *Materialien zu Hermann Hesses 'Siddhartha.'*
9 Gossman, p. 417.
10 Reichert, in Hesse, Gesammelte Werke, pp. 89, 90, 116. Nietzsche was under the care of Dr. Wille in Basel before being transferred to the Jena Clinic under Professor Dr. Otto Binswanger. See also n. 77. Binswanger, a Swiss psychiatrist and neurologist, came from a prominent family of physicians. His father founded the Kreuzlingen Sanatorium, and he was the uncle of Ludwig Binswanger (1881–1966). See "Otto Binswanger," available at: https://en.wikipedia.org/wiki/Otto_Binswanger (retrieved December 28, 2022).
11 Green.
12 Helly's school friend, Emma Zinsstag, also noted her own version of events at the séance. Zumstein-Preiswerk, p. 82.
13 https://www.biapsy.de/index.php/en/9-biographien-a-z/71-nietzsche-friedrich-weilhelm-e (retrieved 31 March 2025).
14 Jung, *Nietzsche's Zarathustra*, vol. 1, p. 544.
15 Jung, *Nietzsche's Zarathustra*, vol. 1, p. 259.
16 Nietzsche titles referenced in the *Black Books* are: *Thus Spoke Zarathustra*, *The Gay Science*, *Beyond Good and Evil*, *Ecce Homo*, and *Dithyrambs of Dionysus*.
17 Later published in two volumes. See Jung, *Nietzsche's Zarathustra*. Among the audience was Prof. Tadeus Reichstein, Nobel Prize winner in 1950 for Physiology/Medicine. Seventy-four people attended the seminars.
18 Jung, *Black Books*, vol. 1, p. 107.
19 See, e.g., Bishop.
20 Jung, *Black Books*, vol. 1, p. 74.
21 Jung, *Black Books*, vol. 1, p. 40.
22 In 2019, the Historical Museum in the Barfüsser Church hosted the exhibition *Übermensch – Friedrich Nietzsche and the Consequences* to commemorate the 175th anniversary of Nietzsche's appointment to the University of Basel. The Artbook Edition of *Thus Spoke Zarathustra* was featured in the exhibition.

FAMILY TREES

1 Jung, *The Red Book*, p. 232.
2 Fischer, "C.G. Jung and the University of Basel."
3 Hannah, pp. 19–20.
4 "Berühmte Freimaurer." Available at: https://freimaurerei.ch/beruhmte-freimaurer/?menu=open (retrieved April 10. 2023).

REFERENCES

Almbladh, Karin. "MS Uppsala O nova 791: A Rediscovered Manuscript of the Arabic Translation of and Commentary on the *Song of Songs* by Japheth ben Eli." *Orientalia Suecana* 61, suppl. (2012): 31–37.

Basilea Reformata. Basel/Liestal: Herausgegeben von den Kirchenräten der Evangelisch-reformierten Kirchen Basel-Stadt und Basel-Landschaft, 2002.

Baumann, Günter. *Der archetypische Heilsweg: Hermann Hesse, C. G. Jung und die Weltreligionen.* Schäuble Verlag, 1999.

Bishop, Paul. "C.G. Jung und Nietzsche: Dionysos and Analytical Psychology." In *Jung in Contexts: A Reader,* edited by Paul Bishop, 199–222. Routledge, 1999.

Bishop, Paul. *The Dionysian Self: C.G. Jung's Reception of Friedrich Nietzsche.* De Gruyter, 1995/2010.

Bitter, Sabine. "Mädchenerziehung durch Arbeit." *Emanzipation: Feministische Zeitschrift für kritische Frauen* 17, no. 4 (1991).

Bonjour, Edgar. *Die Universität Basel.* Helbing & Lichtenhahn, 1960.

Brockway, Robert W. *Young Carl Jung.* Chiron Press, 2013.

Bühler, Hans, et al. *Heimatkunde Binningen.* Liestal, 1978.

Bürger-Korporation Kleinhüningen, Basel. *Kleinhüningen.* Druckerei Dietrich AG, 1999.

Burckhardt, Albrecht. *Geschichte der medizinischen Fakultät zu Basel 1460–1900.* Friedrich Reinhard, Universitätsdruckerei, 1917.

Burkhardt, Bianca. "Der Farbe auf der Spur. Erkenntnisse zu Farbigkeit und Materialität am Basler Münster." In *Basler Zeitschrift für Geschichte und Altertumskunde.* Historische und Antiquarische Gesellschaft zu Basel, 2018, 171–202.

Calian, Georg Florin. "Alkimia Operativa and Alkimia Speculativa. Some Modern Controversies on the Historiography of Alchemy." *Annual of Medieval Studies at CEU* (2010): 167–168.

Degler-Spengler, Brigitte. "Die religiösen Frauen in Basel: Nonnen und Beginen." *Basler Stadtbuch* 111 (1990): 141–144.

Devely, Robert. *Der Breo zu Basel: 3-Phasige Geschichte eines Studentenlokals.* Spalentor Verlag, 2004.

Douglas, Claire. *Translate this Darkness: The Life of Christiana Morgan, the Veiled Woman in Jung's Circle.* Princeton University Press, 1993.

Eggmann, C. "Geduldet aber nicht willkommen." In *D'Studäntin kunnt: 100 Jahre Frauen an der Uni Basel.* Basel, 1991.

Ellenberger, Henri F. *Discovery of the Unconscious: The History and Evolution of Dynamic Psychiatry.* Basic Books, 1970.

Evans, E.P. *The Criminal Prosecution and Capital Punishment of Animals.* College University of Pennsylvania, 1906.

Feldges, Uta. "Das Fischerhaus Bürgin in Kleinhüningen." In *Stiftung pro Fischerhaus, Kleinhüningen: Kleinhüningen gestern und heute,* 2003.

Fiechter, Sandra. "Zur Salon-Wandmalerei von Ernst Stückelberg im abgeganenen Basler Erimanshof: Bedeutung und Beziehungsreichtum einer fragmentarisch erhaltenen Raumgestaltung." *Sonderdruck aus der Zeitschrift für Schweizerische Archäologie und Kunstgeschichte* 80, no. 1–2 (2023). Wolfensberger AG.

Figulus, Benedictus. *A Golden and Blessed Casket of Nature's Marvels.* Translated by A.E. Waite. Vincent Stuart, 1963. Originally published in the 17th century.

Fischer, Thomas. "The Alchemical Rare Book Collection of C.G. Jung." *International Journal of Jungian Studies* 3, no. 2 (September 2011): 169–180.

———. "C.G. Jung and the University of Basel (Abstract)." Presentation at the Joint Conference IAAP/University of Basel, *Theoretical Foundations of Analytical Psychology: Recent Developments and Controversies,* October 18–20, 2018.

Foundation C.G. Jung Küsnacht. *C.G. Jung: Early Visual and Creative Works. Exhibition Guide, Special Exhibition 2020/2021.* July 2020.

Gossman, Lionel. *Basel in the Age of Burckhardt: A Study in Unseasonable Ideas.* University of Chicago Press, 2000.

Green, M.S. *Nietzsche and the Transcendental Tradition.* University of Illinois Press. 2002.

Hannah, Barbara. *Jung: His Life and Work: A Biographical Memoir.* Chiron Publications, 1997/1999.

Hesse, Hermann. "Basler Erinnerungen." In *Kindheit und Jugend vor 1900,* vol. 2. Suhrkamp Verlag, 1978.

———. *"Die dunkle und wilde Seite der Seele": Der Briefwechsel mit seinem Psychoanalytiker Josef Bernhard Lang, 1916–1945.* Edited by Thomas Feitknecht. Suhrkamp Verlag, 2006.

———. *Gesammelte Werke,* vols. 1–12. Suhrkamp Verlag, 1970.

———. *Materialien zu Hermann Hesses 'Siddhartha,'* vol. 1, *Texts of Hermann Hesse.* Edited by Volker Michels. Suhrkamp Verlag, 1975.

Historical Museum Barfüsserkirche. Exhibition materials for the special exhibit *Übermensch – Friedrich Nietzsche and his Afterlife.* October 16, 2019–February 23, 2020.

Hoerni, Ulrich. "Images from the Unconscious: An Introduction to the Visual Works of C.G. Jung." In *The Art of C.G. Jung.* Foundation C.G. Jung, 2018.

Hoerni, Ulrich, Thomas Fischer, and Bettina Kaufmann, eds. *The Art of C.G. Jung.* W.W. Norton & Co., 2018.

Hofmeier, Thomas. *Basels Ungeheuer: Eine Kleine Basiliskenkunde.* Leonhard-Thurneysser-Verlag, 2011.

Hugger, Paul. *Kleinhüningen: Von der 'Dorfidylle' zum Alltag eines Basler Industriequartiers.* Birkhäuser Verlag, 1984.

Jaffé, Aniela. *C.G. Jung: Bild und Wort.* Olten: Walter Verlag, 1978.

———. *Reflections on the Life and Dreams of C. G. Jung by Aniela Jaffé from Conversations with Jung.* Edited with historical commentary by Elena Fischli. Daimon Verlag, 2023.

—. *Streiflichter zu Leben und Denken C.G. Jungs von Aniela Jaffé nach Gesprächen mit C.G. Jung.* Edited with historical commentary by Elena Fischli. Daimon Verlag, 2021.

Jenny, Oscar. *Die Bevölkerung des Kantons Basel-Stadt am 1.12.1910: Mitteilungen des Statistischen Amtes des Kantons Basel-Stadt.* Basel, 1924.

Jung, C.G. *Erinnerungen, Träume, Gedanken von C.G. Jung.* Edited by Aniela Jaffé. Walter-Verlag, 1961/1987.

—. "Instinct and the Unconscious." Paper presented in London, 1919.

—. *Memories, Dreams, Reflections.* Edited by Aniela Jaffé. Vintage Books, 1961/1989.

—. *Nietzsche's "Zarathustra": Notes of the Seminar Given in 1934–1939.* Edited by James L. Jarrett. Princeton University Press; London: Routledge, 1988.

—. *Psychology and Alchemy. Collected Works of C.G. Jung.* Princeton University Press, 1968.

—. *The Black Books of C.G. Jung (1913–1932): Notebooks of Transformation.* Edited by Sonu Shamdasani. Stiftung der Werke von C.G. Jung. W.W. Norton & Co., 2020.

—. *The Red Book: Liber Novus.* Edited by Sonu Shamdasani. Translated by John Peck, Mark Kyburz, and Sonu Shamdasani. W.W. Norton & Co., 2009.

—. *The Zofingia Lectures.* Edited by William McGuire. Princeton University Press, 1983.

—. *Zur Psychologie und Pathologie sogenannter occulter Phänomene.* Dissertation, University of Zürich, 1902. Advisor: Eugen Bleuler.

Jung, C.G., and Aniela Jaffé. *Jung's Life and Work: Interviews for Memories, Dreams, Reflections.* Edited by Sonu Shamdasani, with Thomas Fischer as consulting editor. Translated by Heather McCartney and John Peck. Princeton University Press, forthcoming.

Kessler, M., Kluge M., Häner F., et al. *Leben am Totengässlein: Das Pharmazie-Historische Museum Basel im Haus «Zum Sessel».* Selbstverlag des Pharmazie-Historischen Museums Basel, 2004/2015.

Kieser, Hans-Lukas. "Vischer, Andreas." In *Historisches Lexikon der Schweiz (HLS).* Version from July 31, 2013. Accessed August 27, 2022. https://hls-dhs-dss.ch/de/articles/044905/2013-07-31/.

Koellreuter, Isabel, and Franziska Schürch. "Signaturen der Moderne." In *Die beschleunigte Stadt 1856–1914,* edited by Patrick Kury, 260–311. Christoph Merian Verlag, 2024.

Kurz, Hugo. *Historische Schätze: Einmalige Exponate im Anatomischen Museum Basel.* Reinhardt Druck, 2005.

Lenbachhaus Munich. *World Receivers: Georgiana Houghton, Hilma af Klint, Emma Kunz.* Museum Catalogue. Lenbachhaus Munich.

Liebendörfer, Helen. *Spaziergang mit Hesse durch Basel.* Reinhardt Verlag, 2012.

—. *Spaziergänge zu Frauen und Kindern in Basel.* Friedrich Reinhardt Verlag, 2003.

Lüem, Barbara. *Basel Kleinhüningen: Der Reiseführer.* Christoph Merian Verlag, 2008.

Mellick, Jill. *The Red Book Hours: C.G. Jung's Art Mediums and Creative Process.* Verlag Scheidegger & Spiess AG, 2018.

Michaleas, S.N., K. Laios, G. Tsoucalas, and G. Androutsos. "Theophrastus Bombastus Von Hohenheim (Paracelsus) (1493–1541): The Eminent Physician and Pioneer of Toxicology." *Toxicology Reports* 8 (February 23, 2021): 411–414.

Oeri, Albert. "Some Youthful Memories of C.G. Jung." *Spring* (1970).

Psychologischer Club Zürich, ed. *Die Kulturelle Bedeutung der Komplexen Psychologie: Festschrift zum 60. Geburtstag von C.G. Jung.* Edited by the Psychologischer Club Zürich. Julius Springer Verlag, 1935, 182–189.

Reichert, W. Herbert. "The Impact of Nietzsche on Hermann Hesse." In *Nietzsche's Impact on Modern German Literature: Five Essays,* 88–118. University of North Carolina Press, 1975.

Reichstein, Tadeus. "The Meaning of Alchemy." Inaugural Lecture, ETH Zürich, 21 February 1931. Aldrich Chemical Company, 1991.

—. "Über Alchemy." Lecture presented at the Psychological Club Zürich, April 3, 1968.

Samuels, Andrew. *A Critical Dictionary of Jungian Analysis.* Routledge, 1986.

Shamdasani, Sonu. *A Biography in Books.* W.W. Norton & Co., 2011.

—. Folio. Personal Communication, 2025.

Schwinn Schürmann, Dorothea. "Nebenbauten und Kreuzgänge." In *Das Basler Münster: Die Kunstdenkmäler der Schweiz,* 403. Gesellschaft für Schweizerische Kunstgeschichte, 2019.

Sherry, Jay. "The Basel Painting in the Jung Family Collection." *ARAS Connections,* Issue 1, 2022.

Spycher, Ernst. *Bauten für die Bildung: Basler Schulhausbauten von 1845 bis 2015 im schweizerischen und internationalen Kontext.* Schwabe Verlag, 2018/2023.

Steiner, Gustav. "Die Zunft 'zum goldenen Stern' im 19. Jahrhundert." In *Basler Jahrbuch 1937,* 69–109.

Steiner, Gustav. "Erinnerungen an Carl Gustav Jung." *Basler Stadtbuch* (1965): 117–163. https://www.baslerstadtbuch.ch/stadtbuch/1965/1965_1185.html.

Stoecklin, Lukas M. *Basler Zeitung,* January 23, 1988. «Als die Bottmingermühle ein Eisparadies war.»

Strub, Brigitta. "Bottmingen." In *Historisches Lexikon der Schweiz (HLS),* vol. 2. Schwabe & Co. AG, 2004.

Von Scarpatetti, Beat, et al. *Binningen – die Geschichte.* Lüdin, Verlag des Kantons Basel-Landschaft, 2004.

Van der Post, Laurens. *Jung and the Story of our Time.* Vintage Books, 1977.

Wehr, Gerhard. *Jung: A Biography.* Translated by David M. Weeks. Shambhala, 1985/1989.

Zumstein-Preiswerk, Stefanie. "Aus den Basler Jugendjahren von C.G. Jung." *Neue Zürcher Zeitung,* March 27/28, 1976.

—. *C.G. Jung's Medium: Die Geschichte der Helly Preiswerk.* Kindler Verlag, 1975.

REFERENCES

MAIN INDEX

Abraxas 257
active imagination 201, 238, 262
Ad fontes 145, 201
Adagia 203, 204
alchemy 13, 125, 126, 145, 179, 197, 199, 201, 204–211
Allgemeiner Consum-Verein 149
Alte Universität *See* Old University
Amerbach, Johann 204
analysis *See* psychoanalysis
analytical psychology *See* psychology
anima/animus 14, 258
Antistes 125, 163–168, 169, 227, 239, 242
Antistitium 157, 165, 166
Apollon *See* paintings
Apollonian 169, 262
archaeology 161
archetype 14, 38, 40, 66, 80, 158, 195, 201, 222, 258
Association of Swiss Lunatic Doctors 191
Atmavictu 40, 65
Attila, King of the Huns 51
Augenklinik *See* Eye Clinic
Augustiner Fountain 125
Augustinerbrunnen *See* Augustiner Fountain
Augustinerkloster *See* monastery, Augustinerkloster
Aunt Gusteli *See* Weiss-Preiswerk, (Faber branch), Gusteli

Badestube unter Krämer 199
Barfüsserkirche *See* church, Barfüsser
Barfüsserkloster *See* monastery, Barfüsserkloster
Barfüsserplatz 177, 178, 180
Barfusserplatz infirmary 103
Basel Council 70, 103, 104, 167, 217, 219
Basel Mission 252
Basel Town Hall 211
Basel Zoo 225
Basil Valentinischen 208
basilisk 125–126
basilisk fountain *See* Augustiner Fountain
Basler Nachrichten 219
Basler Rat *See* Basel Council
Basler Stadtbuch 220
Baslerstrasse 116
battles 63, 65, 79, 135, 179
Baumann, Anna 259
Baumannhöhle 259
Beguine 160
Berri, Melchior 105
Bierbrauerei zum Löwenfels 217
Bildersturm 41, 167
Bindschedler & Busch 69, 70
Binningen 25, 144, 163, 231, 233, 240–241, 247
Binninger Mühle 231

Binninger Schloss *See* castles
Birsig *See* river
Birsigtal *See* river
Birsigtalbahn 233
Birsigviadukt 225
Bischofshof 160, 165, 166, 169
Bishop's staff 125
bishops 119, 133, 158, 160, 165, 167, 169
Black Books 196, 206, 261, 262, 263, 265
Bleuler, Eugen 249
Blumenstrasse 231
Böcklin, Arnold 129, 130, 143
Bollingen 25, 90, 123
Bottmingen 163, 231, 233, 235
Bottminger Mühle 144, 229, 231–137, 249
Brändlin 217
Breo 217
bridge
    Dreirosen 93
    Johanniter 95, 111
    Margarethen-Brücklein 228, 231, 241
    Middle Bridge 109, 111, 115, 117
BTB *See* Birsigtalbahn
Bucer, Martin 165
Büchel, Emanuel 79
Bünten 26, 37, 48
Burckhardt, J. R. 183
Burckhardt, Jacob 66, 133, 143, 218, 260
Burg Reichenstein *See* castles
Burg Rötteln *See* castles
Bürgerspital 100, 103–104, 184, 186–187, 191
Burghölzli 193, 223, 238, 249
Bürgin 68–69

C.G. Jung House Museum 40
Carl versus *Karl* *See* Naming Conventions
castle 64, 79, 80, 87, 179, 231, 235
Castle Ruin *See* paintings
castles
    Binninger Schloss 231
    Burg Reichenstein 90
    Burg Rötteln 90
    Château de Landskron 90
    Klybeck Schlössli 89
    Schloss Bottmingen 231
    Schloss Horburg 89
    Schloss Münchenstein 90
    Schloss Wartenberg 90
Catholic 81, 93, 157, 160
cemetery 51, 53–54, 69, 101, 157, 196, 197, 249
cerevis 218–219
Charterhouse of St. Margarethental *See* monastery
Château de Landskron *See* castles

285

Chirurgische Klinik See Surgical Clinic
cholera 217
Chorherrenstift See monastery, Canon's
Christian 66, 172, 174, 179, 222, 255
Christoph-Merian-Wing 103, 186
church
   Barfüsser 177
   Münster See Münster
   Protestant Reformed Church Kleinhüningen 31, 37, 54, 57–60
   St. Alban 51, 163, 245
   St. Leonard's 163, 164, 177, 182, 229, 239
   St. Margaret's 160, 163, 229, 248, 249
   St. Peter's 194, 196–197
   St. Theodor's 59
CIBA 70, 90
citizen-led initiative 95
Clavel Estate 69, 79
Clavel, Alexander 69, 70, 95
Clinic for Children's Diseases 187
cloister See convent
coat of arms
   Basel 63
   Kleinhüningen 51
Collected Works 201, 262, 265
collective unconscious 13, 16, 66
compensation 16, 168
confirmation
   Carl 48, 62, 173, 174
   Schoren Girls 175
convent
   Convent Klingental 112–113, 115, 160
   St. Alban Convent 160
   St. Maria Magdalena Convent 160
cosmology 201
Council of Basel (1431–1448) 160, 169
cousins 44, 46, 90, 151, 227, 236–241, 261

d'Margarete 48, 277
Dance of Death See paintings
De humani corporis fabrica 204
death 56, 196, 263
   Carl's encounters with 52–57, 101, 115, 151
   C. G. Jung 13
   father 43, 54, 57, 72, 151, 236, 243
Death of Gessler, The See paintings
Demian 257
depth psychology See psychology
dialects 13, 117, 132
Die Krone Restaurant See restaurant
Difficult Path, The 257
Dionysian 169, 262
disillusionment 172, 173
dissertation
   C. G. Jung 199, 238, 243, 245
   Paul Jung 165

divinity 201
Dorfstrasse 29–31, 80
Draco Helveticus 125
dragon 63, 65–67, 125, 126, 158, 179
drawing 63, 65, 66, 67, 89, 92, 179, 190, 195, 196, 247, 258
dream
   An Excavation 180–181, 201
   Knight 178–179
   Liverpool 194–198
   Radiolaria 181
Dream Sequence, A 251
dreams 15, 56, 66, 135, 243
Drei Könige See restaurant
Dreirosenbrücke See bridge
dressmaking 242, 245
du Prel, Carl 242
duality 126, 161, 262
dyes/dyestuff 49, 69, 70, 90

ego 15, 66
Einhorn Becher 209
empiricism 11, 222, 243
Golden Well-Fortified Castle, The See paintings
enantiodromic 66
epilepsy sanatorium 271
Erasmus of Rotterdam 145 158, 165, 203, 204, 205, 207
Erimanshof 105–107
eros 258
Evangelical Women's Association 174
evil 66, 126, 158
execution 64
exhumation 54
Eye Clinic 187

factory 59, 62, 69, 70, 99, 175
Factory Act, The 93
fairytale 66, 257
faith 59, 160, 167, 171, 173, 174
family names See Family Name Index, p. 292
Farmers' Houses and Clouds See paintings
father 37, 40, 42, 43, 45, 46, 53, 54, 56, 62, 63, 103, 104, 135, 136, 144, 163, 164, 173, 174, 175, 192, 217, 223, 229, 236, 240, 243, 265,
Father Rhine 89
Faust 259, 262
Feldbergstrasse 93
feminine 237, 238, 243
fischerhaus See fisher house
fisher house 37, 49, 51, 68, 69
fishing 26, 29, 32, 34–35, 48, 49, 59, 61, 69, 74, 88, 132
Flammarion, Nicolas Camille 242
flood 26, 37, 40, 115, 173
Flora See paintings
Foolish Virgin 158
Fortress at Hüningen 78–79
fraternity See Zofingia

Freemason 123. 265
Freud, Sigmund 14, 15, 48. 261
Frey, Emilie Louise 185
Friedhofsgasse 31, 51, 54
Friedmatt Asylum 61, 102, 104, 192, 261
friends
   Oeri, Albert *See* Oeri, Albert
   Sigg, Hermann *See* Sigg, Hermann
   Steiner, Gustav *See* Steiner, Gustav
   van der Post, Laurens *See* van der Post, Laurens
   Vischer, Andreas *See* Vischer, Andreas
Froben, Johann 202, 203, 204, 207
frock coat/black frock coat 26, 38, 40, 45, 53, 173
Fröhlich-Preiswerk, Edmund 82, 163, 270–271
Fröhlich-Preiswerk, Sophie 163, 236, 268–269, 270–271
funeral 53–54, 61, 196

Galen 187, 208,
Geburtshilflich-gynaekologische Klinik *See* Obstetrics and Gynecology Clinic
German
   High 132, 135
   Swiss 48, 132
Gesellschaft für Chemische Industrie Basel *See* CIBA
gnostic 56
god 40, 201, 203
God 45, 66, 158, 171, 172, 261, 263
Goethe 259, 262
gold 87, 126, 171, 207
Gottesäcker *See* cemetery
grail legend 177, 179
Grand Lodge Alpina 123
Grossbasel 115, 117, 132, 160
Guild of the Golden Star 220
Gutzwiller, Sebastian 41
Gymnasium 46, 90, 132, 133, 135
   Oberes 133, 138, 141, 142–143
   Unteres 133–136, 140

Haeckel, Ernst 181
Häfliger, Josef Anton 208–209
Haltingermoos *See* river
Handarbeitsschule 240
Haus zum Sessel 187, 199, 202–207
healing function 195
Helvetic dragon 125
Herbarium 209
Hermes Trismegistus 201
Hermetica 201
Hermeticism 201
hero 66, 158, 257
Hesse, Hermann 254–258, 259, 260
Heuberg 182
Hexentafel 115
His, Wilhelm 186, 218
histological drawings 190

Historical and Military Museum Hüningen 80
Historical Museum Basel 101, 117, 177,
Historisches Museum Basel *See* Historical Museum Basel
Hodler, Ferdinand 130
Hoffmann–La Roche 211
Holbein, Hans the Younger 129, 202, 203, 207
Holy Roman Emperor *See* Kaiser Heinrich II
Holy Roman Empress *See* Kaiserin Kunigunde
Holzpark Klybeck 89
Homer and Classical Philology *See* Lectures, Nietzsche
Hörnli cemetery 54
humanism 145, 201
humanitas 158
Hygiene Institute 186, 193
Hygienisches Institut *See* Hygiene Institute

Iamblichus 201
ideal personality 262
Index Omnium Rerum Achymicarum *See* Index of All Things Alchemical
Index of All Things Alchemical 206
individuation 14, 195, 199, 201, 207, 211, 222, 255, 257, 258, 260
industrialization 49, 54, 56, 175, 183,
Institute of Good Hope 104
integration 196, 263
International Workingmen's Association 93
Introversion 63
Iselin family 37
Isemännli 151
IWA *See* International Workingmen's Association

Johanniterbrücke *See* bridge
Jung, Karl 41, 103, 104, 119–120, 122, 123, 130–131, 182, 183, 186, 192, 265, 267, 268–269, 270–271
Jung, Trudi 42, 45, 46, 151, 227, 236, 237, 240, 241, 267, 268–269, 270–271
Jung (Frey branch), Fritz 53, 267
Jung (Frey branch), Max 53, 56, 267
Jung (Frey branch), Rudolf 53, 56, 267
Jung (Preiswerk branch), Paul† 43, 268–269
Jung-Frey, Sophie 105, 267, 268–269
Jung-Preiswerk, Emilie 25, 41, 42–45, 53, 56, 144, 157, 164, 166, 180, 236, 237, 239, 240, 267, 268–269, 270–271
Jung-Preiswerk, Paul 25, 37, 40, 41, 53–57, 61, 62, 72, 104, 157, 163, 164–165, 166, 173–175, 229, 236, 239, 267, 268–269, 270–271
Jung-Rauschenbach, Emma 25, 157, 179, 245, 268–269
Jung-Ziegler, Ignaz 119, 268–269
Jungian psychology *See* psychology

Kaiser Heinrich II 105, 157, 158
Kaiserin Kunigunde 105, 157, 158
Käppelijoch 115
Kartäuserkloster St. Margarethental *See* monastery, Charterhouse of St. Margarethental

MAIN INDEX

Kaserne 110-111, 113
Kennst du das Land? *See* paintings
Kern, Johann Konrad 217
Kesswil 25
Kinderklinik *See* Clinic for Children's Diseases
Kleinbasel 70, 112, 115, 117, 160
Kleinhüningen 25, 29-35
   coat of arms *See* coat of arms, Kleinhüningen
   origin of name 51
Kleinhüningen historic businesses
   Autino General Grocery 31
   Carpentry Greiner 31
   Gasthaus Drei Könige 31
   Horse-Coach Transport Glockner 29
   Restaurant Die Krone 31
   Restaurant Turnerstübli 31
   Sawmill Herbst 31
Kloster Klingental *See* convent, Convent Klingental
Klostergarten *See* Münster
Klübin *See* castle, Klybeck Schlössli
Klybeck Schlössli *See* castle
Klybeck 49, 72, 73, 87, 89, 90
Klybeckinsel 89, 90
Knabenhaus 255
knight 66, 113, 178, 179
Kohlenberg 126, 177, 178,
Krafft-Ebing 192
Küsnacht 14, 40, 56. 203, 234, 258

Lake Zürich 25
Lällekönig 109, 117
Lambsprinck'schen 208
Landscape with Castle *See* paintings
Lang, Josef Bernhard 257, 258
Lapis Philosophorum *See* philosopher's stone
Laufen 25, 42, 46, 53
lecture(s), C. G. Jung
   Paracelsus as a Spiritual Phenomenon 205
   Paracelsus the Physician 205
   Zarathustra 66, 211, 262
   Zofingia 220, 221-223, 243, 261
lecture(s), Friedrich Nietzsche
   Homer and Classical Philology 132
lecture(s), Tadeus Reichstein
   On Alchemy 211
Leonhardskirchplatz 177, 180, 182, 229
libido 258
Literary Club of Zürich 205
Liverpool dream *See* dream, Liverpool
logos 158
Lohnhof 177, 180
Lunatic Asylum 187, 192
Luther, Martin 165

Mägdlein 144
Magna Mater *See* paintings
Man Dismembering a Dragon *See* paintings
mandala 80, 81, 198, 206, 242
Mangold, Burkhard 29
manikin 38, 40
Margarethen-Brücklein *See* bridge
Marian church 157
Markgräflerhof 153
Matthäus quarter 95
Medical Clinic 186
medical education 120, 183-193, 217, 236, 259
medium 44, 45, 238, 241, 242
Medizinische Klinik *See* Medical Clinic
Mellick, Jill 191
Mercurius 126
Miescher, Friedrich 218
Mietskasernen *See* tenements
Missionsstrasse 255
Mittlere Brücke *See* bridge, Middle Bridge
modernization 161, 185, 186-187, 199
monastery
   Augustinerkloster 160
   Barfüsserkloster 160
   Canon's Monastery of the Augustinians 89, 177
   Charterhouse of St. Margarethental 160
   Predigerkloster 81, 160
   St. Leonard 160
   St. Peter 160
Montagnola, Tessin 258
mother 38, 42-46, 53, 61, 115, 157, 161, 177, 234, 236, 237, 239, 240
Mühlebach 29, 31
Münster 113
   art 105
   benefactors 105, 157
   façade 65, 66, 105, 157, 179
   history 158
   Klostergarten 160, 171
   notable people 158, 169
   Reformation 157
   significant events 119, 157, 160
   structure 41, 133, 137
   turd vision 172
   worship/congregation 162-163, 175
Münsterhof 166
Münsterplatz 133
Münsterschule *See* Gymnasium
muscus pomambra 208
Musée historique et militaire
   See Historical and Military Museum Hüningen
Museum Anatomicum 119, 120, 122, 265
Museum Kleines Klingental 113
Mystery of Humans, The 242
myth 56, 66, 195, 222, 257

MAIN INDEX   288

Naming conventions in this book 17
   Carl versus Jung
   Carl versus Karl
   Samuel Preiswerk versus Samuel Gottlob Preiswerk
   Alliance (Married) Designation
   Multiple Given Names
   Nicknames
Napoleonic Wars 59, 80
Naturhistorisches Museum *See* Natural History Museum
Natural History Museum 127, 129, 181
Neptunbrunnen *See* Neptune Fountain
Neptune Fountain 177
Neuf-Brisach 80-81
Nietzsche, Friedrich 13, 132, 133, 143, 222, 259-263
Nietzsche Fountain 259
Nietzsche's Zarathustra 262
Nobel Prize 211, 255, 257
no-restraint method 191

occult 199, 237-239, 241-243
Oekolampad, Johannes 125, 160, 165,
Oeri, Albert 46, 136, 143, 218-220, 221, 223,
Oeri, Johann Jakob 46,
Oeri-Preiswerk, Hanna 219, 241, 270-271
Öffentliche Kunstsammlung 129
Ohrenklinik *See* Ear Clinic
Old Rhine *See* river
Old University 118-120, 122, 163, 186, 197, 261
On the Mysteries 201
Oporin, Johannes 120, 202
Oporinus, Johannes *See* Oporin, Johannes
Overbeck, Franz 259

Pädagogium *See* Gymnasium
Painter's Family, The *See* paintings
paintings
   Apollon 129
   Basel Landscape 41
   Castle Ruin 247
   David with the Head of Goliath 41
   Death of Gessler, The 109
   Farmers' Houses and Clouds 247
   Flora 129
   Golden Well-Fortified Castle, The
   Kennst du das Land 247
   Landscape with Castle 247
   Magna Mater 129-130
   Man Dismembering a Dragon 65-66
   Painter's Family, The
   Quadrated Circle in the Sky 73-75
   Rütli Oath, The 109
   Tell's Apple Shot 109
   Tell's Leap 109
   Well-Fortified Golden Castle, The 80-81
   Window on Eternity 196, 198
Paracelsus 187, 202, 204-206

paranormal 199, 239, 240
parapsychology 11
parsonage 239
   Kleinhüningen 26, 29, 31, 36-45, 46, 48, 61, 173, 223, 227, 240
   St. Alban 151,
   St. Leonard 182, 229
pastor, social hierarchy 135, 175
pastor's duties 61, 174, 192
pastor's son 53, 54, 62
pastors, family of 151, 157, 161, 163-165, 166, 177, 180, 229, 239, 249
Pathological-Anatomical Institute 186, 188
Pathologisch-anatomisches Institut *See* Pathological-Anatomical Institute
personality 45, 192, 262
Personality Nos. 1 and 2 13, 161
Petersgraben 101, 103, 105
Peterskirche *See* church
Peterskirchplatz 199
Petersplatz 123, 186, 196-197
Pfalz 133
pfarrhouse *See* parsonage
pharmaceutical industry 70, 219
Pharmaceutical Institute 187, 211
Pharmacy Museum of the University of Basel 199, 202, 207-211
philology 132, 145, 164, 208, 259, 260
philosopher's stone 206
Physiological Institute 186, 188
Physiologisches Institut *See* Physiological Institute
plagiarism charge 139, 142
Plattner, Felix 122,
Poliklinik im Spital *See* Polyclinic in the Municipal Hospital
pollution 49, 69, 74
Polyclinic in the Municipal Hospital 187, 188
population growth 13, 49, 69, 70, 77, 93, 96. 132, 183
Porphyry 201
portal 159, 161, 258
poverty 175
Predigerkloster *See* monastery
Preiswerk, Esther 163, 244, 270-271
Preiswerk, Helly 46, 48, 56, 238, 240-242, 245, 261, 270-271
Preiswerk, Luggy 46, 48, 144, 227, 240, 242, 270-271
Preiswerk, Rudolf (the Younger) 227, 270-271
Preiswerk, Samuel 157, 163-166, 168, 177, 180, 182, 242, 265, 268-269
Preiswerk, Samuel Gottlob 151, 163, 236, 242, 245, 270-271
Preiswerk, Vally 239, 244-245, 270-271
Preiswerk-Allenspach, Célestine 44, 46, 227, 241, 242, 245, 270-271
Preiswerk-Allenspach, Rudolf 48, 62, 226-227, 236, 245, 268-269, 270-271

MAIN INDEX

Preiswerk-Burckhardt, Alexander 163, 268-269
Preiswerk-Burckhardt, Anna Maria 163, 268-269
Preiswerk-Faber, Augusta 157, 182, 268-269, 270-271
Preiswerk-Forcart, Lucas 99
Preiswerk-Friedrich, Emma Maria 229, 270-271
Preiswerk-Gerber, Hans 247, 268-269, 270-271
Preiswerk-Oser, Lucas Albrecht 227, 268-269, 270-271
Preiswerk-Vetter, Gustav 233, 234, 236, 237, 241, 268-269, 270-271
Preiswerk-Zinsstag, Wilhelm 46, 48, 240, 270-271
Primary and Secondary School for Boys and Girls See Kleinhüningen, school
primordial images 66
printing
  history of 197, 202, 201, 203-204
  workshop 204, 207
projection 14, 66, 101, 206-207, 211
Psychiatrische Klinik See Psychiatry Clinic
psychiatry 13, 14, 191-193, 261
Psychiatry Clinic 61, 104, 198, 188, 191
psychic well-being 263
psychoanalysis 257, 258
psychological breakdown 261
psychological types 14, 63
psychology 11, 14, 66, 20, 206, 207, 211, 222, 238, 243, 249, 257, 258, 265
  analytic, depth, Jungian 13, 16, 37, 206, 211, 243, 257
Psychology and Alchemy 206
Psychology Club in Zurich 211, 258
psychosomatic illness 45, 136
public health 56, 161, 183, 217

Quadrated Circle in the Sky See paintings

radiolaria 181
radiolaria dream See dreams, radiolaria
Ragaz, Leonhard 175
Rauschenbach, Bertha 43
Realschule 220, 240
Reanimator of Basel Medicine 120
Red Book, The 56, 65, 73, 80, 191, 206, 238, 261-263
Reformation 41, 59, 113, 157, 160, 163, 165, 167, 171,
Reformed Protestant Church See church
Reichstein, Tadeus 202, 211
Reimer-de Lassaulx, Hermann Andreas 271
religion 11, 125, 139, 142, 172, 174
religious socialists 175
Reni, Guido 41
Restaurants
  Bottminger Mühle 234
  Die Krone 31
  Gasthaus Drei Könige 31-32
  Schiff 27, 29
  zum Tell 257, 259
Restaurant Bottminger Mühle See restaurants
Restaurant zum Tell See restaurants
Rhein See river, Rhine

Rhein-Club Basel 48
Rheinbadanstalt 95
Rheinfall See river, Rhine Falls
Rheinsprung 119, 125, 261
Rheintor 117
Rhine See river
Ritter, Wilhelm 235
ritual 38, 40, 45, 53, 61, 123, 173
river
  Birsig 217, 225, 229, 231, 235, 241,
  Birsigtal 178, 235
  Haltingermoos Cover image, 47-48
  Old Rhine Cover image, 47-48, 89
  Rhine 25, 26, 32, 34, 37, 48, 49, 59, 70, 73, 74, 79, 87-90, 95, 109, 111, 115, 119, 133, 169, 180
  Rhine Falls 25
  Wiese 25-27, 29, 32, 34-35, 37, 49, 51, 72, 73, 79, 87, 89
Rotbergstube 168-169
Rütli Oath, The See paintings

sanatorium 56, 104, 192, 235,
Sanatorium für Nervenkranke 235
Sandreuter, Hans 130
Sarasin, Paul 218
Schifflände 109, 117
Schloss Münchenstein See castle
Schloss Wartenberg See castle
Schlossgasse 89
Schneiderin See seamstress
Schnitt, Konrad 126
Schoren Girls 61, 175
Schule auf Burg See Gymnasium
Schützengraben 259
Scrutinies 56
seamstress 245
séances 220, 223, 238, 240-243, 245, 270-271
Seelsorger 174
Seeress of Prevorst: Being Revelations Concerning the Inner-Life of Man, The 242
Seestrasse 25, 40, 19
Seidenhof 105-107
Self 14, 66, 79, 80, 195, 196, 258, 260, 262
self-healing 45
Senn & Co 99
Seven Sermons to the Dead 56, 257
sexual advance 48
shadow 14, 40, 66, 158
Siddhartha 258
Sigg, Hermann 196
silo 49, 51
sister 45, 46, 63, 132, 227, 234, 236, 240
skeleton 101, 120-122
skull 15, 130
Society for Chemical Industry Basel See CIBA
Sonderschulheim See Institute of Good Hope
soul 45, 135, 174, 258, 263
Spalenberg 182, 236

MAIN INDEX

290

Spalentor 160, 197, 259
Spalentorweg 259
Spalenvorstadt 122, 182, 257
spirit 45, 56, 192, 219, 239, 241, 242
spirit of the times/spirit of the depths 13, 74, 161
spiritism 239, 242
spiritualism 238–239, 242, 243
spiritual 160, 161, 173, 174, 201, 205, 239, 263, 265
St. Alban Pfarrhaus *See* parsonage
St. George 65, 66, 67, 158, 179
St. Johann Pharmacy 208
St. Johann quarter 95, 104
St. Johanns-Vorstadt 95, 99, 103
St. Leonhardskirche *See* church, St. Leonard's
St. Margarethenkirche *See* church, St. Margaret's
Staatsexamen 11, 183, 185, 192, 223, 249
Steinenvorstadt 217, 225
Steiner, Gustav 72, 219, 220,
Steppenwolf 257, 258
Stickelberger, Johann Melchior Ernst
  See Stückelberg, Ernst
Stückelberg, Ernst 105–109, 130
suffrage 95
suicide 255
supernatural 239
Surgical Clinic 186, 187
Swedenborg, Emanuel 201
Swiss Confederacy 257
Swiss Federal Constitution 217
**Swiss Society for the History of Medicine and
  Natural Sciences** 206
symbol 66, 69, 74, 80, 123, 125, 126, 157, 187, 196, 201,
  206, 207, 211, 222, 258
synchronicity 14, 199
synod 61, 62

table-turning 239
Telesphorus 40
Tell Chapel 109
Tell, William 257
Tell's Apple Shot *See* paintings
Tell's Leap *See* paintings
tenements 93
tension 11, 73, 74, 158
Theatrum Anatomicum 119, 120, 122
theology 119, 157, 160, 164, 259
Thirty Years' War 57, 59, 217
Thus Spoke Zarathustra 211, 222, 261–263
Tischrücken *See* table-turning
Töchterschule *See* School for Daughters
Totengässlein 187, 194–196, 199, 200
Totentanz *See* paintings
tramway 233
trance 239, 242, 261
transcendent 14, 74
transformation 34, 101

tree
  chestnut 221
  linden 28–29, 31
  magnolia 194, 196
Tripus Aureus 208
Trois Rois *See* Drei Könige
tuberculosis 53, 56, 199, 245
turd vision 171–172
typhoid 175, 217

Uferstrasse 87, 93
unconscious 11, 38, 66, 190, 201, 206–207, 222, 262
unconscious, collective *See* collective unconscious
University Hospital Basel 103
Unterer Rheinweg 111
Unteres Kollegium *See* Old University
Untimely Meditations 261
Urbilder 66

van der Post, Laurens 192, 203
van Wezel, Andries *See* Vesalius, Andreas
Vesalius, Andreas 120, 122, 182, 184, 202
Vesal *See* Vesalius, Andreas
Vesalgasse 122, 162, 193,
Vesalianum 182–183, 185, 186, 188, 259
Vischer, Andreas 193, 218–220
visions *See* turd vision
vivisection 190
von Franz, Marie-Louise 14, 145, 206, 221
von Humboldt, Alexander 120
von Klingen, Walter 113
von Rotberg, Bishop Arnold 169
von Venningen, Bishop Johann 119

Waggis-Basel 132
Walze 218
wax anatomical models 120–121, 122
Weidling cover image, 44, 47, 48
Well-Fortified Golden Castle, The *See* paintings
Weiss-Preiswerk (Faber branch), Gusteli 43, 129, 236,
  239, 266–267, 268–269, 270–271
wholeness 79, 80, 201, 263
Wiese *See* river
Wille, Ludwig 191,
Window on Eternity *See* paintings
Wolff, Gustav 192
World War II 206, 220

Young Seducer 158

Zarathustra Lecture *See* lectures, C. G. Jung
Zofingia 216–223
Zofingia Lectures, The *See* lectures, C. G. Jung
Zumstein-Preiswerk, Stephanie 146–149, 240, 241
Zunft zum Goldenen Stern *See* Guild of the Golden Star
Zwingli, Huldrych 165
Zwingli, Ulrich 167

MAIN INDEX

FAMILY NAME INDEX

**NAMES OF FAMILY MEMBERS
MENTIONED IN THE FAMILY TREES**
Tables 9, 10, 11 (pp. 267–271)

JUNG

Dürk-Jung, Otto
Dürk-Jung (Biedermann branch), **Fanny**

Fiechter-Jung (Frey branch), **Sophie II**
Fiechter-Jung, **Robert**

Fiechter-Wissmann, **Helene**
Fiechter-Wissmann (Jung branch), **Gustav**

Fiechter-Zollikofer, **Paula**
Fiechter-Zollikofer (Jung branch), **Ernst Robert**

Frey (Stickelberger branch), **Johann**
Frey (Stickelberger branch), **Henriette**
Frey (Stickelberger branch), **Karl** †
Frey (Stickelberger branch), **Ludwig** †
Frey (Stickelberger branch), **Rosina**
Frey (Stickelberger branch), **Ludwig** †

Frey-Stickelberger, **Johann Rudolf**
Frey-Stickelberger, **Margareta**

Jung, **Karl Gustav**
   Jung-de Lassaulx (first marriage)
   Jung-Ryenthaler (second marriage)
   Jung-Frey (third mariage)

Jung (Biedermann branch), **Ewald**
   (⚭ Elsa, family name unknown)

Jung (de Lassaulx branch), **Anna Caroline** †
Jung (de Lassaulx branch), **Catharine Franziska Jacobina**
Jung (de Lassaulx branch), **Emma Louise Wilhelmine**

Jung (Frey branch), **Friedrich Daniel Reinhard "Fritz"**
Jung (Frey branch), **Johann Friedrich Max**
Jung (Frey branch), **Rudolf Jeremias Eduard**

Jung (Preiswerk branch), **Johanna Gertrude "Trudi"**
Jung (Preiswerk branch), **Paul** †

Jung (Rauschenbach branch), **Agathe**
Jung (Rauschenbach branch), **Franz**
Jung (Rauschenbach branch), **Helene**
Jung (Rauschenbach branch), **Margaretha "Gret"**
Jung (Rauschenbach branch), **Marianne**

Jung (Ryenthaler branch), **Karl**
Jung (Ryenthaler branch), **Karoline**
Jung (Ryenthaler branch), **Virginie**

Jung-Biedermann (Frey branch),
   Ernst Georg Constantin (first marriage)
Jung-Biedermann, **Fanny**

Jung-de Lassaulx, **Virginie**

Jung-Deutsch, **Julia**
Jung-Deutsch (Biedermann branch), **Ernst**

Jung-Egg, **Anna**
Jung-Egg (Frey branch), **Ernst** Georg Constantin
   (second marriage)

Jung-Frey, **Sophie**

Jung-Preiswerk, **Johann Paul Achilles**
Jung-Preiswerk (Faber branch), **Emilie**

Jung-Rauschenbach, **Emma Maria**

Jung-Ryenthaler, **Elisabethe Katharine**

Jung-v. Pannewitz, **Maria**
Jung-v. Pannewitz (Biedermann branch), **Rudolf**

Jung-Ziegler, Franz **Ignaz**
Jung-Ziegler, Maria Josepha "**Sophie**"

Reimer (Jung branch), **Anna**
Reimer (Jung branch), **Clara**
Reimer (Jung branch), **Emma**

Reimer-Jung, **Hermann Andreas**
Reimer-Jung (de Lassaulx branch), **Anna Charlotte**

Ricklin-Fiechter, **Robert**
Ricklin-Fiechter (Jung branch), **Sophie**

PREISWERK

Faber (Rooschütz branch), **Carl Abraham**
Faber (Rooschütz branch), **Caroline Christina**
Faber (Rooschütz branch), **Gustav Wilhelm**
Faber (Rooschütz branch), **Ludwig Wilhelm**

Faber-Rooschütz, **Johann Carl August**
Faber-Rooschütz, **Karolina Friederika**

Fröhlich-Preiswerk, **Edmund**
Fröhlich-Preiswerk (Faber branch), **Maria Sophia "Sophie"**

Jung-Preiswerk (Faber branch), **Emilie**

Manuel-Preiswerk, **Albrecht Carl Paul**
Manuel-Preiswerk (Faber branch), **Salome Elisabeth**

Oeri-Preiswerk, **Albert**
Oeri-Preiswerk (Vetter branch), **Hanna/Jeanne**

Preiswerk, **Samuel** (Burckhardt branch)
 Preiswerk-Hopf (first marriage)
 Preiswerk-Faber (second mariage)

Preiswerk, **Samuel Gottlob** (Hopf branch)
 Preiswerk-Staehelin (only marriage)

Preiswerk (Allenspach branch), **Bertha**
Preiswerk (Allenspach branch), **Célestine** (the Younger)
Preiswerk (Allenspach branch), **Clara**
Preiswerk (Allenspach branch), **Emilie**
Preiswerk (Allenspach branch), **Ernst**
Preiswerk (Allenspach branch), **Esther**
Preiswerk (Allenspach branch), **Friedrich**
Preiswerk (Allenspach branch), **Helene "Helly"**
Preiswerk (Allenspach branch), **Louise "Luggy"**
Preiswerk (Allenspach branch), **Mathilde**
Preiswerk (Allenspach branch), **Ottile**
Preiswerk (Allenspach branch), **Rudolf** (the Younger)
Preiswerk (Allenspach branch), **Sophie**
Preiswerk (Allenspach branch), **Valerie "Vally"**

Preiswerk (Burckhardt branch), **Alexander**
Preiswerk (Burckhardt branch), **Dorothea**

Preiswerk (Faber branch), **Carl Heinrich**
Preiswerk (Faber branch), **Eduard** †
Preiswerk (Faber branch), **Maria Sophia "Sophie"**
Preiswerk (Faber branch), **Wilhelm Adolf**

Preiswerk (Friedrich branch), **Dorothea**
Preiswerk (Friedrich branch), **Eduard** (the Younger)
Preiswerk (Friedrich branch), **Heinrich**
Preiswerk (Friedrich branch) **Margaretha**

Preiswerk (Gerber branch), **Agnes**
Preiswerk (Gerber branch), **Johannes**
Preiswerk (Gerber branch), **Matthias**
Preiswerk (Gerber branch), **Peter**

Preiswerk (Staehelin branch), **Adolf**
Preiswerk (Staehelin branch), **Charlotte**
Preiswerk (Staehelin branch), **Heinrich**
Preiswerk (Staehelin branch), **Richard**
Preiswerk (Staehelin branch), **Samuel (the Younger)**
Preiswerk (Staehelin branch), **Theodora** †

Preiswerk (Vetter branch), **Augusta**
Preiswerk (Vetter branch), **Bernhard**
Preiswerk (Vetter branch), **Bertha**
Preiswerk (Vetter branch), **Eduard**
Preiswerk (Vetter branch), **Gustav**
Preiswerk (Vetter branch), **Hedwig**
Preiswerk (Vetter branch), **Maria**
Preiswerk (Vetter branch), **Martha**
Preiswerk (Vetter branch), **Paul**
Preiswerk (Vetter branch), **Sophia**

Preiswerk-Allenspach, **Célestine**
Preiswerk-Allenspach (Faber branch), **Rudolf Johannes**

Preiswerk-Burckhardt, **Alexander**
Preiswerk-Burckhardt, **Anna Maria**

Preiswerk-Faber, **Carolina Louisa Augusta**

Preiswerk-Friedrich, **Emma Maria**
Preiswerk-Friedrich (Faber branch), **Eduard**

Preiswerk-Gerber, **Adelheid**
Preiswerk-Gerber (Faber branch), **Johannes "Hans"**

Preiswerk-Hopf, **Charlotte Magdalena**

Preiswerk-Oser, **Rosina**
Preiswerk-Oser (Faber branch), **Lucas Albrecht**

Preiswerk-Staehelin, **Maria Charlotte**

Preiswerk-Vetter, **Anne-Maria**
Preiswerk-Vetter (Faber branch), **Gustav Adolf**

Preiswerk-Zinsstag (Allenspach branch), **Wilhelm**
Preiswerk-Zinsstag, **Emma "Emmy"**

Weiss-Preiswerk, **Emanuel**
Weiss-Preiswerk (Faber branch), **Auguste Dorothea"Gusteli"**

ABOUT THE AUTHOR

Kathrin Schaeppi (MSc, MFA) is a Jungian Analyst and federally licensed psychotherapist with a private practice in Basel. Since 2011, she has been guiding tours on Carl Jung's early years in Basel, expanding her knowledge through ongoing research and uncovering new insights into the historical and intellectual richness of the city—her birthplace and home.

In addition to her psychotherapeutic practice, Kathrin puts her heart and soul into research, teaching, and supervision. At ISAPZURICH, she heads the Picture Interpretation Department, co-founded the ISAPZURICH Picture Collection, and serves as a member of the Zürich Lecture Series team. She regularly teaches both locally and internationally.

Kathrin's previous publications include the family chronicle *Reunion* (Gremper 2002), the prose-poetry collection *Cancer Mon Amour* (Winterling/Dusie Press 2009), and the creative biography *Sonja Sekula: Grace in a Cow's Eye* (Black Radish Books 2011). This work marks her first extended piece of published research. For more information, visit her website: www.kschaeppi.ch.

ACKNOWLEDGMENTS

I extend my heartfelt gratitude to those who supported this project by verifying the accuracy of the historical data and contributing valuable insights.

First, I am deeply thankful to the employees of the Cantonal Archive Basel-Stadt, and specifically to Patricia Eckert and Jasmine Brüderlin, for their assistance in providing access to primary materials.

I am also profoundly grateful to Susanne Eggenberger-Jung (Archivist at the C.G. Jung House Museum and great-granddaughter of C.G. Jung) for her professional support in providing specific images from the Jung Family Archive in Küsnacht. On a crisp, sunny day in February 2023, I had the privilege of meeting Andreas Jung (grandson of C.G. Jung) and his daughter Susanne. Their insightful feedback on the manuscript, shared during our conversation at the C.G. Jung House Museum Archive in development in Küsnacht, was invaluable. I also thank Ulrich Hoerni (grandson of C.G. Jung and resident of Binningen), for generously sharing his extensive knowledge of his grandfather over tea and Basler Brunsli. Klaus and Bea Baumann (grandson of C.G. Jung, also from Binningen) kindly took the time to meet with me in Binningen, offering anecdotes that enriched this work. I am grateful to Carl Christian Jung (great-grandson of C.G. Jung) and Thomas Fischer (historian, past Director of the Foundation of the Works of C.G. Jung, and great-grandson of C.G. Jung), for their insights.

My thanks also go to Bettina Kaufmann (art historian, editor, and Board Member of the Foundation of the Works of C.G. Jung). Special thanks are due to the Basler historian Isabel Koellreuter for her excellent support providing primary research and her friendly feedback during the early stages of the manuscript.

In its later stages, I had the distinct honor of receiving input from Sonu Shamdasani, whose thoughtful feedback and kind gesture of writing the foreword were deeply appreciated.

I am also indebted to the many institutions and private individuals who provided materials to illustrate this book.

A special note of gratitude goes to Vreni Jung for her meticulous transcription of archival documents written in the old German script.

Most importantly, I extend my heartfelt thanks to the editors Lauren Kosinski and Valerie Appleby, with whom I spent many lively hours and retreats discussing and editing. Their friendship, keen insights, and polishing of the manuscript were invaluable. Finally, the superb design and layout by Sibylle Ryser and the work of Robert Hinshaw of Daimon in printing, publishing, and distributing this book deserve special recognition.

Kathrin Schaeppi